# The cultural critics

**International Library of Sociology**

Founded by Karl Mannheim

Editor: John Rex, University of Warwick

Arbor Scientiae
Arbor Vitae

A catalogue of the books available in the **International Library of Sociology** and other series of Social Science books published by Routledge & Kegan Paul will be found at the end of this volume.

# The cultural critics

## From Matthew Arnold to Raymond Williams

**Lesley Johnson**
Department of Education
University of Melbourne

**Routledge & Kegan Paul**
London, Boston and Henley

*First published in 1979*
*by Routledge & Kegan Paul Ltd*
*39 Store Street, London WC1E 7DD,*
*Broadway House, Newtown Road,*
*Henley-on-Thames, Oxon RG9 1EN and*
*9 Park Street, Boston, Mass. 02108, USA*
*Photoset in 10 on 11pt Times by*
*Kelly and Wright, Bradford-on-Avon, Wiltshire*
*and printed in Great Britain by*
*Redwood Burn Ltd,*
*Trowbridge and Esher*


*British Library Cataloguing in Publication Data*

*Johnson, Lesley*

*The cultural critics—(International library*
*of sociology).*
*1. Culture 2. Authors, English—Political*
*and social views*
*I. Title II. Series*
*301.2'0942 HM101 78-41306*

*ISBN 0 7100 7678 9*

# Contents

# Preface

This study focuses on the concept of culture employed by English literary intellectuals since the mid-nineteenth century. This concept has been central to a vital tradition of social criticism which has represented the artistic imagination as a moral force in society and as a fundamental mechanism for social change. The tradition is traced over a period of approximately 125 years through the writings of a number of English intellectuals. Their selection needs some explanation. The three main figures, Matthew Arnold, F. R. Leavis and Raymond Williams, elucidate most clearly the moral critique and social vision associated with the concept of culture. The other writers chosen fall into two categories: those who illustrate the various ways in which the concept of culture was employed and modified over the years; and second, the intellectuals from various areas of specialization who, though not directly associated with the literary tradition, demonstrated similar preoccupations to that tradition. The minor figures were chosen to locate the major writers in terms of the social context of other intellectuals; and further, to provide a broader survey in order to delineate the ideological and political limitations of the literary tradition associated with the concept of culture. Apart from these academic considerations, it will be obvious to the reader that the selection is also subject to my own esoteric interests, an unavoidable factor in making a choice from such a wide field.

For my continuing interest in the study I am indebted to the work of Raymond Williams. His work remains fundamental to the field of cultural studies—theoretical and concrete investigations which stem from the project associated with the literary intellectuals' concept of culture. This field of study has demonstrated the same commitment to a critique of society and a sense of engagement that infused the literary tradition. To indicate clearly my own debt (and that of cultural studies in general) to Raymond Williams I have organized the presentation of the material of this work in a similar style to his book *Culture and Society* (1968). By doing so I have also been able to elucidate how my own approach differs from that of Raymond Williams.

I should like to acknowledge the assistance and encouragement of a number of people. In particular, I am most grateful to Raymond Williams and Terry Eagleton for talking with me about my own work and theirs; Stuart Hall, Richard Johnson, Michael Green and all the people of the University of Birmingham Centre for Contemporary Cultural Studies for their time and their friendliness towards me during my four-week visit there in February 1978; to Peter Musgrave for his constant support and interest in my work; to my family and friends for their warmth and encouragement; and to Martin Sullivan for his assistance, support, and above all for just being there.

# 1 Introduction: intellectuals and their ideas

The history of the concept of culture is complex and tantalizingly ambiguous. Intellectuals from various fields have attempted to disentangle the manifold meanings which have become implicit in the term. These writers have sought to find a basis for one unambiguous concept of culture that either resolves the differences between the existing meanings or replaces these with an entirely new definition of the term. Yet no satisfactory solution has evolved.

Social scientists in the twentieth century have been particularly engrossed in this task, 'culture' being to them an important tool of analysis. But in the nineteenth century the concept of culture was largely the province of the literary intellectuals. They employed this term as a central feature of an important tradition of protest and critical discontent, a tradition of social thought for which they have been primarily responsible in England. The concept of culture expressed these writers' distress at trends in their society and at the same time it articulated a concern to provide a positive vision for that society. Education formed a fundamental part of their social vision, providing both the means to and a feature of the quality of life which they have seen as threatened by modern industrial or mass society.

The critical project underlying the concept of culture in its nineteenth-century form has continued to frame the social analyses of a number of intellectuals in the twentieth century. Most of these writers have represented the concept of culture as central to their commentary on society. Yet they have not succeeded in sustaining the concept of culture in its original form to focus their critical thought or provide the basis of their social vision. They have drawn on other concepts in the attempt to revivify the central thrust of this notion of culture, often totally redefining the term.

In this study the history of this concept of culture is traced over a period of approximately one hundred years. The main concern has been to examine the particular preoccupation with the concept of culture amongst English literary intellectuals during that period. No attempt is made to find a common definition of culture which would satisfy all the demands placed on it, not even those of the literary intellectuals themselves. The central interest lies with the question of how a specific group of intellectuals employs the concept of culture and the ideological field in which it is conceived. An expository history of the concept of culture is not intended, in the sense of an account of the lineage and the specific developments of this idea, but rather a map of the terrain and an analysis of the contours over which the intellectuals have moved.

**The concept of culture**

The notion of culture employed by literary intellectuals in the nineteenth century, according to Raymond Williams, has its roots in the eighteenth century.[1] But its clearest and most forceful expression was given by Matthew Arnold in the mid-Victorian period in England. Arnold deliberately used this term as central to his ideas about society, whereas his predecessors such as Coleridge did not place it in such a dominant position. These writers were inclined to substitute other terms such as 'cultivation'. In his essay *Culture and Anarchy* (1869) Arnold defined culture as:[2]

> a pursuit of our total perfection by means of getting to know, on all the matters which most concern us, the best which has been thought and said in the world. . . .

The commitment to a set of values in such a definition is explicit. It provides the central distinction between this concept of culture and the concept employed by anthropologists and sociologists in the twentieth century. The latter concept stresses a relativistic standpoint or value neutrality and assumes the form of discussions about 'cultures' rather than 'the culture'. Bauman draws attention to this distinguishing feature of what he calls the 'hierarchical concept of culture':[3]

> The term 'cultures', if understood hierarchically, can hardly be used in the plural. The concept makes sense only if denoted straightforwardly as *the culture*; there is an ideal nature of the human being, and *the culture* means the conscious, strenuous and prolonged effort to attain this ideal, to bring the actual life-process into line with the highest potential of the human vocation.

In this sense culture, as it is described by the literary intellectuals in England, invokes the classical ideal of Renaissance humanism. It substitutes the claim by romantic primitivism that man should return to a 'natural' state with the humanistic contention that it is man's distinctive privilege to conceive of an ideal end for himself.

In his work on classicism and romanticism, Bate claims that the classical ideal of perfection requires that man seeks to achieve both the rational and ethical fruition of human nature. Art, he says, is believed to be fundamental to man because its end lies in the revelation and inculcation of this ideal.[4] The concept of culture reflects the influence of such classical notions about art in its stress on the ideal of an end beyond and higher than the individual man. Moreover, it expresses a number of other fundamental principles of classical humanism. For example, Bate demonstrates that humanism from Plato through to the Renaissance believed that to know 'the good' is to do it. Such a belief is implicit in Arnold's statement that perfection is to be sought 'by means of getting to know . . . the best which has been thought and said. . . .' In his views on culture and social action, Arnold relied on the fundamental assumption that men of culture are better or nobler men. Similarly, all claims for the ennobling effect of good art imply an essential connection between knowledge and action. Arnold's reference to 'the best which has been thought and said' illustrates a further instance of the classical humanist influence in this concept of culture. The English literary intellectuals return constantly to this notion which, according to Bate, gained prominence some centuries earlier with the Renaissance humanists. They contended that:[5]

> rational determination of the absolute and ideally good in taste and morality is to be facilitated and made more authoritative by the study of the preferences and the conduct of the best in all ages, and especially in classical antiquity.

These classical influences do not preclude romantic tendencies in the concept of culture. Romantic notions of genius and creativity that depict the artist or intellectual as having a superior vision of the world form an essential feature of this concept. Raymond Williams emphasizes the romantic tradition of the English poets of the eighteenth and early nineteenth centuries as the intellectual heritage of the concept of culture. Poets such as Shelley and Wordsworth, in their poetry and their writings about art, discussed the superior powers of the artists, and the social significance of art. But Williams also recognizes that the idea of culture rests on certain classicist claims about art. He suggests that romanticism and classicism should be understood in this context as 'two sides of the same claim'; they represent two aspects of idealist theories of art.[6]

The interaction between these two tendencies in the concept of culture indicates the framework in which it was originally conceived. In its affirmation of the social role of the artist or the intellectual, the idea of culture repudiated the preoccupation with the individual that became a significant movement in the nineteenth century. The claims of the individual were balanced with the claims of society. Individualism in the form of *laissez-faire* liberalism and the popular 'self-help' philosophy of the time was condemned for its rejection of the claims of society.

Romantic notions about art do not always evince such social awareness. With its assumptions about the artist as a special kind of person, romanticism has a propensity towards individualistic preoccupations. At the turn of the century this negative form of romanticism was predominant in artistic circles. Artists sought to isolate themselves from the rest of society, disclaiming any social responsibility. The moral considerations associated with the concept of culture, its assertion of humane values, were ignored.

Matthew Arnold was adamant that the concept of culture entailed an individual and a social idea. The quality of life in modern industrial society can only be improved by a reassertion of a former unity of the individual and his community. And such a reunion is to be achieved, according to Arnold, if individuals pursue an ideal that takes them beyond their individual selves. The two aspects of culture are thus intimately connected in his thought. Arnold believed culture to be the only antidote for the evils of an industrial society; it was a force to preserve and promote humane values.

As the central focus of the literary intellectuals' critique of society, the concept of culture broke with the dominant intellectual ethos in England in various ways. But any understanding of the development of this concept needs to examine the extent to which its problematic has also been contained within that very same ethos. Tracing the ideological and political limitations of the concept will elucidate more precisely the nature of its relationship to the dominant intellectual ethos of the time. Such an investigation hinges upon an understanding of the role of intellectuals in society, or more precisely of the practice of intellectuals.

## Intellectual practice

Much of the literature on the intellectual centres around three often overlapping issues: the definition of the intellectual; the role of the intellectual in the past and the present; and the intellectual's relationship to society. These questions mark the boundaries of this literature, revealing a number of important features of the very concern itself with intellectuals or intellectual practice. Underlying their discussions is a preoccupation, shared by the majority of writers in this field, with legitimating a particular image of 'the intellectual'. This is true of straightforward dictionary definitions, as it is of the most detailed studies of intellectuals.

*A Modern Dictionary of Sociology*, for example, defines the intellectuals as 'those members of a society who are devoted to the development of original ideas and are engaged in creative intellectual pursuits'.[7] Such a description indicates that the intellectuals are an élite group in society of an asocial, ahistorical nature. It is assumed that this realm of activity is the preserve of certain people rather than all members of society, but no suggestion of the social basis of such a grouping is indicated. The chief weakness of such a definition is that it universalizes what is a specific social and historical phenomenon.

Detailed examinations of the intellectuals have been more conscious of the social context of intellectuals, but they too have attempted to provide an ahistorical definition of this category. Bensman and Lilienfield, for example, argue that the intellectuals have a three-fold, self-selected task:[8]

> (1) to define and assign priority to cultivate value; (2) to criticize society as a means to achieving those values; (3) to defend and attack bearers of values as exemplifying or detracting from the realization of ultimate values.

This definition seeks to distinguish between intellectuals and other members of society on the basis of a preoccupation with 'ultimate values'. A similar distinction is sought by other writers about intellectuals, the basis of which is an examination of what intellectuals do with ideas and the type of ideas with which they work. Intellectuals, it is believed, are preoccupied characteristically with the realm of meanings and values, generating ideas of an abstract rather than concrete kind. The areas of interest most often referred to are the nature of the universe, the rules which govern society and the way in which society could be organized.

Nettl provides one of the most refined analyses along these lines. He claims that the definition of an intellectual must only begin by looking at ideas; it cannot get off the ground if the role of the intellectual in the institutions of society provides the central focus of our discussions. The concept of the intellectual, Nettl argues, must be defined from inside out, from certain types of ideas toward certain categories of idea-articulators. Having established the fundamental nature of the intellectual, we can then begin to ask questions about the institutional attachment of intellectuals and so on. Nettl suggests that we categorize ideas according to two dimensions, the first of which is the essential dichotomy and focuses on the relationship of new ideas to the existing stock of knowledge. He labels the two ends of this dimension respectively that of quality and that of scope, which he defines as follows:[9]

> Quality in this context will be defined as acceptance or rejection of the axio-normative (or value and norm) structures of given systems of thought, a rearrangement of the significance and interrelationship of components. Scope, on the other hand, deals with the broadening of the area of discussion through the addition of genuinely new or at least newly relevant knowledge.

The second dimension which Nettl advances concerns intellectual context and relevance: the particularistic sciences versus the universalistic humanities. This dimension is contingent upon the first for the particularistic sciences are the context in which ideas of scope are manipulated, as are universalistic humanities, the context for the ideas of quality.

Nettl introduces yet another dichotomy to be added to the previous two: the type of social structure. He suggests that the particularistic sciences are most suited to the academic environment because the discovery of something new on a particularistic level initially requires a number of highly skilled 'peers'. This environment facilitates the formulating, testing, validating, and spreading of the ideas of scope, while also limiting the choice of problems by internal, professional considerations. The manner of formulation, acceptance, and diffusion necessary for qualitative ideas is most suited to socio-political movements and environments: 'structures of dissent'. On this basis Nettl argues that:[10]

> the intellectual can be defined from a triple set of dimensions: (1) a profession that is culturally validated, (2) a role that is socio-political, (3) a consciousness that relates to universals.

Nettl stresses the importance of the type of social structure in which the intellectual articulates his ideas, an emphasis which is reiterated in many analyses of the intellectual. The academic environment, Nettl argues, emasculates the intellectual endeavour by the elimination of the universal dimension of their ideas. Ideas are particularized to suit the dominant notion of the disciplines.

Similarly, Bensman and Lilienfield draw a distinction between the intellectual attitude and the academic attitude. The latter, they claim, is narrow and technical, preoccupied with methodology and techniques, and uncritical of the basic values underlying the problems being discussed. The intellectual attitude, on the other hand, decries narrow specialization, adopts a critical stance, and is committed to the expression of values (whereas the academic attitude affects a value-neutrality). They examine the suitability of various social contexts for intellectuals. Contrary to Nettl's adamant statement that only one type of environment is suitable for the intellectual, they claim that a wide range of environments can be suitable, but only if the intellectual retains a certain detachment from his social context. They do not dismiss the difficulty of retaining this detachment in the face of the seductiveness of the institutions which tend to employ intellectuals, but are optimistic about the opportunities for intellectuals to work in at least six areas: the mass media, entertainment, management, research, advisory positions, and education.

The main problem posed by the co-optation of the intellectuals into these various areas, Bensman and Lilienfield claim, has been that the intellectuals have been placed in an uneasy position with respect to their own past. They argue that:[11]

> the traditional position of intellectuals, of being rejected by their society, has resulted in a traditional response of rejecting their society. The acceptance of the intellectuals by their society has undermined a major social support of the intellectual attitude.

This assumption of the importance of rejection by society for the intellectual's critical attitude is fundamental to much of the discussion of the intellectual. It lies behind Nettl's claim that the structures of dissent are the necessary context for the intellectual. Similarly, Mannheim argued that the outsider status of the modern intellectual is essential to his universalizing, critical approach.[12]

Shils adopts a more moderate stance in claiming that intellectuals need autonomy in society. He believes intellectuals to be by nature those who are fascinated by ultimate values with an 'interior need to penetrate beyond the screen of immediate concrete experience. . . .'[13] This sense of quest enables them to resist the influence of external expectations on their ideas while still performing a task essential to their role as intellectuals in the society. Through the production of traditions, by way of example and through their concern with standards, the intellectuals legitimate authority and authority figures; such is one of their central functions in society. Shils depicts the intellectuals' situation as being one of tension between their role and their commitment to 'highest values', 'the sacred'.[14]

Each of these writers is essentially preoccupied with delineating a special role for the intellectuals in society. They each define this specialness in terms of a superior vision and a particular approach to ideas. Such claims are seductive, for they are made by people who are themselves, by implication, intellectuals and they are directed, in the first instance, towards an audience who will respond to the call, who will inevitably be attracted by their claims. But to take these writers at their word is to accept them according to their illusions about their own role in society. A number of assumptions fundamental to their work need to be made problematic.

Each of the writers relies first and foremost on the presupposition that it is possible for certain individuals to reject or overcome the social influences on thought. They generally agree that every society is characterized by a dominant mode of thought, but this only makes the intellectuals' apparent ability to escape this way of thinking of greater social significance. Second, they each refer to the status of intellectuals as having historical justification, the assumption being that the term 'intellectual' can only be legitimately applied to a specific group of people, in the present as in the past. And third, they assume a hierarchy of tasks or functions in the society and that the very nature of the intellectuals' realm of activity places them high in this hierarchy. Intellectual work is regarded as somehow of a fundamentally different nature from other types of work. That it deals specifically with ideas, with the affairs of the mind, sets it apart from other labour.

One writer who has not relied on these assumptions about the intellectual is Pierre Bourdieu. He seeks to elucidate the basis of these type of assumptions throughout his discussions of artists or intellectuals (his category is most broad). The intellectual's work needs to be examined in the context of his society or his age, for it is fundamental, says Bourdieu, that how an intellectual thinks as well as what he thinks about should be determined by his society. An intellectual (or artistic) work, says Bourdieu, leaves unsaid the essential and implicitly assumes what forms its very foundations: 'the axioms and postulates which it takes for granted'. These axioms and postulates, the underlying structures of thought, form what he refers to as the 'cultural unconscious' of our society.[15]

Bourdieu specifies two aspects of the intellectual's or artist's reliance on the cultural unconscious. In the first instance the intellectual's very use of language guarantees that he has been initiated into the cultural unconscious of his society. For through this process of socialization all individuals learn to use the concepts and categories implicit in a language, just as they learn the more obvious ways of thinking associated with that language, often signalled by common expressions, phrases and rhetorical devices. An intellectual, Bourdieu argues, cannot but think within the precepts and assumptions of his society. Second, the significance and 'truth' of an artistic or intellectual work relies on its relationship to the cultural unconscious. The intellectual must be able to communicate to an audience, no matter how small, if his work is to have any meaning. Consequently, the intellectual inevitably expresses his ideas within the basic thought framework of the society, on which even the *avant-garde* relies necessarily for the creation of its own esoteric meanings and values.

Bourdieu is particularly concerned with the relationship between artists themselves (as a broad category) and between artists and the public. He delineates a concept of the intellectual field which is constituted by the complex of agents including 'other artists, critics and intermediaries between the artist and the public such as publishers, art dealers or journalists whose function is to make them known to the public'.[16] The intellectual field ascribes not only the public meaning of an artistic or intellectual work, but also its legitimacy as an area of activity. At any one time activities will be ascribed both legitimacy and status by different types of authorities within that field. He compares the way in which different areas of art will be ascribed legitimacy and status:[17]

> The structure of the intellectual field maintains a relation of interdependence with one of the basic structures of the cultural field, that of cultural works, established in a hierarchy according to their degree of legitimacy. One may observe that in a given society at a given moment in time not all cultural signs— theatrical performances, sporting spectacles, recitals of songs, poetry or chamber music, operettas or operas are equal in dignity and value, nor do they call for the same approach with the same degree of insistence. In other words, the various systems of expression from the theatre to television, are objectively organized according to a hierarchy independent of individual opinions, that defines cultural legitimacy and its degrees.

Bourdieu stresses 'the relative autonomy of the intellectual field'. Creative artists and intellectuals began to liberate themselves economically and socially from the patronage of the aristocracy and the church with the growth of the market economy. The expansion of the 'literary and artistic market' enabled the development of the intellectual field, independent from direct external influences and subject to its own structural logic. Cultural works increasingly competed for legitimacy within the structure of this field rather than seeking the patronage of an external legitimizing agency. Such conditions, Bourdieu suggests, provide the basis for the intellectual's redefinition of himself as independent and indifferent to any demands other than those intrinsic to his creative project.[18]

In the light of Bourdieu's analysis the discussion of the intellectual by writers such as Nettl and Shils appears to be part of the continuing process of redefinition of the intellectual. Such a process, Bourdieu makes clear, should not be interpreted as a compensatory ideology by a social group under threat from particular developments in modern industrial society. He refers to Raymond Williams's discussion of the evolution of notions of the superior reality of art and the autonomous genius in the nineteenth century as coupled with such social changes. Williams's explanation of these ideas works within the illusion of the actors themselves, rather than explaining the source of that illusion itself. Bourdieu seeks to understand the ideology of intellectual autonomy and creative freedom in terms of the support provided for this stance by the structure of the intellectual field and its relative autonomy. His concept of the intellectual field renders all notions of the intellectuals' autonomy, the asocial role of the intellectuals and the superior nature of the intellectuals' work, historically specific.

Similarly Gramsci analysed the intellectuals as historical categories. He insisted that intellectuals as a social group cannot be defined by the nature of the work they do, just as manual workers cannot be defined by the work they do. All men are intellectuals, or philosophers, in the sense that we all think or use our intellect. Rather, he pointed out, if we want to talk of a social category of intellectuals then we need to refer to the social relations in which their work takes place, just as we do with the manual labourers or the workers. Gramsci referred to the intellectuals as a professional category with a specific function in society. This category results from the increasing division of labour and the social differentiation of types of work into tightly defined specialities.

Gramsci distinguished between two types of intellectuals: the organic and the traditional. Organic intellectuals are those created by the development of a particular social class, providing 'homogeneity and an awareness of its own function', he argued, 'not only in the economic but also in the social and political fields'.[19] The traditional intellectuals are constituted by those categories of intellectuals who are historically bound to a previous economic structure. Gramsci instanced the ecclesiastics as the most typical members of this category, but also referred to other groups such a scholars, scientists, non-ecclesiastical philosophers, artists and literary men. The self-assessment of intellectuals as a special group stems from this latter category. According to Gramsci the traditional intellectuals 'experience through an "*esprit de corps*" their uninterrupted historical continuity and their special qualification', on the basis of which 'they put themselves forward as autonomous and independent of the dominant social group'.[20]

Though Gramsci's distinction between traditional and organic intellectuals is an exceedingly fruitful one, his analysis of the traditional intellectuals' self-assessment suffers from a similar problem as Williams's discussion of the ideology of literary intellectuals. Gramsci accepted these intellectuals according to their own illusions about their insistence on their creative autonomy. A sense of historical continuity and special qualification forms an essential part of the ideology of the intellectual rather than a basis for its explanation. Traditional intellectuals as a category are those who are bound by their origins to an earlier social formation, but how they experience these roots is a question of ideology.

Gramsci, then, described intellectuals in terms of their historical formation as specialized categories. He analysed them all as being connected to a social group or class, but the most complex relationship is that between the dominant social group and the intellectuals. Fundamental to this latter relationship, he claimed, is the success of the dominant social group in co-opting the traditional intellectuals:[21]

> One of the most important characteristics of any group that is developing towards dominance is its struggle to assimilate and to conquer 'ideologically' the traditional intellectuals, but this assimilation and conquest is made quicker and more efficacious the more the group in question succeeds in simultaneously elaborating its own organic intellectuals.

Gramsci demonstrated the complexity of this process in a number of brief sketches of the development of the intellectuals in countries such as Italy, France, England, Germany and the United States of America. He pointed out that in America the level of civilization imported in the establishment of the white settlement led to the absence to a considerable degree of traditional intellectuals.

Both Gramsci's and Bourdieu's work suggests that notions of the superior vision and special qualification of intellectuals need to be analysed as part of an ideological language of the intellectuals themselves. Those espousing these notions about the intellectual would appear from Gramsci's analysis to be members of categories of intellectuals who have historical roots in earlier social formations. In Bourdieu's analysis they are members of categories of intellectuals who perceive themselves to have greatest claim to cultural legitimacy. The juxtaposition of these two analyses indicates a complex relationship between various categories of intellectuals and between intellectuals and different social classes.

**English intellectuals**

The literary intellectuals who have sustained the humanist tradition associated with the concept of culture constitute an anomaly amongst English intellectuals. They have eschewed the individualism and pragmatism characteristic of English social thought and contributed to a tradition of social analysis of humanistic concerns in a country where there has been a notable absence of critical, abstract theorizing about the nature of society. A number of writers have commented on this feature of the English literary intellectuals' ideas. For example, Nokes points out that the dominant tradition in English social thought has been reformist (advocating only piecemeal changes), so that no political notions, no positive ideas about what kind of society should be sought, have been forthcoming. Positive visions which went beyond suggestions for removing present injustices and anachronisms, says Nokes, were left to the literary men.[22]

Though there is general agreement about the reformist nature of English social thought, the question of its essential characteristics has provoked considerable debate. Perry Anderson is particularly responsible for engendering interest in this question with his essays 'Origins of the Present Crisis' (1964) and 'Components of the National Culture' (1969); and E. P. Thompson made one of the most significant contributions to the debate with his essay 'The Peculiarities of the English' (1965). Analyses of this question have become increasingly complex, embedded within detailed studies of the structure of the power bloc in nineteenth-century England.

In his essay 'Components of the National Culture' Anderson analyses the essential characteristic of English social thought in terms of the 'absent centre' of its cultural tradition:[23]

> Britain, then, may be defined as the European country which—uniquely—never produced either a classical sociology or a national Marxism. British culture was consequently characterized by an *absent centre*. Both classical sociology and Marxism were global theories of society, articulated in a totalizing conceptual system.

Anderson blames the lack of a total theory of society on the non-emergence of a powerful revolutionary movement of the working class, or more broadly, on the trajectory of the English social structure. English society was never challenged as a whole from within: the dominant class was never at any stage seriously threatened by working-class or radical movements. Any groups seeking change such as the Chartists, the Owenites, or the Utopian Socialists were of a reformist temper. Consequently, the dominant classes and their intellectuals never attempted, or were inclined to attempt, to forge a theory of the total structure of society. It was in their interest that such a problem not be posed so that any ensuing debate, and a possible challenge to their cultural hegemony, could be avoided.

Stedman Jones reinforces this type of analysis in his brief examination of the various responses of English intellectuals to the working class. He too argues that there was no perceived revolutionary threat from the working class in English history. At various stages there was a certain nervousness about the working class, but this class was only ever regarded as a 'social problem', so that the number of intellectuals who turned to, or passed through, socialism was comparatively few. The three main approaches to the 'problem' were: first, a stately reaffirmation of the values of liberal individualism; second, the Fabians with their call for greater state interference; and third, a reaction along lines similar to both the other two positions, these positions including aspects of the welfare state, but moulded in a liberal image. Stedman Jones characterizes English intellectuals in terms similar to Anderson's. Unlike their German or Italian counterparts, he says, English intellectuals have not been alienated in any significant manner from parliamentarist politics. Their social theory has been limited to detailed and concrete proposals for practical reform.[24]

Thompson condemns such comparisons with other countries as being 'inverted Podsnappery'. Referring to articles by Anderson and Tom Nairn, he argues that their analysis relies on 'an undisclosed model of Other Countries, whose typological symmetry offers a reproach to British exceptionalism'.[25] Thompson stresses the uniqueness of the English experience or French experience for any understanding of the history of class relations in these countries. Fundamental to Anderson's and Nairn's failure to understand the uniqueness of this experience, is their assumption that a bourgeois revolution never occurred in England because there was no climactic moment in English history such as the French Revolution of 1789. Thompson shows that the limitations of their historical model in this instance is indicative of their inability to grapple with the complex relations within the English ruling class.

Thompson draws connections between the different types of bourgeois revolutions in France and England and different intellectual approaches in these countries. 'The clarity of confrontation' in France, he suggests, predisposed the intellectuals 'towards systematizing and towards intellectual hierarchy'; in England, on the other hand, with the lack of any direct confrontation with authority the intellectuals were not encouraged to pursue any 'sustained efforts of synthesis' or to develop 'a systematic critique'.[26] But he departs from Anderson's and Nairn's accounts of the English intellectual with his insistence on the vigour of the tradition of dissent in England.

Thompson accuses Anderson and Nairn of failing to recognize the proliferation of intellectual enclaves in the eighteenth century. He points to the way in which these were largely formed outside the ancient universities or self-conscious metropolitan coteries. In a secular sense, he suggests, these enclaves offered a tradition of dissent. Contributions to this revolutionary inheritance came from the gentry, the artisans, the universities of Edinburgh and Glasgow, and the societies of various kinds that arose in the industrial centres throughout England.

These lacunae in Anderson's and Nairn's analyses indicate a fundamental preoccupation. They each draw on an image of the 'true intellectual'. In their criticisms of English intellectuals, in their comparisons with French and German intellectuals, and in their implicit assumptions about the nature of the tasks of an intelligentsia, Anderson and Nairn clearly rely on an idealized notion of the intellectuals. Thompson throughout his essays provides examples of this aspect of their writings and its severe limitations as an attempt to understand the relationship between intellectuals and the ruling class in England. The central weakness in Anderson's and Nairn's analyses of the intellectuals lies in their interpretation of the English ideology in terms of intellectual default. As Thompson points out, such an approach in examining British Labourism is 'as valueless as an account of Russia between 1924 and 1954 which attributes all to the vices of Marxism, or of Stalin himself'.[27] Anderson and Nairn fail to fully grasp the sociological or political context of ideas.

Both Anderson's and Nairn's essays suffer from an inadequate conception of hegemony. Robert Gray takes up this problem in his essay 'Bourgeois Hegemony in Victorian Britain' (1977) in which he provides a careful examination of the nature of the Victorian ruling class. He speaks of the intellectuals in terms of their role 'in the elaboration and reproduction of the dominant ideology' (though he stresses that the relationship between the ruling class and the intellectuals is by no means simple).[28] In accord with Thompson, Gray claims that the industrial bourgeoisie constituted the hegemonic fraction of the ruling class in Victorian England. The intellectuals most centrally involved in the organization of hegemony were 'the urban gentry' (a term employed by Stedman Jones) who were to be found, for example, 'as members of statistical societies and Royal Commissions, writers and readers of the quarterly press, organizers of charity and social discipline'.

Gray describes a hierarchy of intellectuals with the 'urban gentry' uppermost, but in which there were complex links between this group and those others who were not so specifically tied to the dominant fraction.

Contrary to the claim by Anderson and Stedman Jones about the intellectuals' response to the working class, Gray demonstrates a significant degree of social unrest in the nineteenth century. He depicts the urban gentry as playing a central role in 'the attempt to propagate an ideology common to the ruling class as a whole'.[29] The hegemonic influence of the ruling class was sought quite specifically through evangelical movements and the expansion of educational institutions after the social crisis of the 1830s and 1840s. But bourgeois hegemony was not easily won; Gray insists on the need to go beyond a crude social control framework in the understanding of hegemonic processes, as well as an awareness of the way in which bourgeois hegemony had to be renegotiated continually. Thus, to claim the lack of any significant working-class threat, perceived or not, is to attribute too great a stability to bourgeois hegemony in England.

Anderson and Stedman Jones pointed to the quiescence of the working class as the explanation of the particularistic and reformist nature of English social thought. This suggestion has been shown to be quite inadequate by writers such as Thompson and Gray. Leaving aside this question, there still remains the associated problem, posed by various writers, of the literary intellectuals' apparent break from this dominant intellectual ethos. The idea of culture as developed by this group expresses two major preoccupations: first, it provides a moral critique of fundamental trends in modern industrial society; and second, it is an attempt to offer a positive vision of society in which humane values will prevail.

Bradbury describes the literary men as providing a distinctive tradition in English social thought. The English writer in the nineteenth century, he says, was uniquely able to operate somewhere near the centre of the power structure of society, so that he felt able to intervene in the direction it took. The closeness of English literary men to power and rank, their relative concentration and confidence, Bradbury believes, is essentially peculiar to England in the nineteenth century.[30] But this explanation is not sufficient, for closeness to the ranks of power is a feature shared by English intellectuals in general.

Nokes suggests rather that the alternative tradition of social diagnosis and criticism furnished by literary intellectuals was strongly influenced by continental thought and its positive vision of social reconstruction.[31] Such an influence is indeed apparent in the nineteenth century. Both Carlyle and Coleridge were largely responsible for the establishment of a keen interest in continental ideas in literary circles, but this interest was by no means new, for previous lines of communication had been established over the centuries. These earlier networks had been weakened somewhat by the disillusionment and fear which arose in England after the French Revolution. The work of Carlyle and Coleridge established this interest on a firmer basis and for a much wider circle.

These connections suggest the '*esprit de corps*' of which Gramsci spoke. It is not so much that other intellectuals did not have these contacts with continental intellectuals, as the way in which the literary intellectuals experienced the connection. Gramsci described the traditional intellectuals' sense of historical continuity which they experience as an '*esprit de corps*'. The literary intellectuals in England in the nineteenth century articulated such a common interest with continental writers, as well as their predecessors. The poets of the first half of the nineteenth century expressed this most clearly as, for example, did Wordsworth in his poem *The Prelude* (1805). He spoke of the animating faith which holds:[32]

> The Poets, even as Prophets, each with each
> connected in a mighty scheme of truth.

The concern with broad social issues and a humanistic vision of society suggests that the English literary intellectuals can be understood in terms similar to Gramsci's traditional intellectuals. As such they can be contrasted with the urban gentry as organic intellectuals. The literary intellectuals' preoccupation with their role and their belief in their superior qualification to make judgments about society and the way in which members live their lives speak of the self-assessment of traditional intellectuals.

The concept of culture as developed by English literary intellectuals provided the central focus of an ideological language about the relationship between art and society. The language has articulated the way in which literary intellectuals live their relationship to the society. But in representing the image that this group and their craft have a special contribution to make to the society as an ideological notion, the concept of culture is not reduced to a self-conscious attempt to bolster the social importance or status of the literary intellectuals.

Similarly, in looking for the ideological and political limitations of the literary intellectuals' problematic, their role is not being reduced to some notion of the legitimating function of intellectuals. Their ideas in various ways contribute to the organization of hegemony in the society, but not in any direct manner. As Bourdieu stressed, the recognition of the relative autonomy of the intellectual field is fundamental to any understanding of the practice of intellectuals. Without such an insight an investigation into the ideological language of the literary intellectuals or the more general image of the traditional intellectuals would impugn them as suffering from delusions. The relative autonomy of the intellectual field in conjunction with the traditional position of the literary intellectuals in that field have provided fundamental support for their belief in the superior vision of the literary or artistic imagination.

# 2 Matthew Arnold

Writing in the mid-Victorian period in England, Matthew Arnold prefigured much of the social commentary undertaken by English literary intellectuals over the next hundred years. He developed a forceful concept of culture as the basis of his social critique and the focus of his social vision and wrote extensively on educational issues. The combination of these interests may appear on the surface to have been a matter of chance for him. Arnold was a poet of some pre-eminence in his early years, but was not able to earn sufficient by his writing to support himself and his prospective wife. Consequently, he accepted the offer to become one of Her Majesty's Inspectors of elementary schools, a job which he held from 1851 to 1886, two years before his death. Prior to this, however, Arnold was not without some interest in the problem of education, for his father, Thomas Arnold, was the well-known headmaster of Rugby School. This background was consolidated by Arnold's work as an HMI to which, although he found the job tiring and often frustrating, he gave considerable thought. Arnold became a prominent figure in this field, making several official trips to the continent to report to both the Newcastle Commission (1861) and the Taunton Commission (1866) on the state of education there, particularly in France and Germany; and after his retirement he was a witness before the Cross Commission (1886).

Concurrent with his success in this field, Arnold obtained a position of some prestige in the English literary world of the time. He held the Chair in Poetry at Oxford from 1857 to 1867, the customary ten years. He did not continue to write poetry to any great extent after 1858;[1] but turned to literary criticism, establishing many of the guidelines that continue to form that area of activity today. In the main, Arnold is remembered for his literary criticism rather than for his poetry. His poems, on the whole, lack any real inspiration or greatness. Nevertheless, Arnold was a significant literary figure in his time and has had a considerable impact on the tradition of English literary thought.

Arnold's activities in education and literature were combined by him to provide a rich background for his writing on social, cultural and educational matters. But his commitment to these various issues stemmed from a more fundamental basis than simply the accidental pattern of influences and experiences of his own life. Arnold was writing at a time of significant change in society. Debates about education were prominent particularly with the increasing interest of the state in compulsory education. The Education Act of 1870, which introduced education for all, formed part of a more general thrust by the state to intervene in the running of society. Accompanying this shift in the structure of society was the decreasing significance of the church and of religion in the lives of the general population. This development needs to be looked at in this light rather than as the straightforward result of the challenge of science. Scientific debates in the second half of the nineteenth century certainly added to the crisis of the church, but they only aggravated an already existing problem for that institution.

Changes such as these provide the context of Arnold's writings, just as do developments of a more particular nature in the intellectual world which similarly shaped the nature of his concerns. Though science's rising prominence had not yet altered significantly the structure of the intellectual field, some changes were heralded in the types of expectations placed on intellectuals from inside and outside their own domain. For example, pressures towards specialization and professionalism which were to dominate the academic world in the twentieth century offered some challenge to notions which Arnold wished to make axiomatic in his concept of culture. The mass market, too, as represented by large-circulation newspapers and publishing houses which were beginning to flourish placed new demands on the intellectuals. Such changes were embryonic at this stage, but Arnold was certainly sensitive to their potential impact and his ideas need to be examined with this context in mind.

**The state**

The concept of the state was pivotal in Arnold's writings about society. He believed it to be fundamental to democracy which, in accord with the intellectual climate of his time, Arnold claimed to be 'morally neutral':[2]

> This movement of democracy, like other operations of nature, merits properly neither blame or praise. Its partisans are apt to give it credit which it does not deserve, while its enemies are apt to upbraid it unjustly.

Arnold set himself the task of working out how this development could be best employed. On this issue he was very much in agreement with his father, Thomas Arnold. The latter believed that the state was the necessary mechanism to bring out the best in democracy and, indeed, that they implied each other.[3] In accord with these views, Matthew Arnold developed his idea of the state as the ameliorating force necessary in a democratic society.

Arnold argued that the aristocracy was once the force in society which provided guidance and a model to follow for the general population. The aristocracy of England, he claimed, had been the worthiest and most successful of all history. There had been, however, a great change in the aristocracy between the eighteenth and nineteenth century. They lost many of their public and conspicuous virtues: those of lofty spirit, commanding character and exquisite culture. The aristocracy, he lamented, were no longer able to provide true leadership for the rest of the society:[4]

> I cannot read the history of the flowering time of the English aristocracy, the eighteenth century, and then look at this aristocracy in our own century, without feeling that there has been a change. I am not now thinking of private and domestic virtues, of morality, of decorum. Perhaps with respect to these there has in this class, as in society at large, been a change for the better. I am thinking of those public and conspicuous virtues by which the multitude is captivated and led,—lofty spirit, commanding character, exquisite culture.

Arnold rejected Carlyle's suggestion that the aristocracy should rule because of its dignity and politeness. The serenity of the aristocracy, Arnold argued with his quiet sense of irony, is not, as with the Greeks, come from the practice of harmonizing ideas, but from never having had any ideas to trouble them.[5]

Arnold believed that it was vital to have a force in the society to provide leadership. Nations, he claimed, are great only when their members are in the service of an ideal higher than any ordinary man: 'The difficulty for democracy is, how to find and keep high ideals.'[6] Arnold saw the state as the only possible mechanism in a democracy which could both provide these ideals, and promote them in the society.

An additional factor which led Arnold to wish to discover an agency which would provide guidance for the society was his fear of what he called 'Americanization', a fear which was to be echoed in the writings of literary intellectuals over the next hundred years. Trilling described Arnold's fear in terms of a fear of vulgarity, loss of distinction and, above all, that eccentricity of thought which arises when each man, no matter what his training or gifts, may feel that the democratic doctrine of equality allows him to consider his ideas of equal worth with those of his neighbour.[7]

Arnold's apprehension about Americanization stemmed originally from de Tocqueville's warnings about democracy. De Tocqueville, writing about the nature of democracy in 1836, had considerable impact on English social thought in the nineteenth century. He used America as a case study to analyse the possible dangers and trends of democracy. Thereafter in English thought America or 'Americanization' was often seen as the epitome of what was most dangerous in the development of modern industrial society. This theme still appears in discussions today. J. S. Mill in the 1830s, reviewing de Tocqueville's volumes, suggested that the American people represented an exaggeration of the English middle class. Mill, on the basis of de Tocqueville's warnings, modified his faith in democracy. Similarly Saint-Beuve, Renan and Scherer foresaw a wave of Americanism in Europe.[8]

Consequently, while accepting and even welcoming the modern developments towards democracy, Arnold sought to refine and direct it. The state and culture should counteract democracy's weaknesses. They should guarantee that democracy was not just rule by the masses. Through them the masses would be transformed into people; they would be humanized. English democracy would then be one of dignity and intelligence. Arnold feared that:[9]

> When the inevitable course of events has made our self-government something really like that of America, when it has removed or weakened that security for national dignity, which we possessed in *aristocracy*, will the substitute of the *State* be equally wanting to us? If it is, then the dangers of America will really be ours; the dangers which came from the multitude being in power, with no adequate ideal to elevate or guide the multitude.

Arnold continued to return to the concept of Americanism at various stages throughout his writing. As Connell points out, it meant two things especially to Arnold, a tendency towards fragmentariness and an addiction to the banal.[10] Fragmentariness Arnold believed to be the result of an absence of a powerful authority. This phenomenon, he claimed, coincided with the popular doctrine of doing as one likes and a lack of interest in any strict standards of excellence. Consequently, Arnold believed that the society in which he lived was restricted to a concern for the banal. Arnold saw this as a diminution of the stature of man's spirit. Culture is the opposite force, it is the development of man's spirit. The state should promote and facilitate this development.

Arnold's attack on Americanization typified the limits of his critique of society. He attacked the cultural degeneration of this social form as he perceived it without considering the extent to which it stemmed from the basic structure of that society. In so doing he evaded similar questions about his own society and the direction which it appeared to be pursuing. This evasion was by no means deliberate or conscious, but stemmed from the basic problematic underlying all Arnold's writings. His social analysis and social vision were confined to questions of the cultural and moral health of society and its cultural regeneration. He eluded any confrontation with questions about the fundamental structure of society.

The limits of Arnold's concerns were further demonstrated by his attempts to discuss the concept of the state. He relied principally on Burke's definition of the state as '*the nation in its collective and corporate character*'.[11] He was more preoccupied with the question of who would administer and govern the state. The middle class, he claimed, were those most fitted for the task. Once they had been transformed by education to a higher culture, they would be able to rule by means of their best selves. They would be elevated by their contact with the state: given positions of honour they would act with honour.

Arnold avoided any deeper consideration of the nature of the state and its powers through his use of the vague terms, 'best self' and 'right reason'. Their nebulous, ill-defined qualities enabled him to conflate 'the best self' of the middle class with 'the best self' of the nation. His arguments in this case bear resemblance to the German romantic concept of the state developed in the nineteenth century. The 'best self' of the nation, it was claimed, provides a lasting standard in accordance with which the decisions of the state can be made, thereby operating within the framework of 'right reason'. Arnold's discussion of the state was based on a similar claim that the state is the representative of 'best self' and 'right reason'.

Critics of Arnold's writings on the state have suggested that he was confused about how the state would be administered and how it should be defined. Connell argues that Arnold's concept of the state was not formed on the basis of a philosophical theory of the state; rather, it was a practical assessment of the current situation. Connell suggests that Arnold's view of the state can be interpreted as simply a desire to see in England an Academy, not merely of literature but of life. The Academy's function would be educative. It would set ever-advancing standards to form a unifying basis for society and to act as an inspiration towards the perfection which, Arnold believed, should be the goal of all human endeavour. Connell argues that this is the only view of the state which can be salvaged from Arnold's work. He dismisses Arnold's argument that the middle class will be 'elevated' by contact with the state as not very convincing, and Arnold's concepts of 'right reason' and 'enlargement of the mind' as too vague.[12]

These criticisms of Arnold's concept of the state are, on the whole, valuable, but to dismiss these parts of Arnold's concept and to opt for the interpretation outlined by Connell, would be invalid. Arnold's philosophical conception of the state was poorly worked out, but it was, nevertheless, essential to his thought. Similarly, his concept of right reason, though difficult to comprehend, was fundamental to his ideas.[13]

Trilling adopted a different position to that of Connell. He suggested that Arnold's concept of the state was rather like Plato's concept of the Republic. Arnold would not have agreed with such an interpretation, for he would have argued that his attempt to draw up a theory of the state had practical intentions. But Trilling claimed that his attempt does not stand up on logical or political grounds. Arnold's failure is typical of all liberal attempts to form a theory of the state. He could not reconcile questions of power and reason and had to resort finally to 'the Socrates in every man's breast'. Consequently, Trilling argued, it is more useful to see Arnold's concept of the state as a type of Platonic myth. Such an approach makes it possible to judge his notion of the state and the values and attitudes it embodies. 'In these respects', Trilling suggested, 'Arnold's myth is still fertile and valuable—and morally inescapable.'[14]

Trilling's interpretation of Arnold's work on the state is helpful. By seeing Arnold's concept of the state in terms of a Platonic myth, Arnold's notions such as right reason become more acceptable. Their vagueness is part of the general looseness of the theory. Arnold was not concerned to provide a complete model of the state.[15] As Trilling pointed out, the ultimate solution to socio-political questions for Arnold was to rely on the Socrates in every man's breast, and Arnold's belief in the possibility of the middle class governing according to their best self rested finally on this hope.

But neither Connell nor Trilling acknowledges the extent to which Arnold's view of the state was not an uncommon one for that time. His claim for the identity of the general interest and the interests of the middle class formed part of the general thrust to legitimate that class as the hegemonic class in society. The Benthamites were among the first to articulate this move, rejecting the aristocratic class and their claim to be the 'natural' leaders, leaders by birth right, of the society. The middle class were spoken of, instead, as representatives of the nation, rather than having any sacred role to be leaders. Adopting this framework of thought, the vagueness of Arnold's terms allowed him to conflate 'the best self of the nation' with 'the best self of the middle class'. Arnold cannot be accused of any particular illogicality in his discussion of the state; he was expounding on a notion which was prevalent in the society at the time.

Arnold's writings on the state were typical of his approach. They were unsystematic and without a clear or consistent model of society. He analysed some of the major ills of the society as he perceived them at that time and provided some suggestions as to possible directions for remedying these ills. He did not attempt to work out any systematic solutions for these problems. Similarly, Arnold analysed the class structure of English society in the manner more of a poet than a social analyst. He produced a name for each of the three classes he examined: the aristocratic class were the Barbarians; the middle class, the Philistines; and the working class, the Populace. The names indicated the major characteristics of the classes as Arnold saw them. There was a time, he claimed, when the aristocracy was solicitous for the good of their country and its people. At the same time they took it for granted that they were the supreme judges of what constituted this and how to arrange the conditions necessary for it. They were people in '*the grand style*', according to Arnold. But, the superiority of the upper class was no longer so great; nor was the willingness of others to recognize that superiority so ready.[16]

Arnold further criticized the aristocracy on the basis of its lack of interest in ideas. It was only concerned with facts and had lost all its 'culture'. Although Arnold acknowledged that it might recover its interests in culture and intellectual life, his main hopes rested with the middle class. The aristocracy had a basic inaptitude for ideas which made it unsuitable for leadership of the nation; whereas the middle class was characterized by mental fervour. 'The era of aristocracies is over'; he claimed, 'nations must now stand or fall by the intelligence of their middle class and their people'.[17]

The puritanism of our English middle class, Arnold claimed, had kept them back from the pursuit of perfection by casting their spirit in a rigid mould. He called for the establishment of schools for the middle class which would develop the desirable characteristics of a cultured group; their education should aim to develop 'largeness of soul and personal dignity'.[18] Arnold's faith in them was based on what he believed were their chief characteristics of energy and honesty, but he was very critical of the hold which the middle class had over England in his time. In the series of letters called 'Friendship's Garland' (1871), he attacked many of the weaknesses of the middle class as he saw them. Using the persona of Arminius, a Prussian visiting England, Arnold was able to make severe criticisms of the middle class in a tongue-in-cheek manner. English society, he claimed, is continually ruled by the middle class which lives by irrationality. Their emphasis on work precludes any interest in ideas or thought. Arnold complained that, 'your middle class seems to have its sense blunted for any stimulus besides, except religion; it has a religion, narrow, unintelligent, repulsive'.[19] The English middle class, he continued, by the nineteenth century were preoccupied with matters of wealth, and neglected the other two main factors of modern life: love of intelligence and love of beauty. With great enjoyment, Arnold (in the voice of his friend, Arminius) caricatured this class:[20]

> Your middle class man thinks it the highest pitch of development and civilisation when his letters are carried twelve times a day from Islington to Camberwell, and from Camberwell to Islington, and if railway trains run to and fro between them every quarter of an hour. He thinks it is nothing that the trains only carry him from an illiberal, dismal life at Islington to an illiberal, dismal life at Camberwell; and the letters only tell him that such is the life there.

Arnold's view of the lower class, or the populace, is difficult to understand. He was ambivalent about his feelings towards the working class: at times he called them 'raw' and 'less enviable looking', 'lacking in humanity',[21] and at other times, he claimed that the members of this class exhibited wider and more liberal sympathies than those above them.[22] Further, despite his work as one of Her Majesty's Inspectors of Schools, a job which gave him considerable opportunity to observe and think about elementary education, Arnold appears to have been confused about how the masses should be educated. He claimed at one stage that the main aim of the education of the lower classes should be to develop gentleness and humanity.[23] Yet, he also criticized popular literature for teaching down to the mass. Culture, he said, works differently:[24]

> it does not try to teach down to the level of inferior classes. . . . It seeks to do away with classes; to make the best that has been thought and known in the world current everywhere. . . .

Arnold's attitude towards the lower classes is even harder to fathom if we look at his essay 'The Bishop and the Philosopher'. He was accused by his contemporaries of advancing the argument in this work that to bring knowledge to the masses was a crime.[25] Indeed, such an interpretation of Arnold's position can be derived from the essay. He claimed that knowledge and truth are not attainable by the great mass of the human race at all. Yet, in the same paragraph, Arnold indicated that once the great mass is softened and humanized, they too would be able to acquire knowledge and truth.[26]

The basic conflict in Arnold's position appears to be between his liberal commitment to the idea of equality and his basic fear, or nervousness, about the masses. This was to be a constant feature of liberal social thought in England over the next hundred years. Arnold's commitment to the idea of equality was expressed strongly and clearly in *Culture and Anarchy*. He argued that culture is a social idea and that men of culture are the true apostles of equality. Elsewhere he asked: 'Can it be denied, that to live in a society of equals tends in general to make a man's spirits expand, and his faculties work easily and actively. . . .'[27] Yet the very title of his essay *Culture and Anarchy* illustrates one of his main preoccupations. He expressed commitment to the French Revolution, to the idea of equality, yet at the same time was apprehensive about the consequences. He feared the masses.

This fear surfaced with, or at least was exacerbated by, the Hyde Park riots of 1866; and it was shared by many Victorian liberals. With the fear of the reality of the society in which he lived hanging over him, Arnold readily adopted ideas about the necessity of initial humanization of the masses. As can be seen in his writings on education, Arnold accepted one of the principal arguments for the need for popular education at that time. Couched in terms of the need to humanize or civilize the masses, education was turned to as a major means of ensuring the incorporation and control of the working class.[28]

Arnold has been diagnosed as a reactionary by a number of authors. Trilling examined the evidence for these claims in various aspects of Arnold's work. For example, he claimed, through the vagueness of his theory at a time when the political consciousness of the working class seems to have increased, Arnold failed to acknowledge the very real feelings for the state-idea which the proletariat possessed. Similarly, Arnold passed over the remarkable sense of Europeanism of the working class, which, until frightened by the Commune of 1871, had had a real sense of internationalism.[29] In addition, Trilling commented on Arnold's intellectual tradition, which, although it proved nothing, suggests much. He referred to Arnold's connection with the romantic prophets of philosophical reaction, Burke, Coleridge and Wordsworth; and further, to the influence of Plato and Aristotle, which could scarcely make Arnold a partisan of democratic hope. Finally, Trilling suggested, Arnold's own coupling of democracy with Protestantism, and of Protestantism with anarchy, and his placing of authority with reason, suggest reactionary strains.

However, Trilling acknowledged that while Arnold worked from the tradition of Burke, he also belonged in the tradition of Rousseau. Rousseau's 'general will' can be seen to have similarities with Arnold's concept of the 'best self' of a nation. Like Rousseau, said Trilling, Arnold failed to solve the problem of the self in relation to society, a problem which can only be solved in absolutist terms, for example those developed by Marx. But Trilling's main argument against calling Arnold a reactionary was to point to Arnold's actions. He examined the four political issues which Arnold discussed in *Culture and Anarchy*.[30] Arnold's concern for the poor and his wish to give them a 'fair chance', Trilling claimed, gave sinew to his theory and rescued him from charges of vagueness and reactionariness.

Other writers have seen Arnold's development in a different light. Walcott argues that Arnold's position developed from one of benevolent rational authoritarianism to one far more accepting of the principle of democracy.[31] There is some evidence to support this view in Arnold's increasing estrangement from Carlyle.[32] Arnold did not trust in the benevolence of the 'hero' as did Carlyle; yet he never shook off his fear of the brutishness of democracy in later years. He continued to warn against the Americanization of Europe throughout all his work. In addition, Arnold was always concerned about the dangers of the state, as he demonstrated in his criticism of France, where he believed the state had too much control.[33]

Rather than interpreting Arnold's political development as one of a steady progression towards democratic theory, it appears more useful to view Arnold as moving between two traditions as Trilling suggested. On issues such as reason and authority, and the individual and society, Arnold found these traditions difficult to resolve. His only solution was to rely on the goodness of the individual and more generally, on his conception of culture; the ideal which leads man beyond himself so that the conflicting demands of the individual and society are subordinated to higher concerns.

## Culture

Arnold's work on the concept of culture is perhaps the best known of his social and educational writings. In his own time he was dubbed 'the prophet of culture'.[34] Very early in Arnold's published work he claimed a need for culture. In his first report as one of Her Majesty's Inspectors of elementary schools in 1852, he complained of the lack of mental 'culture' in pupil teachers. He called for the requirement that pupil teachers should study portions of the 'best English authors'. This type of education, Arnold contended, would tend to elevate and humanize pupils. The prevalent type of schooling, he claimed, placed too great a store on information.[35]

Arnold continued to develop these ideas, their most clear expression being given in *Culture and Anarchy*. He claimed that culture was the pursuit and study of perfection. He argued that there are three aspects to perfection: that it be harmonious, general, and carried out in action. Culture is the development of all sides of human nature. Arnold recommended:[36]

> culture as the great help out of our present difficulties; culture being a pursuit of our total perfection by means of getting to know, on all the matters which most concern us, the best which has been thought and said in the world; and through this knowledge, turning a stream of fresh and free thought upon our stock notions and habits, which we now follow staunchly but mechanically, vainly imagining that there is a virtue in following them staunchly which makes up for the mischief of following them mechanically.

The above statement reveals three main features of Arnold's concept of culture: first, that it is a social idea; second, the notion of getting to know the best that has been thought and said; and third, the need to turn a stream of fresh and free thought upon our stock notions and habits.

Arnold emphasized in the early chapters of *Culture and Anarchy* that culture is concerned with the general perfection of mankind. Unless the individual promotes this general perfection, his own perfection will be stunted. Arnold was particularly concerned to stress this feature of his concept of culture in order to counter criticisms of dandyism levelled at him by contemporaries, such as Frederic Harrison, the social critic, and the *Daily Telegraph* of the time. Arnold claimed:[37]

> there is of culture another view, in which not solely the scientific passion, the sheer desire to see things as they are, natural and proper in an intelligent being, appears as the ground of it. There is a view in which all the love of our neighbour, the impulses towards action, help, and beneficence, the desire for removing human error, clearing human confusion, and diminishing

human misery, the noble aspiration to leave the world better and happier than we found it—motives eminently such as are called social,—come in as part of the grounds of culture, and the main and the pre-eminent part.

But towards the end of the book, Arnold appeared to change his stance. He argued that culture should lead us to adopt a position of inaction. Describing a number of social actions connected with issues arising from parliamentary bills or policies, Arnold claimed that such reforms led more to injustice than justice. On this basis Arnold recommended cultivated inaction, while we pursue for ourselves the frame of mind more able to suggest schemes for fruitful reform. Arnold concluded that men of culture should adopt a similar role as that of Socrates who, by his disinterested play of consciousness upon 'stock notions and habits' provided an excellent example for the rest of society. In this manner, Arnold claimed, he had an incomparable influence. Men of culture if they were to follow this example, would be the sovereign educators: although their influence may not be felt now, it would be in the immediate future.[38]

It seems, then, that Arnold changed his position, for at first he claimed that social concerns were a part of culture. Yet, later in the same work, he recommended that action should not be undertaken until one has *become* a man of culture. And even then it appears, one should not engage in direct action. Having discounted his critics at the beginning of his work, Arnold appears to have failed to carry the argument through to the end.

Arnold's position adopted at the end of *Culture and Anarchy* faces a major difficulty. He claimed that reform should not be undertaken until the proper frame of mind has been developed. Yet it is difficult to discern when, in Arnold's opinion, this frame of mind would be considered to have been achieved. There seems to be a disparity between Arnold's personal policy and his theoretical position: Arnold himself engaged quite significantly in social action, but argued for cultivated inaction.[39] It would seem that he did not have the patience which he recommended to others.[40]

It is crucial to recognize that Arnold did not equate culture with 'the best which has been thought and said'. This was the basis of culture, but not an end in itself. To accept such a view would be to confine culture to a notion of the arts, the very concept of culture which Arnold set out to dispute in *Culture and Anarchy*. He argued instead that we should study the best which has been thought and said, so that we might critically examine our thoughts and ideas.

Arnold's notion of studying the best which has been thought and said has been criticized frequently. His contemporary, Frederic

Harrison, pointed out that Arnold spoke of the *best* ideas, the *best* knowledge, the *best* principles, but provided no means by which we could recognize these.[41] In other words, Arnold failed to acknowledge that disputes occur about what exactly is the best which has been thought and said in the world.

Some indication of how Arnold believed such disputes could be settled, can be found in his discussion of the relative merits of literature and science. He argued that if he was forced to make a decision in favour of studying either literature (humane letters) or science, he would choose the former. The criteria which Arnold provided in this case were first, that 'letters will call out their being at more points, will make them live more'; and second, the humane letters and art are a 'criticism of life by gifted men'.[42] Moreover, Arnold compared the intellectual powers of science and literature in terms of their access to truth. Poetry, he asserted, 'thinks emotionally' and as such enables us a greater grasp on the truth than science which relies solely on our logical thought.[43] The best which has been thought and said is, then, that which enables us to draw on all our intellectual and emotional resources to throw out those ideas based purely on habit.

In making these claims Arnold was defining the role of the literary intellectual in society as existing at two levels. In terms of their craft or their products, they provided the material for others to study—the 'criticism of life by gifted men'—in order critically to examine their own thoughts and ideas. But at a second level, the literary intellectuals were the obvious embodiment of Arnold's men of culture through whose example others would be led to pursue culture: they were the modern Socrates, the mentors of their age.

Arnold argued that the study of the best which has been thought and said induces flexibility of thought. He employed the term 'Hellenism' to signify this aspect of culture. Hellenism is the turning of 'a stream of fresh and free thought on our stock notions and habits', it is the concern to 'see things as they really are'. To this Arnold added the concept of 'Hebraism', whose chief concerns are conduct and obedience. Arnold argued that the aim of both Hellenism and Hebraism is the same, but they pursue this aim by different courses: 'The governing idea of Hellenism is *spontaneity of consciousness*; that of Hebraism, *strictness of conscience*'.[44] Arnold believed that at various times in our history we emphasize one or other of these modes of action and that in his own time, Christianity promoted Hebraism in the society. Arnold was concerned to extol the virtues of Hellenism to redress the balance, for he claimed that culture calls for both Hebraism and Hellenism to be of equal importance. Hellenism's lack of prominence was responsible for the confusion and anarchy which he observed in the society at that time. The over-emphasis on Hebraism had led to conduct being considered as an end in itself, just as there was a general preoccupation with an obviously more instrumental attitude: for example, in questions of manufacture, population increase and religious organization.

Alexander argues that Hellenism really meant for Arnold all his hopes for the perfection of mankind.[45] Hebraism is scepticism about the capacity of men for perfection and his consciousness of their inherent weakness; Hellenism is a positive ideal. The ideal of culture in *Culture and Anarchy* is the ideal of Hellenism; Hebraism merely provides the groundwork. Such an interpretation of Arnold's notion of culture is inadequate, for it fails to recognize that Arnold claimed to place a greater emphasis on Hellenism only because of its serious absence in English society at that time. If Hebraism was lacking, rather than Hellenism, then it would follow, from Arnold's argument, that he would have been more concerned to place Hebraism in a positive light. In some senses, by stressing the forces of Hellenism in his concept of culture, Arnold was reacting to the strong puritanism and earnestness of the early Victorian period which his father epitomized. But his ideas need also to be looked at in the context of his religious commitment. When Arnold first formulated his ideas on culture at the end of the 1860s, he displayed very little intellectual interest in examining religious issues. In *Culture and Anarchy* he claimed that 'culture goes beyond religion'. Culture is the harmonious development of all sides of human nature, whereas religion looks at conduct only.[46] Seven years later in *Literature and Dogma* (1876) culture had been very much reduced in stature. In this instance Arnold claimed that conduct or Hebraism, which is religion's province, is 'three-fourths of human life'; and culture, or Hellenism, is 'one-fourth'.[47] Culture was no longer concerned with development of all sides of human nature, combining both Hebraism and Hellenism, but only with the latter aspect of human nature.

In *Culture and Anarchy* Arnold was concerned to find a force which would unify the society and give guidance to the individual's life. He claimed that religion should be subservient to culture at this stage in his writings because he believed the middle class, his target audience, to be too preoccupied with religion and its puritanical outlook on life. But by the late 1870s Arnold was becoming increasingly concerned with the need to promote religion in English society.

The shift in Arnold's ideas can be explained at a number of different levels. In personal terms, his letters show a growing commitment to his father and an awareness of a marked similarity between himself, as he grew older, and his father, who had been a very religious man.[48] And at the societal level, science was threatening the whole basis of religion. Darwin's *Origin of Species* was published in 1859 and, as interest in his work gained momentum, the implications for religion began to be discussed. The considerable interest shown in the debates between figures such as T. H. Huxley (who was dubbed Darwin's bulldog) and Bishop Wilberforce demonstrate the extent of this challenge to religion.

Arnold adopted a distinctly secularized view of religion in which he claimed that the Bible should be read as a work of poetry and as an attempt to lead us to righteousness, rather than as a work embodying great truths. To stop the masses from being increasingly sceptical about the Bible and its religion, Arnold argued, we must change our approach. We must stop forming our statements on the basic assumption about the Great Personal First Cause and talk instead of something that is verifiable. He suggested that we should adopt the attitude that: 'There rules an enduring Power, not ourselves, which makes for righteousness, and *therefore* study your Bible and learn to obey this.' The Bible's peculiar value rests, Arnold claimed, on the power of its poetry to make us feel its message.[49]

Arnold's secularized view of religion formed part of a general attempt to maintain a dominant position for religion where increasingly its traditional outlook was losing its hold. His change of focus to the questions of religion in society suggests not only a shift in his central concerns, but also demonstrates the seriousness with which he took his role of prophet. He believed that he could be an important source of opinion and authority in society, providing guidance in all areas of social problems of the age, including religion. It also indicates that he was aware that there were threats to the centrality of the social vision which he espoused. Arnold perceived these threats to come primarily from modern industrial society, its emphasis on individualism and lack of concern for standards of excellence. The challenge to religion by the scientific world view was a further threat to the values, attitudes and way of perceiving reality which formed Arnold's vision.

Arnold in his ideas on both culture and religion was concerned to promote the view that man should be committed to something beyond himself. In religion this commitment is to God, and He is the embodiment of the ideal of perfection which Arnold developed in his ideas on culture. There are a number of different interpretations of what it means, according to Arnold, for the individual to pursue this ideal of perfection. Alexander argues that he was concerned with the Goethean ideal of seeking a complete and harmonious development of one's nature.[50] Connell suggests that Arnold's concept of perfection was to develop the potentialities of each individual to their fullest extent.[51] Such a notion is akin to the romantic ideal, developed, for example, by Rousseau. But Bantock argues that Arnold's whole preoccupation with culture was a reaction to the romantic idea that the source of enlightenment lay within the self. Culture, he claims, is a reassertion of the classical ideal of perfection, which looks to an external discipline.[52]

As can be seen, it is extremely difficult to interpret Arnold's conception of the ideal of perfection. The following passage illustrates the difficulty of adopting any one interpretation:[53]

> culture may with advantage continue to uphold steadily its ideal of human perfection; that this is *an inward spiritual activity, having for its characters increased sweetness, increased light, increased life, increased sympathy.*

Such a statement could be interpreted as supporting any one of the suggested interpretations. Nor does Arnold's intellectual background provide us with any suggestions on this matter. In his notebooks, Arnold provided indications of influences from the romantic tradition, but also from the classical humanism of the Renaissance and its interest in Greek thought, particularly Plato.

At one stage Arnold did make an explicit connection between the concept of perfection and the individual attaining his fullest development.[54] Yet in *Culture and Anarchy* this notion of perfection does not appear to have been adequate. Arnold used the Greek word EVØVIA to clarify what he meant by perfection.[55] This word is defined as: In accordance with some standard of natural goodness or rightness. Arnold went on to say that perfection is the development of all sides of human nature, to be guided by a standard of harmonious perfection. It is perfection which combines beauty and intelligence, or sweetness and light; it is a finely tempered nature.[56] The term 'nature' when it is used in this context does not mean that which exists in a primitive state, but is an ideal about what man can be.

A further suggestion that Arnold developed his concept of perfection along the lines of a more classical ideal is provided by Williams's discussion of Arnold's relationship to the tradition of Newman and Coleridge. Arnold's concept of culture was developed within this tradition. It is a tradition, according to Williams, which puts up an ideal of perfection against the utilitarian concept of education. In Newman's words, the ideal of perfection is:[57]

> There is a physical beauty and a moral: there is a beauty of person, there is a beauty of our moral being, which is natural virtue; and in like manner there is a beauty, there is a perfection,

> of the intellect. There is an ideal perfection in these various subject-matters, towards which individual instances are seen to rise, and which are the standards for all instances whatever.

The notion of perfection developed by Newman, which Arnold also seems to have adopted in at least some of his writing, is a demanding ideal. Culture is the pursuit of an unattainable ideal consisting of suprapersonal values. The way in which Arnold sought to have this ideal recognized was through education.

**Education**

In the most simple terms, Arnold believed education to be the promotion of culture.[58] He was opposed to the instrumental view of education. Education, he claimed, is a humanizing process whose aim coincides with that of culture: the pursuit of perfection. Culture, however, differs from education in that its goal is wider. Culture is not only the pursuit of perfection, it is the concern that perfection should prevail.

At the organizational level, Arnold claimed that education was the province of the state. He argued vehemently against prevalent '*laissez-faire*' attitudes towards education. In pragmatic terms he pointed out that if the state did not take a hand in education, England would soon lag even further behind Germany in industrial matters.

A programme of universal education is basic to the economic progress of the country.[59] In more general terms, Arnold also claimed that education performs the fundamental function of the state, for it serves to unify and humanize the society. As a humanizing process education would counteract the interest in the banal which characterizes 'Americanism'. On these grounds, Arnold argued that the continuing suspicion of state involvement in education must be overthrown. Jealousy and suspicion of state action may have once been prudent, but it no longer remained so under the prevailing circumstances in England.[60]

Of primary importance to Arnold was the education of the middle class, for it was they whom he viewed as the hope of modern civilization. The existing academies, he claimed, were totally inadequate. The establishment of secondary schools for this class was an urgent task, in order to develop in them that 'fine culture' or 'living intelligence' essential to their role as leaders of the nation. State organization of secondary schools would be the only way to provide an effective system of education, so that England could attain the level of secondary instruction already given to the middle class in schools on the continent. In addition, by giving the schools a national character, they would achieve a greatness and nobleness of spirit which the middle class themselves would be unable to provide, for they lacked these characteristics as yet.[61]

The existing schools for the middle class, the academies, were inadequate, Arnold claimed, on a number of accounts. They were lacking in any true appreciation of the idea of systematic knowledge and science and were generally weak intellectually.[62] They failed too to give students social or governing qualities. The public schools were the only educational institutions in England of which Arnold approved. He wished the middle class to receive a similar type of education as these schools provided.

Arnold extended his criticism of middle-class education to the state of the universities. Referring to Oxford and Cambridge, Arnold called the universities of England 'hauts lycées'.[63] The standard in England was such, he claimed, that the degree of the Bachelor of Arts was only equivalent to the final year of schooling in Germany and France. Students were not being brought into contact with first-rate teachers in English universities. In 1868, therefore, Arnold made the plea, 'Organize your secondary and your superior instruction'.[64]

By this time Arnold believed that the principle of state involvement in popular education had been accepted and he had turned much of his attention to the education of the middle classes in secondary and tertiary ('superior') instruction.[65] But he did continue to write extensively on elementary education. An issue which particularly concerned him in this area was the introduction in 1862 of the Revised Code, which was to have a considerable impact on the type of education offered by the elementary schools in England. Under this system the schools received payments according to the performance of their pupils in the 3Rs: 'payment by results'. It was the task of inspectors to test all pupils and determine the payment.

Arnold brought out an anonymous pamphlet in 1862 called 'The Twice Revised Code', in which he viciously attacked the Code and its originator, Robert Lowe.[66] Arnold criticized the Code initially for having introduced mechanical instruction into the schools. Teachers seeking good results concentrated on teaching the 3Rs and employed rote methods of teaching. Pupils came to know only what was set for them and even this they knew only in a very shallow manner. In addition, Arnold was bitter about the way in which the Code had changed the Inspector's role. The Inspector was no longer seen as a guide and advisor. His function was merely one of examiner; he had no time to fulfil any other role. In his report for 1863, Arnold outlined the two main effects of the Revised Code as he saw them: first the change in the Inspector's role, and second, the effect on the higher intellectual life or culture of the school.[67]

On his return to England from the continent in 1865, Arnold was struck by further changes in the schools. He saw a significant decline in the morale of teachers and pupil-teachers and a reduction in the numbers of teachers in the profession. Arnold had always been very concerned with the welfare of teachers, for from them he felt he detected a desire for a better culture. This threat to the teaching force in England, which he attributed to the introduction of the Revised Code, was consequently most distressing for him.[68]

Arnold's letters to his mother reveal the considerable thought he gave to the way in which he should fight against the Revised Code. He chose a path of political expediency in which he did not seek the complete abolition of payment by results because, as he argued before the Cross Commission in 1886, 'with the tastes of England' at the time of 1862 it 'might have been a good thing'.[69] He relied instead on the code being beaten in parliament by the actions particularly of Spencer Walpole, the Conservative Home Secretary.[70]

Arnold's participation in the fight against the Revised Code exemplified his concern to act in accordance with the principle of the 'Zeitgeist', as he called it. His commitment to this idea led him to modify and revise his position on issues which deeply concerned him for the sake of political expediency.[71] In his desire to get things done, Arnold did not always stay to consider the inconsistencies in his position. Such an approach is indicative of the way in which Arnold unhesitatingly operated within the power structure of his society, despite his claims for the need for 'cultivated inaction' in *Culture and Anarchy*. The vagueness of his concepts in his writings on culture facilitated his stepping from the role of prophet to active social reformer without confronting the inconsistencies or actual conflicts within his different works.

Arnold was particularly distressed by the way in which the Revised Code promoted an increased emphasis on learning by rote. He did not believe that such a technique could further the cause of culture in the schools. Yet paradoxically, it would seem, he favoured 'learning by heart'. The distinction in Arnold's mind appears to have been mainly one of the content: learning by rote applies to the 3Rs; learning by heart to familiarity with masterpieces. Arnold argued that passages of classical poetry chosen carefully should be learnt by all students: 'To learn by heart first-rate pieces of poetry and of prose must surely do a child good'.[72] Arnold criticized the recitation of lessons in the schools because insufficient care was given to the choice of passages to be learnt. Nor were pupils taught enough about the sense and allusions of what they recited. Recitation, he claimed, should be turned into a literature lesson. Learning by heart, for Arnold, was an important way of introducing pupils to the 'best which has been thought and said'.[73]

Bantock criticizes Arnold's belief in the importance of learning poetry by heart. He is dubious whether, if Arnold had known then all that we know now in learning theory, he would have favoured rote learning at all. Such a hypothetical point seems hardly justified as a criticism of Arnold's ideas. Bantock's general criticism of Arnold, which he makes following on from this point, is more interesting. He suggests that Arnold should have been more observant in schools he was inspecting. If he had, says Bantock, he would have gained a better understanding of the child's mind and would have seen many of the bad features of education at that time. Such observation was not beyond the Victorians, Bantock claims, as George Eliot has shown us. There is little apparent overflow, he concludes, between Arnold, the Inspector and Arnold, the social critic. Arnold never saw the system as a whole, nor made the connection between the state of the nation's education and the state of its culture.[74]

Although it may be true that Arnold showed less observation and insight than George Eliot, we should note in his defence that the rate at which Arnold had to work scarcely gave him time to be the sensitive observer that George Eliot was. His letters reveal, particularly after the introduction of the Revised Code, how little time he had to sit and observe in the schools. Visits to the schools were brief and his time was taken up with official duties, a fact much bewailed by him. Nor does the second criticism made by Bantock appear to be justified. Arnold was acutely aware of the importance of the nation's education to the state of its culture. He showed this in all his arguments for the need for a better middle-class education. Similarly, Arnold believed that elementary education was of fundamental importance to the humanization of the masses, a process which he saw as being a preliminary to the pursuit of culture. Arnold argued that these two areas of education were indispensable for the improvement of the general culture of the society. He was particularly concerned that public instruction should be undertaken in the area of secondary education so that we might have 'a cultured, liberalized, ennobled, transformed middle class'. Arnold was optimistic that this principle would eventually be accepted and implemented:[75]

> Children of the future, whose day has not yet dawned, you, when that day arrives, will hardly believe what obstructions were long suffered to prevent its coming! You who, with all your

> faults, have neither the aridity of aristocracies, nor the narrow-mindedness of middle classes, you, whose power of simple enthusiasm is your great gift, will not comprehend how progress towards man's best perfection—the adorning and ennobling of his spirit—should have been reluctantly undertaken; how it should have been for years and years retarded by barren commonplaces, by worn-out clap-traps.

An uplifting vision, indeed!

# 3 Arnold's contemporaries

In the period 1850 to 1890, social, cultural and educational issues were discussed by intellectuals from a wide variety of backgrounds. The problem of the quality of life in modern civilization, or 'the condition of England question' as it was sometimes called, which formed the focus of the social critique of literary intellectuals such as Matthew Arnold, also preoccupied many scientists, utilitarians, artists and socialists.[1] Never again was there to be such a wide range of perspectives on this problem.

The idea of the professional or the expert was not yet dominant in the English intellectual world. Scientists, for example, did not consider it at all improper to discuss issues concerned with the quality of life. They did not trouble themselves with questions about whether they were qualified to speak on such matters, nor whether they were encroaching on someone else's domain. Moves to promote specialization and professionalism as a way of clearly defining boundaries between areas of intellectual endeavour were beginning to impinge on the universities particularly, but they had not yet established definite expectations about the intellectuals' mode of approach to social or cultural issues.

This dominant attitude about the intellectual's domain reinforced the closeness of the intellectual networks at this time. Annan, in his essay 'The Intellectual Aristocracy' (1955), shows how these networks were maintained along fairly close and established lines through a propensity to inter-marriage and a common educational background.[2] This pattern of recruitment was sustained by the traditional expectations about the role of the intellectual. Once new roles emerged and different types of intellectuals proliferated these features of the traditional intellectual networks in England were considerably undermined. But while these intellectual networks continued to persist they promoted discussions between different groups about the social issues of the time.

The rapid social change which marked the Victorian age promoted the quality of life as a central concern amongst the intellectuals. The degree to which social change was more dramatic at this time than at any other time is a topic of considerable debate amongst historians, but there is general agreement that there was a significant degree of change. The quality of life issue was particularly pertinent for the intellectuals because the developments that were occurring were seriously challenging traditional patterns of life. For example, the increasing industrialization of society, the challenge to religion and the thrust by the state into the social arena on questions such as education for all members of society were just some of the changes which were part of a general shift in the structure of the society. Established ideas about the relationship between the individual and society, the values which should provide guidance for conduct, and the expectations which various groups had about their lives were challenged throughout the society.

J. S. Mill, Herbert Spencer, T. H. Huxley, John Ruskin and William Morris represent the various types of intellectuals who participated in the debates about social and cultural issues in this period.

## J. S. Mill

As a utilitarian with leanings towards poetic concerns, John Stuart Mill provides a valuable example of some of the conflicts which intellectuals of the period experienced. Like Arnold, Mill promoted the middle class as the desirable leaders of the nation and yet he had some yearnings for the society of the past in which the aristocracy clearly dominated. This tension in his ideas set Mill apart from other utilitarians of the first half of the nineteenth century, among whom his father, James Mill, was a dominant figure.

De Tocqueville's writings on democracy had contributed to Arnold's awareness of the dangers which could accompany its evolution, but they had a far more profound effect on J. S. Mill (though at first this appeared not to be the case). Reviewing de Tocqueville's first volume on *Democracy in America* (1836), Mill had argued that the criticisms levelled at democracy in this work were really only criticisms of America.[3] Five years later Mill was not as optimistic, for he was no longer so much under the influence of his father's thought. Himmelfarb suggests that Mill was trying to please James Mill in criticizing de Tocqueville's first volume.[4] After the death of his father in 1836, Mill's thought changed significantly; he became more of a heterodox conservative than a utilitarian (in the sense that James Mill and Jeremy Bentham were utilitarians). In 1840 Mill wrote a review of de Tocqueville's second volume on democracy, *Democracy in America* (1840), in which he was far less critical. Mill suggested that de Tocqueville's fear of the tyranny of the majority was probably well based and he argued (as did Arnold too) that the American people, as shown by de Tocqueville, were an exaggerated version of the English middle class. The Englishman, Mill claimed, was more and more concerned to improve his condition than enjoy it: the spirit becoming ascendant amongst the English, he believed, was American. Summing up his anxieties about democracy, Mill wrote:[5]

> The remainder of the tendencies which M. de Tocqueville has delineated, may mostly be brought under one general agency as their immediate cause, the growing insignificance of individuals in comparison with the mass.

Mill articulated the fear which echoed through much of the social and political thought of the mid-Victorian period in England, the central problem being to reconcile the claims of the individual with the claims of society. Various solutions or approaches were offered but all writers seemed to have shared one basic assumption. The inevitability of democracy itself was never questioned; the claims of the individual and the claims of society were always looked at within this context.

Mill's solution was representative government, but in terms of government by the wisest few. The wisest few would be the servants; the people would be the masters employing the more skilful than themselves for their own benefit.[6]

> In no government will the interests of the people be the object, except where the people are able to dismiss their rulers as soon as the devotion of those rulers to the interests of the people becomes questionable.

Such a claim represented a belief which appears to be quite different from Arnold's, that the middle class should rule, according to their 'best selves'. Mill's argument is more akin to Spencer's claim that government should be ruled by experts.

Through government by the wisest few Mill hoped to avoid what he referred to as the tyranny of the majority, a tyranny which he feared both in the realm of politics and in the realm of culture. This was a fear which he believed to be justified by what was happening in America. In politics the individual was waning in significance compared to the claims of the mass; in the cultural sphere, Mill claimed, the actual destruction or dissipation of the arts and the traditional high culture was imminent. This threat to art and the cultural tradition emanated from two sources. First, society increasingly was placing very little value on its intellectual and artistic tradition.

Second, the cultural products of this society, in the form of books and newspapers, undermined the cultural preserve of this tradition. As early as 1836, Mill wrote:[7]

> Hence we see that literature is becoming more and more ephemeral: books, of any solidity, are actually gone by; even reviews are not now considered sufficiently light; the attention cannot sustain itself on any serious subject, even for the space of a review article. . . . As the difficulties of success thus progressively increase, all other ends are more and more sacrificed for the attainment of it; literature becomes more and more a mere reflection of the current sentiments, and has almost entirely abandoned its mission as an enlightener and improver of them.

Mill went on to claim that the price we pay for civilization may be the decay of individual energy, the weakening of the influence of superior minds over the multitude, the growth of charlatanerie and the diminished efficacy of public opinion as a restraining power.

Similar claims were to be made by Arnold over thirty years later. Mill's interest in the problem of the onslaught of 'mass culture' on the traditional culture of the arts appears to have stemmed from the influence of Coleridge. At the age of twenty, Mill went through what today would probably be called a nervous breakdown, which he described quite poignantly in his *Autobiography* (1873). He was tormented by the lack of humanity, of human warmth, in the tradition of strict utilitarianism which he had inherited from his father, and poetry, particularly that of Wordsworth, had been of great importance in his recovery. It is on this basis that Mill began to look at the issues which were later to preoccupy Arnold. Coleridge had a considerable influence on Mill in this area of his ideas.

Coleridge's influence is palpable in Mill's use of the term 'culture'. In his discussion of university education, Mill argued that as well as intellectual and moral education in schools and universities, there should be a third ingredient of 'human culture' necessary to the completeness of the human being—the aesthetic branch: 'the culture which comes through poetry and art. . .'; the 'education of the feelings'; the 'cultivation of the beautiful'. Mill called on the audience whom he was addressing to 'let us strive to keep ourselves acquainted with the best thoughts that are brought forth by the original minds of the age. . . .'[8]

There is a marked similarity between this notion and that of Arnold's which called for the study of the best which has been thought and said, but the similarity exists mainly on the surface, a point which is brought out by Williams's analysis of the relationship between the ideas of Coleridge and Mill. Not only was Mill selective of the ideas from Coleridge on which he drew, but, Williams points out, the ideas which Mill selected were not those which Coleridge was offering.[9] For example, Mill used the term 'culture' as Coleridge used the term 'cultivation', to denote a general condition, a 'state or habit' of mind. According to Mill, this condition could be adequately catered for by the extending system of national education. The full force of Coleridge's conception of culture (or cultivation) was emasculated; there was no suggestion of the standard of perfection, of the 'harmonious development of those qualities and faculties that characterize our humanity' which was not merely to influence society, but to judge it.

A similar disparity is evident between Mill's and Arnold's concepts of culture. Arnold envisaged culture as an active force in society; Mill, on the other hand, placed more emphasis on change within the political structure of society to achieve his ends. Arnold was concerned that society be changed, but this was always to be done with reference to culture. Mill, on the other hand, had no such vision or court of appeal guiding his claims for reform, except the notoriously unsatisfactory principle of 'greatest happiness for the greatest number'.

This lack of a vision guiding Mill's discussion of social reform is manifest in his ideas about education. No clear programme emerged from Mill's writing on educational issues, although he did believe that education had an important social role. He adopted de Tocqueville's belief that popular education should be used to counteract the evils attendant on the development of a democratic society. He advocated the formation of a national system of education, but did not believe this sufficient. He suggested that in the political sphere a class of persons should be created who would be responsible for the formation of the best public opinion. It would provide social support for opinion and sentiments different from those of the mass. The shape of this body of people, Mill claimed, would be determined by circumstances, but the element composing it should be: an agricultural class, a leisured class, and a learned class. The agricultural class was included in this membership because Mill believed its natural tendencies to be generally the reverse of the manufacturing and commercial classes. All classes mentioned represented the middle class or above; Mill did not consider the working class as possible members at all.[10]

This notion of a body of persons responsible for high sentiments and opinions in the society resembles Coleridge's concept of the clerisy, Arnold's Academy and Ruskin's aristocracy. Mill claimed it necessary to introduce such a mechanism for the improvement of society because he did not believe a national system of education sufficient to promote tolerance and liberal-mindedness in the community. His main preoccupation when he did write about education was with university education, a further indication that he did not believe national education could be a cogent force in society. The education which he saw as being for the élite, at the university level, occupied his attention, for it was the élite upon whom he relied for the improvement of society.

Mill opposed what he saw as the current trend at that time to dismiss logic and the classics from educational institutions such as Oxford and Cambridge, Eton and Westminster Schools. He did not agree with the view which was beginning to be voiced that modern languages should be introduced and that studies be made to have a closer connection with the business world. Indeed, Mill advocated that classics and logic be taught more extensively and on a deeper level than they were at the time. And on the broader issue, he expressed antagonism to any development in the existing educational system which might have brought it closer to the business world.[11]

In addition, Mill criticized what he saw as being the chief emphasis in university education at that time, the preoccupation with the opinions held by a person, rather than the manner in which he arrived at these opinions. He recommended that:[12]

> The very corner-stone of an education intended to form great minds must be the recognition of the principle, that the object is to call forth the greatest possible quantity of intellectual *power*, and to inspire the intensest *love of truth*. . . .

As a concomitant to this belief, Mill claimed that the university should not be an institution for professional education. Its object was to make capable and cultivated human beings, so a general education should be undertaken at the university. Too limited a conception of man's capabilities of learning is held, Mill argued: an individual should be able to study both literature and science. Mill asked what was to happen as knowledge increased: men would know nothing outside their narrow discipline. Knowledge of only one area of study, he claimed, narrows and perverts the mind no matter what the area.[13]

In order to reform the university, Mill proposed that the following subjects form the basis of its curriculum: history, logic and the philosophy of mind, sciences (including mathematics), sciences of human nature (for example, philosophy of morals, of government, of law, of political economy, of poetry and art), and religion (in a catholic spirit). Through this scheme Mill hoped to regenerate the character of the higher classes, but, in the end, Mill always saw certain fundamental social changes being necessary before the higher classes would be improved. In particular, he believed it necessary to put an end to every kind of unearned distinction, so that the only road to honour and ascendancy would be that of personal qualities.[14]

In arguing for the elimination of any form of unearned distinction Mill was challenging the fundamental basis of the aristocracy in society. Yet at the same time, as can be seen in his writings on education, he sought to perpetuate a style of institution which had more in common with aristocratic notions of a liberal, general education than with the middle-class concern for professionalism. This tension pervaded his work particularly in his later writings as he became more conservative and less optimistic about the way in which society was progressing.

**Herbert Spencer**

By way of contrast Spencer typified Victorian optimism and confidence. He was a self-educated man who began his career as engineer on the railways in England. He was an individualist, often bordering on being an eccentric, who can be frequently irritating to read (particularly when he wrote of himself in his autobiography); but his prodigious influence on people such as T. H. Huxley and Beatrice Webb requires that he be treated with some respect.

Spencer, like Mill, argued that society should be governed by experts or the 'wisest few' and that in order to implement such a system the individuals of greatest intelligence or learning must be permitted to rise up to the highest level of society. Spencer railed against the lack of qualifications of those in government, claiming that legislators should only act on the basis of sound knowledge. In his characteristically aggressive manner he pointed out that:[15]

> Unquestionably among monstrous beliefs one of the most monstrous is that while for a simple handicraft, such as shoemaking, a long apprenticeship is needful, the sole thing which needs no apprenticeship is making a nation's laws!

Spencer recommended the study of comparative sociology and the history of law-making to ensure that the prospective legislator should learn about social organization and the mistakes of previous legislative actions.

But Spencer did not share Mill's belief in the importance of the state's intervention in the management of society. Spencer was a fervent advocate of a *laissez-faire* style of politics. He argued that Liberalism in his time was becoming more like Toryism: instead of advocating freedom for the individual from as much interference as possible, Liberalism was becoming increasingly equated with the idea of state interference. This argument highlights the central focus of Spencer's ideas: the fundamental importance of the freedom of the individual. On the basis of this assumption, Spencer claimed that the government of a country is simply a committee of management with no intrinsic authority. The divine right of majorities, he argued, is just as fallacious an idea as the divine right of despots. The government in whatever form has no right to interfere in the actual direction which society might take. The only way in which the society could be improved, according to Spencer, was by the improvement of individuals. The experts that were to govern the country should confine themselves to the barest minimum of action or involvement in the direction of the society. In this way the degree of state interference in the life of members of society would be eliminated as much as was feasible.[16]

Spencer's attitude to the state interference was not at all unusual in the mid-Victorian period in England. In politics *laissez-faire* policies still gained a great deal of support and in the general life of the nation the *laissez-faire* position still held considerable sway. The enormous popularity of Samuel Smiles's book *Self Help*, which was published in 1859 and sold 20,000 copies in the first year, epitomized the influence of this view. Arnold was amongst the smaller group of people who stridently opposed its dominance over people's attitudes to the state and to the moral issues of the time.

Spencer's beliefs that the only means of social reform was through the progress of individuals were reflected in his ideas of culture and education. Of culture in Arnold's sense, he had very little to say. Occasionally he used the concept in the sense of cultivation or growing something: 'The worth of any kind of culture, as aiding complete living, may be either necessary or more or less contingent.'[17] Or again, he claimed that 'As a final test by which to judge any plan of culture, should come the question,—Does it create a pleasurable excitement in the pupils?'[18] In the latter usage of the term, Spencer used the term in a manner synonymous with the term 'education'.

Spencer's concept of culture differed markedly from the concept which was being developed by Arnold at this time. Spencer lacked any interest in what he called 'aesthetic culture'. He admitted that this type of 'culture' in conjunction with the appreciation of the beauties of nature were conducive to happiness, but, he claimed, they are not fundamental requisites:[19]

> Accomplishments, the fine-arts, *belles-lettres*, and all those things which, as we say, constitute the efflorescence of civilisation, should be wholly subordinate to that instruction and discipline in which civilisation rests. *As they occupy the leisure part of life, so should they occupy the leisure part of education*.

In delegating the 'fine-arts' to the leisure part of life, Spencer was a forerunner of the view of culture as 'the arts'. Culture is equated with the actual objects which make up the arts, rather than the state of mind which comes from studying and appreciating the arts. Williams's work shows that this view of culture became quite popular in about the 1870s. It arose in part as the outcome of artists defiantly exiling themselves and asserting the value of art for its own sake, but this stance did not become prevalent until the turn of the century. Spencer's work demonstrates that it can also be seen to be partly the outcome of certain groups of people forcing the arts into the background.

Spencer's bias against the arts is evident in his writings on education. Art or general education play no part in his ideas in this field. Although he wrote extensively on education, his interests were extremely narrow, his chief preoccupations being the promotion of individual liberty and the advancement of science. Spencer was greatly influenced by Pestalozzi, who claimed that education should be child-centred. As long as we continue to equate education with the acquisition of knowledge, he argued, it will remain repugnant to them and be rejected as a life-long process. The main preoccupation of children in this situation, said Spencer, is to be free of schools, masters, teachers, parents, as soon as possible, whereas if education was self-instruction and pleasurable children would wish to continue with it for the rest of their lives. The central principle of educational theory should be the development of the individual's potential.[20]

Spencer had most impact on educational debates in his ideas about science. His essay 'What Knowledge is of Most Worth?' came out in 1859, the same year as Darwin's *The Origin of Species*.[21] Spencer was in the forefront of the controversy about science which was to continue for the next twenty years. He claimed to be reacting against the current character of education:[22]

> Not what knowledge is of most real worth, is the consideration; but what will bring most applause, honour, respect—what will most conduce to social position and influence—what will be most imposing. As, throughout life, not what we are, but what

> we shall be thought, is the question; so in education, the question is, not the intrinsic value of knowledge, so much as its extrinsic effects on others. And this being our dominant idea, direct utility is scarcely more regarded than by the barbarian when filing his teeth and staining his nails.

The learning of Latin and Greek is purely for decorative purposes, the education of a 'gentleman', Spencer claimed, rather than for any intrinsic value. The function of education, he said, is to prepare the individual for complete living. For this reason he set out a classification of what he believed to be the leading kind of activities which constitute human life:[23]

> They may be naturally arranged into: 1 those activities which directly minister to self-preservation; 2 those activities which, by securing the necessaries of life, indirectly minister to self-preservation; 3 those activities which have for their end the rearing and discipline of offspring; 4 those activities which are involved in the maintenance of proper social and political relations; 5 those miscellaneous activities which fill up the leisure part of life, devoted to the gratification of the tastes and feelings.

Education, Spencer claimed, should aim for the preparation of the individual in each of these activities in proportion to their relative importance. Science is fundamental to all of them, including the activities to be carried out in the leisure part of life, the arts or aesthetic culture. The highest art of every kind, Spencer believed, is based on science. Art objects are all more or less representative of objective or subjective phenomena; and they are good only in proportion as they conform to the laws of these phenomena. We can only appreciate the arts on the basis of a scientific knowledge, just as the cultivated man gains greater enjoyment from a poem because of his wider acquaintance with objects and actions.

In this essay 'What Knowledge is of Most Worth?', Spencer extended his definition of science in a way that he did not make explicit, nor did he attempt to justify it. Science in the arguments outlined appears to be the observation of phenomena, but it is not clear whether he seriously wanted science to be interpreted as this broad area of activity, or whether for polemical purposes he extended the meaning of the word to gain acceptance for science as an important realm of intellectual endeavour.

Spencer justified science as a fundamental aspect of the school curriculum in terms of the provision of mental training, a common claim amongst scientists at the time.[24] Science, he argued, does more than languages, for it both trains the memory and understanding, and cultivates judgment. In addition, science encourages independence of thought. The study of languages, he claimed, tends to further the individual's respect for authority, whereas science makes the individual appeal to reason. The uniform reply to the question 'What Knowledge is of Most Worth?' is, Spencer concluded, science.

Spencer's claims for science reveal very strikingly the assumptions about science at the time and indicate the basis upon which science was to struggle towards recognition in the late nineteenth century. His preoccupation in his educational writing with advocating the importance of science should be contrasted with the wide range of Arnold's interests. Education was central to Arnold's thought; he believed it to be of fundamental importance to society and its reform. Spencer's interests were more narrowly focused. His main concern was with improving the status of science both in the intellectual field of the time and in the society generally. His educational writings expressed this concern most blatantly; not only was science desirable to education, it was the essence of education. Huxley displayed a similar preoccupation in all areas of his writing.

### T. H. Huxley

Huxley was a scientist, humanist and educationalist, but he is probably best known for his promotion of Darwin and his theories. Although of a scientific background, Huxley in many ways was quite opposed to Spencer's views, most noticeably in the realm of politics. Huxley argued strongly against the view of the state which Spencer propounded. Huxley did not believe that the state should act simply in the role of policeman, as the protector of the people against aggression. He claimed that such a view of the state did not have the logical consequences which its advocates saw it as having. This view can be extended, he pointed out, to include the rejection of state interference in drainage and vaccination, as well as education. He argued in favour of state intervention in the activities of society:[25]

> The higher the state of civilization, the more completely do the actions of one member of the social body influence all the rest, and the less possible is it for any one man to do a wrong thing without interfering, more or less, with the freedom of all his fellow-citizens. So that, even upon the narrowest view of the functions of the State, it must be admitted to have wider powers than the advocates of the police theory are disposed to admit.

Huxley adopted John Locke's maxim that 'the end of government is the Good of Mankind'.[26] With this in mind he suggested that the state should guarantee the happiness of everyman as long as it did not diminish the happiness of his fellow man. Such happiness is derived from a sense of security or peace; from wealth, or commodity, obtained by commerce; from Art—whether it be architecture or sculpture, painting, literature, or music; from knowledge, or science, and finally, from sympathy and friendship.

In all his writing Huxley appears to have been a very thoughtful man, far less dogmatic and more humane than Spencer. Yet, Huxley did not perceive any threat to, or deterioration in, the quality of life of men in modern industrial society. Neither he nor Spencer was critical of or remarked upon any increasing stress on individualism and materialism in society. Huxley was optimistic about the way in which society was developing, an attitude which he exhibited quite explicitly in his reaction to America. He was filled with optimism and exhilaration by his visit there. Describing his first sight of America, he remarked on the excitement he felt on seeing the towers and buildings of the post office and other communication centres, instead of the spires of churches. Huxley interpreted this first sighting as symbolizing the Americans' interest in knowledge rather than superstition.[27]

Huxley's exhilaration about America contrasts sharply with Arnold's fear of Americanization. Bibby, in his book on Huxley, *Scientist Extraordinary—T. H. Huxley* (1972), notes the difference between Arnold and Huxley as also being on a more general level: Huxley found 'the spirit of the age pregnant with exciting possibilities' and viewed the Americans as having great 'cultural potentialities'.[28] Neither Huxley nor Spencer had regrets about the decline of the past form of society, its structure or its cultural form. They were firmly committed to modern society and to the developing social form which America epitomized. As scientists their influence lay with this developing society; it was natural that they proclaim its virtues. In so doing intellectuals such as these were to play a vital role in legitimating the changes in society in terms of the progress of reason.

Culture in Arnold's sense was, then, irrelevant to Huxley's vision of society. He did use this term in a manner which on the surface appears similar to Arnold's usage of it. Huxley talked in terms of culture as the criticism of life, as did Arnold; culture, he claimed:[29]

> implies the possession of an ideal, and the habit of critically estimating the value of things by comparison with a theoretic standard. Perfect culture should supply a complete theory of life, based upon a clear knowledge alike of its possibilities and its limitations.

Culture, according to Huxley, appears to be the way in which an individual finds meanings and guidance for his actions in life. Art provides an important basis for culture in Huxley's view, but he dissented from Arnold's assumption that art, or more narrowly literature, could alone supply that foundation. Our whole theory of life, he claimed, is now influenced by the general conceptions of the universe which have been forced upon us by the physical sciences. Consequently, he argued, culture would be incomplete without both scientific and literary education.

To some extent, no doubt in order to adapt to the changing emphasis in the intellectual field of the time, Arnold had conceded this point in his later writings. The more fundamental difference between Huxley and Arnold was that Huxley did not envisage culture as an active force in society. He saw culture as something that the schools should promote; but he did not regard it as a way of changing society. He spoke of it in terms only of the individual. Huxley placed his hopes in the progress of mankind on the increasing predominance of reason and tolerance in the society:[30]

> If we ask what is the deeper meaning of all these vast changes I think there can be but one reply. They mean that reason has asserted and exercised her primacy over all provinces of human activity: that ecclesiastical authority has been relegated to its proper place; that the good of the governed has been finally recognised as the end of government, and the complete responsibility of governors to the people as its means; and that the dependence of natural phenomena in general on the laws of action of what we call matter has become an axiom.

Huxley believed reason to be applicable and vital to all spheres of human activity. He claimed that:[31]

> The end of society is peace and mutual protection, so that the individual may reach the fullest and highest life attainable by man. The rules of conduct by which this end is to be attained are discoverable—like the other so-called laws of Nature—by observation and experiment, and only in that way.

The centrality of reason to Huxley's social thought was fairly unusual. In all Victorian thought there was a belief in the importance of the search for truth, but the truth was not always seen in empirical terms.[32] Even Spencer, despite his commitment to science, did not place such an emphasis on reason (the idea of the individual's freedom was the central point in his beliefs). The belief in reason became a faith to Huxley, for he could give no evidence that reason would provide rules of conduct. He, like many Victorians, was searching for a guiding principle for his life which would replace or at least bolster up religion. For Huxley, this principle was to be found in the individual's quest for knowledge based on the scientific examination of experiments and observation; for Arnold, the principle was sought in culture at both the individual and the social levels.

In education, Huxley argued that no boy or girl should leave school without possessing a grasp of the general character of science, and without being disciplined, more or less, in the methods of all sciences. He justified the importance of science as essential to the school curriculum in a number of different ways. On the one hand, he claimed science to be fundamental to the way in which the individual operates in the world:[33]

> Leave out the Physiological sciences from your curriculum, and you launch the student into the world, undisciplined and in that science whose subject-matter would best develop his powers of observation; ignorant of facts of the deepest importance for his own and others' welfare; blind to the richest sources of beauty in God's creation; and unprovided with that belief in a living law, and an order manifesting itself in and through endless change and variety, which might serve to check and moderate that phase of despair through which, if he take an earnest interest in social problems, he will assuredly sooner or later pass.

In these arguments Huxley displayed his strong belief in the need for a faith in science or reason, both for the individual and the society as a whole. His claims for science as a guiding principle went beyond those which would be found credible today.

On another level, Huxley also made the claim for science which Spencer and others had made, that it provided both mental training and a love of nature. Science's great contribution to mental training, Huxley argued, is by the teaching of induction; the mind is brought directly into contact with the facts. In using this type of justification for science, Huxley was attempting to show that science could make a similar contribution to education as literary and classical studies, which were regarded as providing fundamental discipline for the mind.[34] Similarly, as Layton points out, Huxley's advocacy of science as activating a love of nature was an attempt to justify it in terms of another set of socially acceptable objectives.[35]

Huxley reacted against what he saw as the common mode of thought at the time which regarded education as a panacea for all social problems. Education, he said, is suddenly believed to be vitally important for the masses if they are to govern in the future. Huxley claimed to favour a different view of why the masses should be educated. They should be educated, he said, because they are men and women with unlimited capacities for living, doing, and suffering, and 'that it is as true now, as ever it was, that the people perish for lack of knowledge'.[36]

In advocating such a basis for the education of the masses, Huxley moved away from the prevalent view of the time which saw education as a way to humanize the masses. Such an approach made it possible for him to escape the problems of other scientists who had attempted to have science introduced as central to the curriculum. Layton, examining the difficulties encountered by scientists, points to one of the main reasons as being the conviction of many educators that science did not touch on humane values. If the function of education is seen as a humanizing agent, then science cannot compete with literary studies. By claiming that all people should have education just because they are people and not because it would humanize them, Huxley escaped this problem.[37]

Huxley advocated a liberal education, that is an education which develops the individual in all different aspects of his being:[38]

> That man, I think, has had a liberal education who has been so trained in youth that his body is the ready servant of his will, and does with ease and pleasure all the work that, as a mechanism, it is capable of; whose intellect is a clear, cold, logic engine, with all its parts of equal strength, and in smooth working order; ready, like a steam engine, to be turned to any kind of work, and spin the gossamers as well as forge the anchors of the mind; whose mind is stored with a knowledge of the great and fundamental truths of Nature and of the laws of her operations; one who, no stunted ascetic, is full of life and fire, but whose passions are trained to come to heel by a vigorous will, the servant of a tender conscience; who has learned to love all beauty, whether of Nature or of art, to hate all vileness, and to respect others as himself.

Neither elementary education nor middle-class education, Huxley claimed, approached this ideal.

It is difficult to ascertain Huxley's feelings about the different type of education given to the middle class and the working class at that time. In his statements about the education of the masses, Huxley appears to have thought that there should be no distinction in the type of education given to individuals in the society. In addition, he attacked what he referred to as the 'caste argument', which claimed that the poor should not be educated because it will make people discontented with being labourers. It is ironic, Huxley pointed out, that the people who put forward this argument are the middle class who most favour upward mobility for their own kin. But, Huxley's chief objection to the 'caste argument' was that there was no proof that education as such would make men unfit for or incapable of carrying out rough and laborious, or even disgusting occupations. All men should be given an education and, most importantly, all artificial props in the society should be removed so that capacity can rise from bottom to top and incapacity can go from top to bottom.

In these claims Huxley advocated that all classes should receive the same education, but his egalitarianism was not so evident in his discussions of technical education.[39] He did not acknowledge the difference between middle-class education and elementary education. Quite disparate opportunities were opened up for children undertaking these two types of education available at the time. Huxley accepted this disparity by assuming that from elementary education the young boy would automatically pass into technical education. Agreeing with the common tenet at the time that entrance into the work force by these boys should not be delayed, Huxley recommended that technical education should be engaged in only on a part-time basis in evening classes.[40]

Huxley did not recognize that such ideas about education were tantamount to streaming children on the basis of class rather than ability. Nor did he realize that educating the different classes in different schools was fundamental for the maintenance of the existing social structure. Social mobility through education required far greater organizational changes than Huxley was prepared or able to acknowledge.

Huxley wrote considerably on technical education, but he was also very concerned with the universities and the type of education they were providing. Like Arnold, he was critical of English universities, comparing them unfavourably with German universities. His ideal for universities was that they:[41]

> should be places in which thought is free from all fetters; and in which all sources of knowledge, and all aids to learning, should be accessible to all comers, without distinction of creed or country, riches or poverty.

The universities, in Huxley's view, ought to have been the fortresses of the higher life of the nation. He wanted to see painting, sculpture and architecture in the university just as there was already music, and he recommended that there be a professor of fine arts for every university. It was a mark of Huxley's depth and openness of mind that, in his moves for university reform, one of his most vehement attacks was on Oxford for its use of the

Merton Chair of English Language and Literature as a chair of philology. But of paramount importance for Huxley was the establishment of a faculty of science.[42]

Huxley's readiness to advocate the burgeoning of these different faculties in the universities demonstrates the way in which he saw little problem with the increasing emphasis on professionalism and specialization in educational institutions. Although he advocated a liberal education, he did not recognize any conflict with these two concerns. In contrast, Arnold was not so quick to proclaim the virtues of having a chair of English language and literature. Bibby comments on the strangeness of Arnold's tepid protest about the use of the Merton Chair.[43] But the move to have a chair of English language and literature was part of the move towards specialization in the universities, which ironically would undermine the traditional status of English literature as something which all people (or at least, all gentlemen) would naturally read. Arnold's tepid protest indicates the ambivalent position of the literary intellectuals of that time.

**John Ruskin**

Ruskin first made his name as an art critic and wrote several major works on architecture. He was associated with the Pre-Raphaelite movement[44] in art in England and was a most useful spokesman for their ideas in his early years, but his interests became increasingly opposed to those of many of the members of this group.

The Pre-Raphaelite movement, which at various times attracted both Ruskin and William Morris, had many features of a sect. It tended to withdraw from society, to maintain a set of doctrines which all its members ascribed to, and to follow a style of life which was contrary to the way in which most people in the society lived at that time. Their withdrawal in this manner was essentially a reaction to the society's indifference to art. These artists wanted to be more than just the portrait painters for the upper classes. To assert their independence from the demands and expectations placed on them by the society and to find a sense of importance for themselves in their chosen tasks, they had set themselves apart from the rest of society and established intellectual networks of their own.

Neither Ruskin nor Morris found this alternative attractive for very long. Ruskin became more and more concerned with the problem of the individual and the society (although his ideas in this realm were greatly coloured by the medievalism which pervaded the Pre-Raphaelite movement). He wanted a return to what he believed had been the dominant mode of human relationships in medieval times: social affection. This concept was central to his essays *Unto this Last* (1866) in which he claimed that even though the interests of masters and their men were different, these groups do not have to be antagonistic to each other. He called on manufacturers to treat all working men as if they were their sons. The traditional relationships between a master and his domestic servant, and the commander of a regiment and his soldiers, exemplified for him the ways in which social affection can and did exist. Such affection is a part of the justice which must pertain in all human relationships. It is the '. . . affection as one man *owes* to another. All right relations between master and operative, and all their best interests, ultimately depend on these.'[45]

Ruskin's reliance on social affection for the creation of a more humane society was only partial. The success of this principle was dependent on the action of the aristocracy. Ruskin was continually critical of the existing aristocracy for its indolence and materialism, but he relied on them to be the rulers of society. The aristocracy, he believed, needed to be reconstituted to form a highly cultivated and responsible minority, a notion very similar to Coleridge's concept of a clerisy.

In Ruskin's vision of society each class would be properly trained in its function and form part of a rigid class structure. This notion of the social function of each class emerges at various times amongst English literary and artistic intellectuals. The basis of class is depoliticized and it is claimed that instead of each class being purely an economic category, it can be seen to have a special task to fulfil in the society. By organizing the society in this way, it is claimed, each individual will be more fully integrated as members of that society and the society would be organically formed.

Ruskin divided society into two classes. The upper classes, consisting of landowners, merchants, manufacturers, scholars and artists, would perform the function of keeping order in the society and raising their inferiors to a level as near to them in their lives as possible. To find an image of the organic society he envisaged Ruskin turned his attention to medieval times. He idealized the way in which society functioned at this time, suggesting that social relationships were based on social affection. Through the image of medieval society, he tried to give some concrete basis to his view of a society in which it was possible that members all act in accordance with their function, and in which there was a sense of community, of social unity. As Williams points out, Ruskin's interest in medievalism was essentially backward-looking. William Morris, employing a similar image of medievalism, contributed an element of future orientation through his utopian socialism.[46]

Ruskin was a socialist to a certain extent, but his lack of faith in the working class meant that all his ideas on society were of an authoritarian or paternalistic nature. Quentin Bell analysed Ruskin as being an authoritarian socialist who was against revolution because he could not entrust his programme to the masses.[47] But such a description of Ruskin is too static. Ruskin himself claimed to be a communist, 'of the old school—reddest of the red'. This entailed two major beliefs, first that all property is to be shared or is common, and second, that all men must work in common. Nevertheless, Ruskin was against revolution because of the violence and destruction it caused. He was particularly bitter about this in later years because of the burning of the Louvre in the Paris Commune of 1871. In addition, Ruskin became more and more authoritarian, as he became convinced that the alternative for society was between the scramble for the wealth of capitalism and authoritarian socialism.[48]

Ruskin was opposed to the idea of democracy for, he argued, equality of individuals is neither a possible nor desirable principle for society:[49]

> My continual aim has been to show the eternal superiority of some men to others, sometimes even of one man to all others; and to show also the advisability of appointing such persons or person to guide, to lead, or on occasion even to compel and subdue, their inferiors, according to their own better knowledge and wiser will.

However, Ruskin's assumption of a paternalistic attitude to the working class had different implications for the way in which he treated them than did Arnold's implicit paternalism. Ruskin frequently addressed himself to the working class; whereas Arnold only ever addressed himself to the middle class. Despite his vision of a paternalistic society, Ruskin appears to have had more respect for and faith in the capabilities and intelligence of the masses than Arnold, who paid lip-service to the idea of an egalitarian society.[50]

Ruskin took up the question of how society should be because of an increasing sense that art could only flourish when society had improved. In Ruskin's terms, not only had the artist to have noble motives, but the society too had to be noble, if the art was to be good:[51]

> Art is neither to be achieved by effort of thinking, nor explained by accuracy of speaking. It is the instinctive and necessary result of power, which can only be developed through the mind of successive generations, and which finally burst into life under social conditions as slow of growth as the faculties they regulate.

If the society is not noble, Ruskin claimed, then art is unlikely to communicate to us feelings or thoughts of a peaceful or beautiful nature.

Early in his writings Ruskin advocated the need to return to the beauty of the Gothic style in architecture. He was later to have serious regrets about this stance, in so far as he was important in popularizing what was to become a Gothic revival in architecture. He found many of the buildings inspired by this movement grotesque and he turned vehemently against his audiences who had invited him to advise them on designing their buildings. Speaking at Bradford, he attacked his audience who had asked him to speak to them about the design of their proposed new Exchange building: 'I do not care about this Exchange,—because *you* don't; and because you know perfectly well I cannot make you.'[52] He went on to explain why he did not wish to advise them on the building of their Exchange:[53]

> Now pardon me for telling you frankly, you cannot have good architecture merely by asking people's advice on occasion. All good architecture is the expression of national life and character; and it is produced by a prevalent and eager national taste, or desire for beauty.

Until the people of Bradford gave up worshipping the 'Goddess-of-getting-on', Ruskin believed, they would never have beautiful architecture.

The Gothic revival for Ruskin was a dramatic example of how a form of art could be corrupted by a society whose way of life was antagonistic to art. Consequently, he turned his attention increasingly to advocating fundamental changes in society. Once everyone is fed, dressed, and housed well, he claimed, then good art will naturally follow. Ironically, Ruskin argued, if noble art existed amongst us, we would not have any need to talk about art. The fact that he was asked to talk about art meant to Ruskin that there was something wrong about art at that time.[54]

In these statements Ruskin was expressing his frustration and feelings of failure as an art critic. Through his advocacy of a Gothic revival he had been responsible for some atrocious developments in architecture; his championing of Turner's painting had led to his being asked to arrange a series of drawings for the National Gallery, which had never been hung; and his arguments about the necessity of noble motives for noble art had been misinterpreted as suggesting that the individual's motive behind an art work is the only criterion for judging its artistic merit. In societal terms he had been successful, because he was frequently invited as an art critic to give lectures, but he had the perception to see through this appearance of success and to realize that his ideas were not having the impact he desired.[55]

Throughout his life Ruskin became less and less convinced that art or the artistic imagination could be an ameliorating force in society. Like Arnold, he wished to assert his particular realm of art as having a special role in society. But Ruskin became convinced that there was no hope of persuading people in general at that time of the importance of the arts. His only hope was that society would change so that the value of art would no longer be problematic.

Williams suggests that Ruskin's work provides evidence of a shift in the meaning of culture: there was a transition from 'culture' as the state of mind of the individual to 'culture' as a 'whole way of life'. Although this interpretation has some validity, it does not give sufficient credence to the different levels of meaning in Arnold's concept of culture. Arnold was not totally preoccupied with the individual's perfection or state of mind; he stressed the extent to which this was inter-dependent with the general condition of society and its members. The difference between Arnold and Ruskin was a matter of emphasis. In Arnold's ideas culture is an active force; in Ruskin's ideas culture is passive or totally dependent on social change. This transformation was to have significant implications for Morris's ideas.

Underlying the contrasting emphases in Arnold's and Ruskin's ideas about culture were their specific commitments to particular realms of artistic activity. Arnold, concerned primarily with the literary imagination, held a secure position in the intellectual field of the time and had a strong sense of historical continuity with the literary tradition of England. In the wider society, too, the literary intellectuals retained a position of status and influence as central figures in the social networks of the time. Ruskin, on the other hand, exhibited none of Arnold's confidence that he could be a prophet of the age. His success as an art critic was, as far as he was concerned, an illusion, for he could not effect those changes that he desired. The visual arts were not respected by the general community, except in the form of portraiture for established members of the society and nor were they central to the intellectual field of the time. The visual arts were not taught in the schools and a chair of fine arts in English universities was not set up until 1869 (a position at Oxford which Ruskin first held).[56]

Ruskin's lack of conviction that art could play a prominent role in society was manifest in his ideas on education. He neither placed art in a central position in his ideas about education, nor did he regard education as an ameliorating force in society. Education, according to Ruskin, works mainly at the individual level:[57]

> the entire object of true education is to make people not merely *do* the right things, but *enjoy* the right things: not merely industrious, but to love industry—not merely learned, but to love knowledge—not merely pure, but to love purity—not merely just, but to hunger and thirst after justice.

Ruskin provided very little indication of how he would institute these ideas, though he did set out the way in which he saw the education of the two sexes differing. He paid particular attention to the education of women. The material of a girl's education should be basically the same as a boy's, he claimed, but it should be quite differently directed. A woman should be familiar with the various fields of knowledge only in so far as it allows her to sympathize in the pleasure of her husband and his best friends. Women were very much merely for the pleasure and comfort of men in Ruskin's view.[58]

In his ideas on education, Ruskin displayed a similar concern to Arnold in the studying of the best which has been thought and said:[59]

> the first use of education was to enable us to consult with the wisest and the greatest men on all points of earnest difficulty. That to use books rightly, was to go to them for help: to appeal to them, when our own knowledge and power of thought failed: to be led by them into wider sight, purer conception, than our own, and receive from them the united sentence of the judges and councils of all time, against our solitary and unstable opinion.

Ruskin in this statement adumbrated a number of ideas which also appeared in Arnold's writings on education: the study of the best which has been thought and said; the widening of our thought and increasing its flexibility; and the importance of tradition as a countervailing force against anarchy or instability. He did not expound much further on his ideas about education, a feature it would seem of the lack of centrality of education in his ideas about society and art. William Morris, who was greatly influenced by Ruskin, especially in his youth, exhibited a similar lack of commitment to education. His ideas in this sphere were determined, like Ruskin's, by his ideas about society and art.

## William Morris

Early in his life Morris, with the help of some of his Pre-Raphaelite friends, set up a company which designed tapestries, stained glass windows, tiles and cloth. Through this company Morris developed and practised many of his ideas about the artist as craftsman. Men in the workshop were responsible for designing and crafting their products. In putting this policy into effect, Morris displayed his deep respect for working men and their capabilities. His respect for these people was reinforced by the success of his enterprise, providing a firm basis for Morris's continuing faith in the working class as the new hope of society.

In his earlier writings Morris had been concerned to encourage the middle class to participate in changing the direction of society, in order to ensure that the transformation took a peaceful rather than a violent course. The fundamental impetus lay with the working class, but Morris had some hopes of persuading others of the justness of their cause. Towards the end of his life he was more reconciled to the revolution which he believed to be imminent.[60]

The different elements in Morris's ideas have been a matter of considerable debate, the main problems being with Morris's utopianism and his Marxism. Some authors have argued that Morris was essentially a romantic utopian, whereas others have claimed him to be an orthodox Marxist. E. P. Thompson, in a recent essay, has attempted to demonstrate that these two traditions were welded together successfully by Morris. Thompson refers to Morris as a utopian communist.[61]

Morris's utopianism is clear. He looked forward to the time in which:[62]

> there should be neither rich nor poor, neither master nor master's man, neither idle nor overworked, neither brain-sick brain workers, nor heart-sick hand workers, in a word, in which all men would be living in equality of condition, and would manage their affairs unwastefully, and with the full consciousness that harm to one would mean harm to all—the realization at last of the meaning of the word COMMONWEALTH.

Morris avoided considering problems about the mechanisms of how this change was to occur or how it would be organized once it had occurred, but, as a vision of how things ought to be, it is strikingly different from the ideas of other writers in this period. Utopian writing formed a significant aspect of Morris's exploration of revolutionary ideas. In *News from Nowhere* (*1891*), for example, he described a society in which people worked and lived in happy coexistence: an organic community.

Morris's utopian vision was distinctly medievalist in its depiction of how people dressed, their houses and the crafts they were engaged in. These images derived initially from Ruskin's influence and from Morris's continuing interest in medieval tales and sagas from Ireland and Norway. But Morris did not wish society to return to some past form. He rejected Ruskin's paternalism and relied on images of medieval life only in so far as they provided illustrations of how people could work and live in a manner quite distinct from that which prevailed in the second half of the nineteenth century. The simplicity of cultural forms and the lack of distinction between work and enjoyment by the craftsmen of medieval times particularly appealed to Morris.

Though he admired certain aspects of medieval life, Morris did not condone the social structure of that society. The organic community, which he envisaged, could not be based on feudal social relations; it would arise with the abolition of private ownership of the means of production. In developing these ideas Morris turned to Marxism in the middle years of his life. He described this transition as being a fairly simple progression in his thinking:[63]

> the consciousness of revolution stirring amidst our hateful modern society prevented me, luckier than many others of artistic perceptions, from crystallizing into a mere railer against 'progress' on the one hand, and on the other from wasting time and energy in any of the numerous schemes by which the quasi-artistic of the middle classes hope to make art grow when it has no longer any root, and thus I became a practical Socialist.

The continuity in Morris's ideas was sustained by his critique of society, which throughout his life relied on the moral critique of Ruskin and Carlyle. As Thompson points out, this romantic tradition was transformed by Morris as he embraced Marxism, but he did not reject this background. His attack on commercialism was couched in terms similar to Ruskin as he denounced its destruction of the beautiful countryside and its creation of millions of unhappy workers. And he was particularly concerned with the problem of the quality of life in English society at that time, as were all writers in this romantic tradition. Morris employed Carlyle's phrase 'the condition of England' to draw attention to this problem.[64]

The moral critique of the romantic tradition continued to play an active role in Morris's ideas because of his commitment to questions of art in society. The writings of Marx and Engels were noticeably inadequate in this area. Morris was distressed by the preoccupation with materialism and individualism in his society and he believed these trends to be having a deleterious effect on art. The commercialism of capitalist society had killed popular art, the art done by the ordinary workman; and the stress on individualism had cut the intellectual artists off from their colleagues and their tradition, and deprived them of sympathetic audiences. As long as the system of competition in production and exchange continued, Morris argued, the degradation of the arts would go on. Art would be doomed and die, and hence, civilization would die:[65]

> our civilization is passing like a blight, daily growing heavier and more poisonous, over the whole face of the country, so that every change is sure to be a change for the worse in its outward aspect. So then it comes to this, that not only are the minds of great artists narrowed and their sympathies frozen by their isolation, not only has co-operative art come to a standstill, but the very food on which both the greater and the lesser art subsists is being destroyed; the well of art is poisoned at its spring.

Morris's critique of society and his analysis of the threat to the intellectual and artistic tradition by the dominant trends in that society clearly illustrate his involvement and commitment to the romantic tradition of which Arnold and Ruskin were prominent members. His approach differed, as he himself pointed out, in the solution he suggested to the 'condition of England' question. His revolutionary position had significant implications for his analysis of the future of art. On the basis of his claim that art is a product of man's happiness in his work, he insisted that art could not flourish until society changed. Art not merely reflected the quality of life of the people, their state of moral culture, as Ruskin claimed; art to Morris was a thing of the people. 'That thing which I understand by real art,' he proposed, 'is the expression by man of his pleasure in labour.'[66]

Nineteenth-century art was not 'real art' according to Morris, because it was the product of a few men, divorced from their true base. In the organic community, which he envisaged, art would not be the product of the few, it would be a basic part of all men's work: there would be no distinction between art and craft. Morris wanted a reassertion of the lack of distinction between intellectual art and popular art of medieval times. Intellectual art in modern society is the art produced by the group of men in society called artists and in that side of art which tends to our mind. Popular art is that side of art which is, or ought to be, done by ordinary workmen as part of their ordinary work. A workman would naturally decorate the products of his labour if he had the necessary time and interest in his work. Morris was adamant that this distinction must be eliminated and art be seen once more as the expression of man's joy in his labour:[67]

> I believe that art has such sympathy with cheerful freedom,

> open-heartedness and reality, so much she sickens under selfishness and luxury, that she will not live thus isolated and exclusive. I will go further than this and say that on such terms I do not wish her to live.

The unrelenting note in Morris's attitude to art in modern society highlights the transformation which had occurred in his ideas. He was prepared to do without art if it continued in the same form. For Arnold, Mill and Ruskin the overriding consideration was that the general population should learn to appreciate and wish to study the arts. For Morris, an active interest in the arts was not enough; he wanted all people actually to participate in art, to be artists.

Ruskin had departed from Arnold's claims about culture by his greater emphasis on the way in which the quality of the cultural life of each member of society was dependent on the general state of society and its cultural health. This was an important shift, but Ruskin still retained the view that élites had to be retained in the society: that art was the product of a skilful, inspired minority, and that the general population had to be guided by a special class of people. Morris totally rejected such élitism. The cultured few, he claimed, have no viability:[68]

> The truth is, that in art, and in other things besides, the laboured education of a few will not raise even those few above the reach of the evils that beset the ignorance of the great mass of the population: the brutality of which such a huge stock has been accumulated lower down will often show without much peeling through the selfish refinement of those who have let it accumulate. The lack of art, or rather the murder of art, that curses our streets from the sordidness of the surroundings of the lower classes, has its exact counterpart in the dullness and vulgarity of those of the middle classes, and the double-distilled dullness, and scarcely less vulgarity of those of the upper classes.

'The murder of art' will not cease, Morris asserted, until the whole basis of society has been changed. Society must be organized on the basis of the principle that:[69]

> It is right and necessary that all men should have work to do which shall be worth doing, and be of itself pleasant to do; and which should be done under such conditions as would make it neither over-wearisome nor over-anxious.

The working people themselves, Morris believed, were the only ones who could institute these changes. He was one of the few writers of the romantic tradition to display any regard for the working class of other than a paternalistic nature. Neither Ruskin nor Arnold was able to regard the working class as capable of having responsibility for their own destiny.

Morris's commitment and faith in the working class enabled him to contemplate the fundamental restructuring of society. He discarded all concern to find a special role for art and artists in the society, believing that art's healthy existence could only be secured when it belonged to all people and arose out of their joy in their work. This stance constituted a significant break from the romantic tradition which was very much preoccupied with legitimating a special role for art and its intellectuals, a role which would provide them with a position of power and influence in the hierarchical structure of society.

It has been suggested by a number of writers that there was a steady progression in Morris's ideas from art to socialism as a means for the salvation of society. Jackson, for example, analysed Morris's desire to combat the evils caused by technical progress:[70]

> He first thought of achieving his object through the Church, but soon abandoned that idea for Art, and when Art failed to overthrow the commercial system which he loathed, he turned to Socialism, upon which he endeavoured, without success, to graft his idea of salvation by the arts and crafts. But whatever means he adopted he never ceased to be an artist seeking an artist's paradise, not in some dim future, but here and now.

While Morris may have always been an artist seeking an artist's paradise, it is an over-simplification that Morris's thought developed in such a clear-cut manner. Art and socialism were always inextricably involved in his ideas; the only change being that Morris became clearer about his socialism with his increasing involvement in that movement in the 1880s.

Bradbury claims that Morris exemplifies the endless hunt by literary intellectuals, particularly after the 1870s, for new styles and mannerisms. The confidence and unity of the intellectual world was shaken, not simply by the publication of Darwin's work, or the growing bulk of social and political problems attendant on expansion and industrialism, but largely as the result of the capacity of the growth and development in society to outrun the control of thought and art, of culture in general. Morris, according to Bradbury, pursued 'a dream of aesthetic restoration, of dandyism for all'.[71]

To accuse Morris of dandyism in this manner suggests that Bradbury has only a limited knowledge of his work. As Morris grew older he became less and less preoccupied with 'aesthetic restoration', so much so that he could claim to prefer art to disappear than to be retained at the cost of the continued greed and selfishness of the existing society. But Bradbury's analysis of the social context of Morris's ideas has more credibility. His turn to socialism was part of the search for alternatives by literary intellectuals whose role had become problematic within the society because of the particular nature of social changes at that time. Thompson provides a more authoritative interpretation of the development of Morris's ideas. He argues that Morris effected a transformation of the romantic tradition of the literary intellectuals. Morris did not simply progress from art to socialism; he took the moral critique of this tradition and drew out and extended those criticisms which were consonant with the Marxist analysis of capitalist society. In so doing, he developed a powerful diagnosis of the alienation of our cultural life attendant on this type of social process and escaped the framework of Victorian thinking to create 'a new kind of sensibility'.[72]

Thompson displays an overwhelming admiration for Morris. He insists on the need for Marxists to turn to Morris with a sense of humility to learn something of his moral concerns in 'the interests of socialism's heart'. This may indeed be a valuable move to counter some of the excesses of contemporary Marxists today, but Thompson's claims for Morris as a transformed romantic do not sufficiently counter criticisms of humanistic moral critiques of capitalism as being limited or contained by the very terms of that social form itself.[73] But to raise the possibility of such a limitation operating in Morris's thinking is not to dismiss the particular force of his critique of society nor of his vision for its reconstruction. His ability to step outside many of the major preoccupations of his age and the humanity of his concerns do command our particular attention.

In the field of education, both Morris's distinction and his limitations were displayed. He penetrated to the heart of one of the basic injustices of the existing educational provisions when he analysed the contrast between the types of education received by the working class and the other classes: the very terms 'liberal education' and 'elementary education', he pointed out, typified the inequities of a system which assumed that the working class should only be educated on a very basic level. Morris did not seek to have 'the scraps of ill-digested knowledge which constitute much of so-called liberal education' extended for all to acquire; rather, he suggested that the real contrast lay in:[74]

> the taste for reading and the habit of it, and the capacity for the enjoyment of refined thought and the expression of it, which the more expensive class really has (in spite of the disgraceful

> sloppiness of *its* education), and which unhappily the working or un-expensive class lacks.

Morris suggested that the possession of leisure is fundamental for the acquisition of the extensive type of education which is assumed by the term liberal education. He argued, therefore, that the prevalent assumption amongst social reformers that the working class should be content with their lack of leisure must be rejected.

Morris believed education to be important, but it was not a primary concern for him. He saw it as neither a way of changing society, nor a way of promoting art in society. Though he was the most radical of the intellectuals considered in this period, he did not propose any significant changes in the type of education to be offered to all members of society. Only Spencer in any way suggested a significant departure from the educational practices of the time. This seems to be in part a reflection of the way in which he educated himself; the other intellectuals examined were educated more traditionally. In part it also reflects Spencer's rejection of those areas of intellectual endeavour which formed the basis of English education at the time. Morris, on the other hand, did not reject these areas, though he did not believe that their cultivation would in any way improve society.

# 4 Entr'acte: 1890–1920

The Victorian spirit in many ways still dominated English thought in the period 1890 to 1920. Yet it was a period with its own peculiar vitality. It is often overlooked as being at the end of one great age and only edging on the period which is referred to as being modern. But beginning in the 1890s some important trends in ideas about the question of the role of the arts in modern industrial society were being clarified. Two quite separate streams of thought with implications for this concern can be traced. On the one hand, a remarkable literary and artistic renaissance early in the 1890s provoked a great deal of discussion about art. Ideas about art for art's sake became pre-eminent. On the other hand, the socialist movement gained momentum. A number of groups were established, in particular the Fabian Society. These two trends continued throughout the period with various modifications and offshoots.

The Victorian spirit of optimism was apparent in both movements, but it began to subside with the decline of liberalism before the First World War.[1] And it received a deathly jolt with that war. A number of intellectuals refer to the awakening that occurred at this time. Democracy was no longer regarded as inevitable. Despotism and militarism had been shown to be viable, though not necessarily attractive, alternatives. Clive Bell, for example, insisted that had he written his essay *Civilization* (1928) before the war, he would not have considered the possibility of any other form of government than democracy.[2]

> The war has changed all that. The war, with its attendant catastrophes, has revealed the, to my generation, startling, fact that military despotism is not only a still possible, but, during the next fifty years, a probable form of government. The war

> has reminded us that the true source of power remains what it ever has been: not the will of the people, but a perfectly armed and disciplined body of men which can be trusted to execute unquestioningly the orders of its officers.

Apart from this change in the intellectual climate during the period a further important process was begun. Contact with European thought was firmly established. Ibsen's plays in the 1890s had a profound effect not only in literary circles, but throughout the whole society. The first post-Impressionists' exhibition in 1910 brought to England by some of the members of the Bloomsbury group, caused widespread reverberations. As Hynes points out:[3]

> England's relation to Europe changed during the Edwardian years, and that change is probably the most important of all the transformation that took place in England before the war. It was a change that was vigorously resisted by the conservative forces of Edwardian society, for whom Europe was an infection and isolation was splendid. The liberating movement in this case was the sum of the efforts expended to persuade the English to become Europeans, or at least to take seriously what Europeans were doing.

It would be wrong to over-emphasize the isolation from European thought before the 1890s. In intellectual circles previously there were important contacts. Indicative of the type of contact which existed was Matthew Arnold's interest in and visits to Germany and France. The difference between England's relationship to the continent in the Edwardian and the Victorian periods was that the European influence became more widespread. The whole society was increasingly aware of the intellectual foment which had been going on in Europe for some time.

On the basis of the number of changes occurring in the English intellectual climate in the period 1890 to 1920, it would seem natural to expect that significant developments would arise in the debate about mass society, culture and education. Yet, no spokesman in the humanist tradition of Arnold was forthcoming. The concept of culture, in the sense which was of such importance in the mid-Victorian period, seemed to hold no sway in this period. In fact, on first glance, the whole issue appears to have gone underground. Literary or artistic intellectuals from 1890 until the late 1920s appeared to be unaware of the vital tradition, its moral critique or social vision, to which they were the natural heirs. The question of culture in modern industrial society was no longer relevant to these groups.

But the question of the role of art and its intellectuals in society did emerge in other forms amongst literary and artistic intellectuals. The aesthetic and socialist movements dominated the social thought of these groups; the liberal tradition, though it did still exist, was struggling.

**The eighteen-nineties**

The 1890s can be examined as a separate period in the turn to aestheticism by a number of artists and writers. Holbrook Jackson in his book *The Eighteen Nineties* (1913) provided a fascinating account of artistic movements in this decade. One of its major characteristics was the emphasis on novelty. This was partly a splintering of the Victorian tradition. Variety and difference were encouraged as a reaction to the heavy hand of Victorian attitudes and conventions. Novelty was also part of the *fin de siècle* movement. Jackson discussed this trend:[4]

> The Eighteen Nineties were so tolerant of novelty in art and ideas that it would seem as though the declining century wished to make amends for several decades of intellectual and artistic monotony. It may indeed be something more than coincidence that placed this decade at the close of a century, and *fin de siècle* may have been at one and the same time a swan song and a death-bed repentance.

At the basis of the concern for novelty were movements which consisted of emphases on both renaissance and decadence in art. By the middle of the decade, according to Jackson, the literary outlook in England was exceedingly bright. A vitality pervaded the publishing world which was even beginning to extend to those involved in the stage. Accompanying this was an interest in decadence in both life and art. This aspect of the artistic movement of the time was characterized by a perverse and finicking glorification of the fine arts and mere artistic virtuosity.

Decadence did not consist simply of an obsession with tricks of style or an over-emphasis on art for its own sake. It came to stand for a definite phase in artistic consciousness, a desire to discover the quintessence of things. In this sense it was the obvious outcome of the romantic movement in art. The rights of personality, of unique, varied and varying men formed the basis for its ideal. A doctrine which was quite disparate to the idea of culture. Jackson examined the social roots of the decadent movement:[5]

> It is, of course, permissible to say that such outbreaks of curiosity and expansion are the result of decay, a sign of a world grown *blasé*, tired, played-out; but it should not be forgotten

that the effort demanded by even the most ill-directed phases of decadent action suggests a liveliness of energy which is quite contrary to the traditions of senile decay. During the Eighteen Nineties such liveliness was obvious to all, and even in its decadent phases the period possessed tonic qualities.

The establishment of the little magazine reflected the vitality of the literary and artistic world. This type of magazine was a phenomenon, according to Gross, comparatively unknown in England before the 1890s. It was a decade of ornate periodicals and exotic reviews—the *Yellow Book* and the *Savoy*, as well as the lesser known—the *Dome*, the *Pageant*, the *Quarto*, the *Hobby Horse*, the *Chameleon*, the *Rose Leaf*, and others even more obscure.[6] The *Yellow Book* was symbolic of this whole period. It was first published in April 1894, its editor being Henry Harland and its art editor, Aubrey Beardsley. The content was mainly *fin de siècle*, but not exclusively. It was an instant success as Jackson described it:[7]

> The first number was in the nature of a bombshell thrown into the world of letters. It had not hitherto occurred to a publisher to give a periodical the dignity of book form; and, although literature had before then been treated as journalism, it was quite a new thing in this country for a group of lesser-known writers and artists to be glorified in the regal format of a five-shilling quarterly. But the experiment was a success even in the commercial sense, a circumstance aided no doubt by its flaming cover of yellow, out of which the Aubrey Beardsley woman smirked at the public for the first time. Nothing like *The Yellow Book* had been seen before. It was newness in *excelsis*: novelty naked and unashamed. People were puzzled and shocked and delighted, and yellow became the colour of the hour, the symbol of the time-spirit. It was associated with all that was *bizarre* and queer in art and life, with all that was outrageously modern.

Jackson portrayed the intellectual excitement of the 1890s most evocatively in this passage.

The ideas which dominated these movements stemmed from the notion of art for art's sake. It was a restatement of the French principle *l'art pour l'art* and had been heard in England at various times before the 1890s. Oscar Wilde made the phrase prominent. The dandyism which is often held to characterize the 1890s stemmed from extreme interpretations by certain groups. But to accuse all advocates of this approach to art of dandyism and to condemn the period as being dominated by such affectations is unwarranted. In the words of Hough, it would be a great mistake to dismiss it as 'an era of green carnations and ethical eccentricity'.[8]

The argument, art for art's sake, is an attempt to justify art purely in terms of aesthetic values. The moral values which a work of art conveys are held irrelevant to any judgment of its value. Most importantly, art is regarded as quite separate from society. This view was partly a retreat by the artist from his society; but partly also, as Jackson pointed out, an expression of a vision of an electrifying ecstasy, which is the essence of human life. Artists were still concerned with the question of 'how to live', as were Arnold and his contemporaries. In the 1890s the solution appears to have been of a more individualistic and isolationist nature. Artists in the aesthetic movement believed they should throw themselves into their work and live by that, not concerning themselves with how the mass of mankind was to live.

This is not to say that all artists in the 1890s took this approach. There were those who did not accept the principle of art for art's sake. For example, Bernard Shaw and H. G. Wells employed their art for social purposes. As in the subsequent decades, two quite distinct approaches to the role of art were prominent. Jackson summed up these two views in the context of the 1890s:[9]

> Art for art's sake had come to its logical conclusion in decadence, and Bernard Shaw joined issue with the ascendant spirit of the times, whose more recent devotees have adopted the expressive phrase: art for life's sake. It is probable that the decadents meant much the same thing, but they saw life as intensive and individual, whereas the later view is universal in scope. It roams extensively over humanity, realising the collective soul. The decadent art idea stood for individuals, and saw humanity only as a panoramic background. The ascendant view promotes the background to a front place; it sees life communally and sees it whole, and refuses to allow individual encroachments.

The social reformers continued to develop their position, but the world of the decadents received a dramatic shock in 1895. The arrest of Oscar Wilde is generally believed to have been responsible for a sudden retreat of this artistic movement. On the one hand, the artists were severely shocked that the society could control them so effectively; and on the other hand, the general public, still very staunchly Victorian, found the revelations of the trial too much to cope with. Jackson described the reaction:[10]

> The general public first realised the existence of the decadence with the arrest and trial of Oscar Wilde, and, collecting its wits

> and its memories of *The Yellow Book*, the drawings of Aubrey Beardsley, and the wilful and perverse epigrams of *A Woman of No Importance*, it shook its head knowingly and intimated that this sort of thing must be stopped. And the suddenness with which the decadent movement in English literature and art ceased, from that time, proves, if it proves nothing else, the tremendous power of outraged public opinion in this country. But it also proves that English thought and English morality, however superficial on the one hand and however hypocritical on the other, would neither understand nor tolerate the curious exotic growth which had flowered in its midst.

The exoticism and eccentricities of members of the decadent movements, which often deteriorated into dandyism, reflected the basic isolation in which they existed. They were defiantly so. Stories abound of the way in which figures such as Oscar Wilde and Aubrey Beardsley went out of their way to draw attention to their disengagement from general society. They attempted to capitalize on what they felt was their isolation from the society by forming clubs at which they were to discuss poetry and life. But, as Jackson pointed out, it was a very half-hearted attempt. It failed to revive the literary taverns of the eighteenth century which, ironically, had flourished at a time when the literary men were far from feeling isolated from the rest of society.

The pattern of behaviour of the members of the aesthetic movement suggests a group who, finding themselves on the periphery of society, attempted to maintain their identity by emphasizing their very outsiderness. They adopted attitudes and values which were contrary to those which were basic to the society and its traditional world view. Yet this does not explain why they should feel so isolated. They appeared to have no less access to the society than artists in previous periods; nor were their feelings apparently shared by all artists at the time.

Their attitude becomes intelligible when they are examined in terms of being an extension of certain trends in ideas about art of the nineteenth century. Ruskin and Morris were two prominent figures who expressed an overwhelming pessimism about the social efficacy of art and the role of art in society generally. Art in their view merely reflected the society. Such pessimism may engender a commitment to change society so that art may flourish. Such was Morris's and Ruskin's approach. On the other hand, this pessimism may lead to a defiant attitude to society and art being justified in terms of its intrinsic merit, rather than in terms of its social function. The members of aesthetic or decadent movements adopted the latter approach and succumbed to the pressures of a society which were redefining the social and cultural preserve of the intellectuals and artists in general. They accepted that they should be on the periphery of society and tried to turn it to their favour.

Coincident with the decadent or aesthetic movements was an increasing preoccupation with social reform amongst other groups of artists and their intellectuals. The contrast was very marked. Writers such as Shaw and Wells sought to use their art in order to develop and promote their socialist ideas. They rejected Arnold's type of argument which held art to have special powers to make men better, to lead them on to nobler things and adopted the view that art was a direct means of promulgating ideas, of persuasion. The artistic nature of their work was often secondary to the ideas expressed.

**George Bernard Shaw**

Shaw needs to be seen in the context of his membership of the Fabian Society. It was through the dialogue and debates of this group that Shaw developed his ideas and gained confidence in himself as a propagandist. One of the first developments in the Fabian Society's doctrine, according to Pfeiffer, was its rejection of utopian socialism. They discarded any notion of founding socialist colonies as romantic and futile as a way of changing society.[11] Shaw was scathing of any utopian doctrines. His approach to politics was overwhelmingly practical: an aspect of Shaw which often led to his being unpopular.[12] His discussion of the question of poverty illustrates his style of attack on problems. He refused to romanticize the poor:[13]

> the blunt truth is that ill used people are worse than well used people: indeed this is at bottom the only good reason why we should not allow anyone to be ill used. . . . We should refuse to tolerate poverty as a social institution not because the poor are the salt of the earth but because 'the poor in a lump are bad.' And the poor know this better than anyone else.

He criticized the socialism of 'lovers of art and literature' who, he claimed, make the poor seem saintly (an obvious attack on people like Ruskin and Morris). They assume that all that is needed is to teach socialism to the masses.

Shaw attempted to be eminently practical, in his solution to the problem of poverty. He did not advocate revolution nor even any major restructuring of society. Neither did he take the nineteenth-century approach of seeking a moral solution. He talked in terms of money. Money, he claimed, is the basis of life:[14]

> For the two things are inseparable: money is the counter that enables life to be distributed socially: it *is* life as truly as sovereigns and bank notes are money. The first duty of every citizen is to insist on having money on reasonable terms; and this demand is not complied with by giving four men three shillings each for ten or twelve hours' drudgery and one man a thousand pounds for nothing. The crying need of the nation is not for better morals, cheaper bread, temperance, liberty, culture, redemption of fallen sisters and erring brothers, nor the grace, love and fellowship of the Trinity, but simply for enough money. And the evil to be attacked is not sin, suffering, greed, priestcraft, kingcraft, demagogy, monopoly, ignorance, drink, war, pestilence, nor any other of the scapegoats which reformers sacrifice, but simply poverty.

The stress on money rings a strangely materialistic note in the writings of a socialist. Money symbolizes so much of the capitalist society, that it appears incongruous to accept it as a means of establishing the egalitarian society which Shaw envisaged.

Shaw confounds us even further by his interpretation of his own play *Major Barbara*. In his preface Shaw argued that the industrialist, Undershaft, is the hero of the play. Shaw condoned his hard-headed realism, rather than the day-dreaming idealism of some of his other characters. Undershaft, Shaw claimed, has simply grasped the fact that poverty is a crime. Because he had the choice between poverty or a lucrative trade, Undershaft opted for the latter. Shaw accepted industrialism as a necessary step in the evolution of society and, on this basis, he was prepared to think in the terms set by society: in this case, money. His technique was to use the terms set by that society to bring about the next step in its evolution. Undershaft was the hero because he had recognized how to do this to his own advantage. Shaw wanted to take this further so that everyone would seek the advantages that Undershaft had accrued for himself. Shaw explained how this would bring about the next stage of the evolution of society (once again he was criticizing the type of approach taken by Ruskin and Morris):[15]

> They call on the poor to revolt, and finding the poor shocked at their ungentlemanliness, despairingly revile the proletariat for its 'damned wantlessness' (verdammte Bedürfnislosigkeit).
>
> So far, however, their attack on society has lacked simplicity. The poor do not share their tastes, nor understand their art-criticisms. They do not want the simple life, nor the esthetic life; on the contrary, they want very much to wallow in all the costly vulgarities from which the elect souls among the rich turn away with loathing. It is by surfeit and not by abstinence that

> they will be cured of their hankering after unwholesome sweets. What they do dislike and despise and are ashamed of is their poverty.

Shaw believed that the masses must be given all the advantages that this society can offer, before we can begin to talk to and persuade them of the value of a new type of society, a view that had something in common with Beatrice and Sidney Webbs' dictum of the inevitability of gradualness.

The Webbs in many ways typified the fundamental beliefs of the Fabians, whereas Shaw tended to share only certain of their principles and, particularly in his later years, developed his own esoteric solutions to society's problems. Shaw's attitudes to industrialism and poverty were held in common with the Webbs, but his overriding principle in his consideration of these questions was quite distinct. Shaw proposed that we look at social change in terms of 'creative evolution'. Arguing against the pessimism of the Neo-Darwinists and Mechanists, Shaw proclaimed that there was significant hope for human improvement. He did not believe that we are dominated solely by the winds of fortune:[16]

> But this dismal creed does not discourage those who believe that the impulse that produces evolution is creative. They have observed the simple fact that the will to do anything can and does, at a certain pitch of intensity set up by conviction of its necessity, create and organize new tissue to do it with. To them therefore mankind is by no means played out yet.

Shaw's belief in 'creative evolution' should not be confused with the Victorian idea of progress. As McBriar points out, Shaw began increasingly to doubt that man would progress towards any sort of millennium. His hope, particularly in later years, was pinned to the idea of the Superman. 'Creative evolution' would depend on a race of beings whose rationality was developed far beyond ours. They would be able to guide and to will the process of evolution in the most desirable direction. The race of Supermen bears great resemblance to the samurai order which Wells envisaged. As a concept it can be traced back to the notion of a clerisy devised by Coleridge, or even further to Plato's notion of Philosopher Kings.

Shaw went so far as to suggest that 'creative evolution' should become a religion. Civilization needs a religion, he argued, as a matter of life and death. 'Creative evolution' provided the belief in humanity, strengthened by its basis in scientific principles. Established religion, according to Shaw, is at present inadequate for civilization's needs, for it is duped by the powerful and the rich. It can be bought by the rich, as Andrew Undershaft shows of the

Salvation Army in *Major Barbara*. By its charitable concerns it removes the insurrectionary edge of poverty and persuades the masses to be content with hopes of a better life in the next world, rather than this. Thus Shaw proposed his own religion as one which would be a counterpoise to the establishment in society.

Crampton suggests that Shaw's search for a religion belongs to the tradition of Carlyle and Ruskin, who believed that social instincts could only be vital and courageous if based on religious connections rather than on logic or self-interest. These men, according to Crampton, sought to purge theology of supernaturalism, Biblical literalism and popular salvationism. Creative evolution for Shaw was thus a creed by which men can live, as well as a way of changing society. But Shaw's religion differed from Carlyle's and Ruskin's creeds in that it relied on modern technology and made no reference to their central concern, the social need for art.[17]

Yet this is not to suggest that Shaw did not envisage an important role for the artist in society. In fact, as Colin Wilson points out, one of the dominant themes in his works is that of the relation of the poet to a society run by practical men.[18] The practical men in Shaw's plays are shown to be ultimately inadequate; it is the poets who will eventually have to take the responsibility of changing society. But, Shaw did not believe that artists should be given a privileged position in society. McBriar outlines Shaw's idea of the place of the artist in the socialist state:[19]

> he insists that the State can do no good by regulating or pampering its artists, and the only solution is to give them some employment that will leave them plenty of leisure (which will bring them into contact with community life, and yet leave them free to pursue their art).

Shaw's sentiments on this issue were not necessarily shared by other members of Fabian or socialist circles of the time. Wells, for example, believed that artists should be allowed the special privilege of a leisured existence. Shaw proposed that artists have a significant role in society, but that they must remain distinctly within that society. Their role it would seem, judging from his own behaviour, should be one of idea-mongers.

Shaw's policy that artists should be part of the society bore personal significance for him. Wilson discusses at some length Shaw's battle against the feelings of his youth that he as an individual was not part of society. At this stage of his life Shaw perceived himself as an outsider, outside society, politics, sport, and the church.[20] He undertook deliberate measures to combat this sense of outsiderness. He consciously chose to become a central figure not only in the artistic and intellectual circles of the time, but a prominent person in the society itself. He rejected the alternative adopted by many of his contemporaries who had similar feelings of being outsiders and who set out to capitalize on that as a matter of status. Shaw chose to become involved in society, to attempt to change it so that art would attain her appropriate position of influence.

In opting for this approach, Shaw aligned himself with the Fabian Society's rejection of the idea of the individual seeking perfection. He described this development in the doctrine of the Fabian Society:[21]

> The Fabian Society was warlike in its origin: it came into existence through a schism in an earlier society for the peaceful regeneration of the race by the cultivation of perfection of individual character. Certain members of that circle, modestly feeling that the revolution would have to wait an unreasonably long time if postponed until they personally had attained perfection, set up the banner of Socialism militant; seceded from the Regenerators; and established themselves independently as the Fabian Society.

The Fabians' rejection of the idea of the perfection of the individual as the basis of the development of a nobler society constituted a significant break with one of the major tenets of Victorian thought. Arnold had advocated this principle as central to his notion of culture, just as others had regarded it as the only possibility for social change.

Shaw's rejection of the notion of the perfection of the individual provided a basis for the peculiar twist in his ideas on education. He advocated what now could be called 'de-schooling'. He admitted the need for elementary education so that children may learn the basic skills of expression, but beyond that point he believed it would be better to leave children to educate themselves:[22]

> The real remedy lies in the direction of enabling young people to educate themselves very much as the Fabians educated themselves, by giving them money enough and freedom enough to choose their own subjects and organize their own instruction, and employ their own teachers. It may be taken as a sound general rule that it is waste of time to teach secondary subjects to anyone who does not want to learn them.

Schools, Shaw said, for many parents are just a pretext to avoid the trouble of looking after their children. Yet schools are not even necessary for learning, and indeed quite often inhibit it. Shaw proposed:[23]

> Give every laborer's family a thousand a year tomorrow, and at the same time close all the secondary schools and hang all the school teachers, and you will soon have more secondary education than you have ever had before, with voluntary colleges and popular teachers rivalling great preachers and politicians in popularity, and a public opinion that will make it as difficult for a young man to do without secondary education as it is now to do without fashionable clothes.

Shaw did not show any interest in education as a way of developing the individual in terms of an ideal or a fundamental preoccupation; and because he eschewed such claims, he had no interest in anyone paying particular homage to the traditional sources of that ideal: the basis of Matthew Arnold's concept of culture. Rather Shaw criticized education for its reliance on traditional material. The standards of gentility, he suggested, remain out of touch with developments in modern society; in particular, the modern, democratic, humanitarian movement.[24]

> As modern ideas are not taught in the schools, they can spread only among those who are not at school, or who, being at school, are neglecting their school work and reading books which are either forbidden or else hinder their readers instead of helping them in the school work of winning scholarships and passing examinations. On the other hand, feudal ideas, mercantile ideas, snobbish ideas, are steadily inculcated and embraced. Thus secondary education is an obstacle to modern culture and therefore a danger to the Labor Party.

Such a cavalier attitude to education was not shared by other members of the Fabian Society; the Webbs were particularly committed to education, advocating compulsory and free education at the elementary and secondary levels, and a scholarship ladder to the university level. The spread of knowledge and wisdom throughout the community, they claimed, is fundamental to the functioning of a democracy.[25] Similarly, H. G. Wells stressed the function of education as a means of initiating social change.

## H. G. Wells

Wells, who is probably best known for his novels, fiction and science fiction, was a prominent member of the Fabian Society for some years. He shared their emphasis on education and went so far as to stand as a Labour candidate for London University in the 1922 and 1923 elections, simply to have the opportunity to give public lectures on the importance of education.[26] Throughout his life he was concerned with education and sought to advance this cause through the publication of general textbooks in different areas of human knowledge: an outline of history, written by himself in 1919; an outline of biology, and outline of social and economic science, both produced with the help of collaborators. These books, particularly the first, were an outstanding success. Wells had been inspired to write the educational textbooks through his involvement in the move to create the League of Nations towards the end of the First World War:[27]

> My League of Nations Union experience had enforced my conviction that for a new order in the world there must be a new education and that for a real world civilization there must be a common basis of general ideas, that is to say a world-wide common-school education presenting the same vision of reality.

Wells was as critical of the existing curricula of the different schools as was Shaw, but he did not criticize the actual existence of formal educational institutions. He believed them to be fundamental to the diffusion of modern ideas.

Perhaps Wells insisted on the value of formal educational institutions because he had changed his own life so much through his schooling. He saw it as a social mechanism to enable individuals to achieve success, to go beyond their class background. Shaw, on the other hand, gave no consideration to this aspect of education. He, too, seemed to reflect his own background in this instance, for he had received no formal schooling. Shaw's success as an artist and public figure was more attributable to his own efforts between the ages of 20 and 30. He carried out a concerted programme for the establishment of a persona, public and artistic, in which he did not once turn to an institution of formal education. Ironically, he provided an excellent example for the Victorian advocates of the principle of self-help and, in some ways, his own ideas need to be examined as confined within a similar framework.

Wells's commitment to education as a means of individual social mobility did not mean that he accepted the present system. He was very critical of it, calling it a 'jerry-built' system, in which the resistance of the established respectable educational organizations, the old universities and the schools with prestige and influence, prevented any real change or adequate growth taking place in the national system of education. Indeed, Wells was hostile to the whole basis of the Education Act of 1870. The National Schools, he claimed, remained inferior to the middle-class establishments[28] which still persisted alongside them:[29]

> In spirit, form and intention they [the National Schools] were

> inferior schools, and to send one's children to them in those days . . . was a definite and final acceptance of social inferiority. The Education Act of 1871 was not an Act for a common universal education, it was an Act to educate the lower classes for employment on lower-class lines, and with specially trained, inferior teachers who had no university quality.

T. S. Eliot (and others who held similar ideas about education and the state of society as Eliot) would have done well to note these sober reflections by Wells. Eliot viewed the Education Act with panic, believing it to be the beginning of the end for tradition and the Christian society. In fact, as Wells so ably argued, the Education Act was not an attempt to promote equality in the society. It was an attempt to maintain the status quo, to arrest social mobility between classes. Shaw added to the condemnation of the Act. He claimed that Disraeli saw it as a way of inculcating in the working classes all the beliefs and prejudices that were in danger of dissipating due to increased individual freedom.[30]

Wells not only criticized the education provided by the National Schools, but also the education provided by the public schools. He saw all existing education as inadequate for modern society:[31]

> How absurd is the preoccupation of our schools and colleges with the little provincialism of our past history before A.D. 1800! 'No current politics', whispers the school-master, 'No religion—except the coldest formalities. *Some parent might object.*' And he pours into our country every year a fresh supply of gentlemanly cricketing youths, gapingly unprepared—unless they have picked up a broad generalization or so from some surreptitious socialist pamphlet—for the immense issues they must control, and that are altogether uncontrollable if they fail to control them.

Wells believed that education was not promoting the qualities needed for leadership. Education, he claimed, should exist for no other purpose than to 'give our youths a vision of the world and of their duties and possibilities in the world'.[32]

Wells was obviously interested in a meritocratic system of education. The upper classes, he believed, have become inadequate as rulers and mentors for the society. What we wanted was a new governing order. Education would be the means by which we could develop individuals who would be fit to join this order:[33]

> We want the world ruled, not by everybody, but by a politically-minded organization open, with proper safeguards, to everybody. The problem of world revolution and world civilization becomes the problem of crystallizing, as soon as

> possible, as many as possible of the right sort of individuals from the social miasma, and getting them into effective, conscious co-operation.

He called the governing order of the future the samurai.

Wells acknowledged the similarity of his idea of the samurai to the Guardians or Philosopher Kings in Plato's *Republic*. His reading of Plato in his youth had persuaded him of the necessity of social reconstruction. But this notion of the samurai also needs to be examined in the context of the tradition of English thought. There are strong resemblances with Coleridge's clerisy, as well as with the utilitarian notion of rule by experts. Wells explained the functioning of the samurai in his *A Modern Utopia*:[34]

> Typically, the *samurai* are engaged in administrative work. Practically the whole of the responsible rule of the world is in their hands; all our head teachers and disciplinary heads of colleges, our judges, barristers, employers of labour beyond a certain limit, practising medical men, legislators, must be samurai, and all the executive committees, and so forth, that play so large a part in our affairs are drawn by lot exclusively from them.

The samurai will be selected on the basis of education and willingness to observe the austere rule of living which would be required of them. Membership would be voluntary.

Wells's discussion of the ruling order of society suffered from some ambiguity. In the main he advocated the establishment of the samurai, yet at times he seemed to have believed that the old ruling classes could successfully fulfil the role which he envisaged for this group. This may have been merely an alternative which he was offering to the society, but one which he did not favour himself, but such an interpretation is not clearly upheld by an essay he wrote in 1912 entitled 'Labour Unrest'. In this work he encouraged the aristocracy to take on their old roles of mentor and guide:[35]

> I have tried to suggest that, whatever immediate devices for pacification might be employed, the only way to a better understanding and co-operation, the only escape from a social slide towards the unknown possibilities of Social Democracy, lies in an exaltation of the standard of achievement and of the sense of responsibility in the possessing and governing classes. It is not so much 'Wake up, England!' That I should say as 'Wake up, gentlemen'—for the new generation of the workers is beyond all question quite alarmingly awake and critical and angry. And they have not merely to wake up, they have to wake

> up visibly and ostentatiously if those old class reliances on which our system is based are to be preserved and restored.

By 1912, then, Wells resorted to a claim very similar to that of Arnold and Ruskin: a connection he himself acknowledged. The ruling classes were accused of no longer being involved in their traditional function in society; but some hope was held that they may be jolted into taking up their function once again. An increasing sense of urgency and frustration led Wells to abandon ideas of a samurai order formed on the basis of education. The existing ruling orders would have to be co-opted into leading the society in the face of growing social unrest.

When Wells first proposed the samurai order in *A Modern Utopia*, he appeared to advocate a meritocratic system of social organization. Yet at times he was inconsistent even at this stage. Wells argued that inheritance is not a good basis on which to select future members of the governing order. But he also believed that inheritance of money may be still permitted in his utopia on a limited basis. Such a scheme he believed would allow a lucky few to be free of the need to work, a necessary system in order to encourage some sectors of the society to be involved in pure intellectual activity, in philosophy and in experimentation.[36]

Wells emphasized the practicality of his utopia in comparison to Morris's. He disputed the value of ideas which did not accept that man would be perpetually aggressive. But he did not allow the need for practicality to dominate him to the extent that he became reconciled to the status quo.

The Fabians, he argued, had made this mistake. After some bitter disputes he severed himself from that group in 1908 and the English utilitarian tradition. He accused the Fabians of being quite content with the existing social order, with no real interest in changing society in any fundamental way. Wells decided that it was not enough to provide merely a protest rather than a plan. He disclosed the Fabians' essentially Victorian frame of mind in his analysis of the tenor of their discussions at William Morris's house at Hammersmith, in the 1880s:[37]

> The prevalent sub-consciousness of the time was not a perception of change but an illusory feeling of the stability of established things. That Hammersmith gathering shared it to the full. It needed such a jolt as the Great War to make English people realize that nothing was standing still. There they all felt and spoke as if they were in an absolutely fixed world, even if they thought that it was a world in which stable social injustices called aloud for remonstrance, resistance and remedies.

The Fabians believed in the essentially immutable nature of the existing social structure and the possibility of a steady, unalarming progress within that structure.

Wells opposed any notion of a revolution to institute his vision for society, the New Republic. He dismissed such a method as belonging to the 'riff-raff'—misfits, or more eccentrics of society. He turned to the middle class to ensure that social change should occur without revolution; he did not trust the working class, the 'proletarian masses'. Not only did Wells reveal his similarity to other English literary intellectuals in his reliance on the middle class and distrust of radical change, but he demonstrated this even further in his description of the New Republic:[38]

> The central conception of this New Republicanism as it has shaped itself in my mind, lies in attaching pre-eminent importance to certain aspects of human life, and in subordinating systematically and always, all other considerations to these cardinal aspects. It begins with a way of looking at life. It insists upon that way, it will regard no human concern at all except in that way. And the way, putting the thing as compactly as possible, is to reject and set aside all abstract, refined, and intellectualized ideas as starting propositions, such ideas as Right, Liberty, Happiness, Duty or Beauty, and to hold fast to the assertion of the fundamental nature of life as a tissue and succession of births.

Wells wanted to escape from the use of abstract ideas and notions. He developed a vision for future society in his description of utopia, but he clung to pragmatic terms of reference. Abstract ideas and notions were studiously and consciously avoided, a predilection exhibited very generally by English intellectuals.

The major force for change, Wells believed, was education. Education could provide the communality of beliefs and ideas which he saw as fundamental to the establishment of the new society. The writer, the man of literature, has a similar function through the promotion of a widened discourse and the preparation of members of society for the new society. His view was essentially the same as that of Shaw, who ascribed the function of the promulgation of ideas to the writer and the artist, but Wells was sensitive to the possible allegation that he was merely bolstering his own interests. To counter such claims, he argued that:[39]

> We who write are not all so blinded by conceit of ourselves that we do not know something of our absolute personal value. We are lizards in an empty palace, frogs crawling over a throne. But it is a palace, it is a throne, and, it may be, the reverberation of

> our ugly voices will presently awaken the world to put something better in our place. Because we write abominably, under pressure, unhonoured and for bread, none the less we are making the future. We are making it atrociously no doubt; we are not ignorant of that possibility, but some of us, at least, would like to do it better.

Wells evinced none of the confidence of Matthew Arnold. The literary men might still be depicted as prophets, but Wells was not so certain that this would be acceptable to the general society.

Nevertheless, he was sufficiently convinced of their social function to argue for the subsidy of authors. Only by freeing authors from the demands of the market, Wells claimed, could they adequately discharge their functions in the modern state. Wells sought the position of outsider for artists and writers in contrast to Shaw. He believed such a status to have been of advantage to himself, enabling him to evaluate critically the total structure of society. Unless writers, artists and intellectuals existed in this relationship to society, they would lose all willingness to undertake their critical task.[40]

Wells did not condone the attitude which proclaimed art as existing quite separate from society. He refused to play the 'artist', as he himself expressed it, for he was opposed to the aesthetic valuation of literature. He preferred to call himself a journalist to avoid being associated with this movement. In his earlier days he had not been certain and had been torn between sympathy with the social reformism of the Webbs and the attraction of the notion of the divinity of the artist. But as he grew older, he drew further and further away from the aesthetic attitude, so that by 1930 Wells had abandoned all attempts at art, his writing now being purely polemical.

The transition in Wells's ideas reflected an increasing sense of urgency and frustration. He had now abandoned any notions of the role of art or its intellectuals resembling those developed by Arnold or other writers of the romantic literary tradition. Art was still regarded as an ameliorating force in society, but not through any inherent quality, only as a direct statement of ideas about society. Neither Wells nor Shaw believed art to have any indirect moral impact on its audience; its value to society could only be assessed through its usefulness in the dissemination of ideas.

### C. F. G. Masterman

Masterman was one of the few intellectuals in this period who attempted to sustain a critique of English society emulating

Arnold's social analysis.[41] He wrote *The Condition of England* in 1908–1909 when he was a minor member of the government of the time. His book attracted considerable attention. It articulated the apprehension of a significant proportion of the population at the apparent threat to English liberalism and the society it represented. Masterman sought to maintain the old system, unaware of the fundamental nature of the social changes which were occurring in England. He was convinced that England could be returned to her glorious position of the mid-Victorian era.

Masterman was no more than a distorted echo of Arnold. In this guise he remained confined to the terms of analysis of society employed by Arnold and his solution to the problems he diagnosed was a mere shadow of Arnold's social vision. He was totally unable to extend Arnold's social analysis, to assess critically the significant changes which had occurred since the mid-Victorian period. Yet, in many ways, his writings are more indicative of the trends in general thinking of society at that time than are the social reformers or the aesthetic movement.

Masterman's debt to Arnold and his literary tradition was expressed in the title of his essay, though 'the condition of England question' was also a commonly used phrase at this time.[42] He reproduced Arnold's *Culture and Anarchy* in this work in a number of obvious ways, but most noticeably in his analysis of the class structure in England. Society was divided into the 'Conquerors'—the aristocratic class; the 'Suburbans'—the middle class; and the 'Multitude'—the working class. This classification imitated Arnold's providing distinctive labels for each class as he perceived them. Masterman added a fourth group, the 'Prisoners' —a category of 'human failures', such as the prison population, vagrants, asylum occupants and the unemployed.

Masterman criticized the different classes on similar grounds to those used by Arnold. He accused the aristocracy of having abrogated their traditional social function. They had become obsessed with living up to elaborate standards, Masterman claimed, compromising their intellectual energy and vigour of the past. The middle class, or suburbans, on the other hand, exhibit soullessness and a concern for the trivial. They have no vision of life which they can employ to judge what is trivial or what is heroic:[43]

> Beyond these incorrect standards of value there is a noticeable absence of vision. Suburban life has often little conception of social services, no tradition of disinterested public duty, but a limited outlook beyond a personal ambition. Here the individualism of the national character exercises its full

> influence: unchecked by the horizontal links of the industrial peoples, organizing themselves into unions, or by the vertical links of the older aristocracy with a conception of family service which once passed from parent to child.

And of the 'Multitude', Masterman was most disturbed by their potential anarchism. He revealed the same fear of the working class, particularly when they came together in large groups, in a crowd, as Arnold. His other criticisms of this class were largely in terms of their preoccupation with matters of material comfort and everyday existence. The multitude, he said, were not at all interested in the social millennium.

Masterman revealed yet a further acceptance of Arnold's terms of reference in his discussion of the middle class as the most hopeful promise of England. Any modern analysis, he claimed, regards the middle class as representative of England. They are the ones who are losing their religion; and they are the ones with whom the seed of unrest continues, driving them out to be the frontiersman of all the world. The middle class, Masterman decided, contains both the good and bad characteristics of England. To them we must turn to lead us to a clean and virile life.

The central problem for the condition of England question, Masterman claimed, was the disparity between the material progress of the society and its spiritual progress. Yet he proffered no specific solution to this problem. Education played no part in his ideas, instead he merely provided a weak plea to the middle class to take up the leadership of society and trusted the rest to a vague hope of religious revival.

Yet even religion for Masterman seemed to have lost its specific identity. He wished simply that a religion prevail so that society in general could have something to believe in, even if that belief was a rather arbitrary one. In Arnold's writings religion had taken on a secularized form; Masterman stretched the process to its extreme limits. Discussing the crowd who go delirious at a football match, he argued:[44]

> Among all of these—and they comprise in all classes the overwhelming majority—the place of a Philosophy or a Literature must be taken by a Religion. And the question of the survival of a Religion—in the most liberal interpretation of the term—is the question of the survival of any extra-material ideal in the civilisation of the twentieth century.

His preoccupation with a common faith for all members of society was shared by other intellectuals. Beatrice Webb depicted this search as one of the characteristics of the time.[45]

Beyond his hope for a religious revival Masterman had no other solution to the condition of England question. He rejected both literature and science; literature, he argued, is inadequate as a force for social change:[46]

> Literature—at its highest estimate—is, however, only the luxury of the few. It influences a strictly limited class. It is produced by a still more limited class. It is so little operative upon the general life of the nation that its very claim to be considered in a survey of the 'condition of England' is doubtful.

Science, on the other hand, Masterman claimed, cannot change society because of limitations inherent within itself. It makes no claim to remedy human ills. Indeed, said Masterman, it makes no claim to exercise any kind of influence on human life. It does not reveal, and nor does it profess to reveal, the secret meaning of the universe. All that can be deduced from Masterman's work is that what England needed was, as Hynes phrases it, a change of heart.[47] Masterman's failure to find any solution is revealed by his own conclusion:[48]

> Humanity—at best—appears but as a shipwrecked crew which has taken refuge on a narrow ledge of rock, beaten by wind and wave; which cannot tell how many, if any at all, will survive when the long night gives place to morning. The wise man will still go softly all his days; working always for greater economic equality on the one hand, for understanding between estranged peoples on the other; apprehending always how slight an effort of stupidity or violence could strike a death-blow to twentieth century civilisation, and elevate the forces of destruction triumphant over the ruins of a world.

No panacea for changing society was provided.

Masterman was essentially a politician. He had no particular intellectual activity for which he felt strong allegiance. Consequently, he did not seek to promote literary, scientific, economic or sociological pursuits as being fundamental to the improvement of society. Nor did he have any other solution to offer. His motivation to write *The Condition of England* appears to have sprung from a deep sense of unease, but he could neither grasp the source of that feeling, nor dispel it through an overriding vision of how society needed to change. The success of his book suggests that he articulated a general attitude of mind in the society of that time.

**Clive Bell and the Bloomsbury group**

Clive Bell in his essay *Civilization* (1928) expressed attitudes of a liberal nature bearing similarities with those of Masterman and Arnold. Yet he had been a prominent member of the Bloomsbury group, the inheritors of the aesthetic movement of the 1890s. Bell's essay provides some useful insights into the tensions which existed in the ideas of that group.

There are many doubts as to when the Bloomsbury group existed or even whether they ever actually existed as such. Setting aside such questions, a number of ideas relevant to the issues of the artist in modern society and the quality of life of that society can be said to be attributable to at least certain members of the group. Holroyd analysed the general tenor of these ideas:[49]

> They were alike in their determined opposition to the religious and moral standards of Victorian orthodoxy; and in their work they represented more truly than anything else the culmination and ultimate refinements of the aesthetic movement.

Drawing on Greek ideals, the Bloomsbury group turned to concepts of 'beauty' and 'pure aesthetic value'. They attempted to argue that art should be valued for its own sake. These ideas were often taken to extremes, so that accusations of dandyism could be made, just as they were made against the aesthetic movement in the 1890s. The group deliberately isolated itself from society. They were men and women either of aristocratic background or acceptably upper middle class with the correct university background. Mostly they had—even though meagre—independent means, so that isolation (or insulation) from the ordinary life of society was a feasible alternative for them.

Holroyd claims that this isolation had both good and bad features. Members of the Bloomsbury group were attempting to transport the intellectual vitality of Cambridge to London and a non-institutional setting. But, there was an element of over-cultivation which gave many of their claims a shrill thinness. They wished to establish a society of people who would be responsible for the arts, to promote and encourage the arts even in the face of a hostile society. This group of people would be committed to the search for truth and beauty, maintaining and promoting standards of excellence to provide the necessary atmosphere in which the artist could flourish. Bloomsbury's dictum was that the artist could be, and should be, totally independent from society. Yet as a self-conscious 'modern' movement they failed to sustain their convictions or even to separate themselves from the past. Holroyd views the Bloomsbury group as a failure:[50]

> For all their elegant and ingenious tinkerings, most of the Bloomsbury writers and artists were unable finally to sever the

> umbilical cord joining them to the inherited traditions of the past. Theirs was a tenuous transitory mood, largely barren and inbred, a suspension bridge that now forms our authentic link back to the solid cultural traditions of the nineteenth century. They modified, romanticized, avoided those traditions with varying degrees of success. But rather than being the real founders of a new and originally conceived civilization as Virginia Woolf supposed, they were, in the words of Roger Fry himself, 'the last of the Victorians.'

Just how tenuous the break from Victorian traditions was for the Bloomsbury group is clearly revealed by the extent to which Clive Bell fell back on them in his essay after the Great War. He rejected the idea of art for art's sake and acknowledged that artists should be seen in the context of their society. Artists will flourish in any society, he claimed; their quality of work is not affected by the society, but the means by which they achieve their ends are.[51] Bell was embracing a view of art essentially similar to Arnold's traditional Victorian stance. Ruskin's or Morris's analysis of the relationship between art and society constituted too significant a break with Bell's previous allegiance to the principle art for art's sake.

Art, according to Bell, should still be valued for its own sake. But this claim had taken on a different meaning. It was no longer a matter of art being judged in purely aesthetic terms:[52]

> He who possesses a sense of values cannot be a Philistine; he will value art and thought and knowledge for their own sakes, not for their possibile utility. When I say for their own sakes, I mean, of course, as direct means to good states of mind which alone are good as ends. No one now imagines that a work of art lying on an uninhabited island has absolute value, or doubts that its potential value lies in the fact that it can at any moment become a means to a state of mind of superlative excellence. Works of art being direct means to aesthetic ecstasy are direct means to good.

Art as a means of achieving a desirable state of mind was a fundamental precept in Arnold's concept of culture. In the romantic tradition of English literary intellectuals it formed the central tenet of their claim for the social function of art in general.

Bell developed his notion of civilization in terms largely Victorian. He set out to define the characteristics of a civilized man by first analysing those characteristics which do not define him. He came to the conclusion that civilization, to be civilized, is an artificial phenomenon. Its essence lies in morality and intellectual development, both of which, he argued, are to be achieved through education. Similarly, Arnold had espoused an overriding commitment to the pursuit of truth in spiritual and intellectual spheres. Passages of prose in Bell's essay are frequently couched in similar terms to Arnold's writing.

Bell advocated the formation of a 'civilized nucleus', a group of civilized individuals to act as examples for the rest of society. He believed that it was not possible to disseminate civilization through forcing people into the desirable mould. Such a group, then, could not be constituted in the Bloomsbury fashion, as separate and insular. The 'civilized nucleus' must have power and influence in society. With reasons similar to H. G. Wells, he claimed that a leisure class must be maintained by society as the basis for this group:[53]

> As a means to good and a means to civility a leisured class is essential; that is to say, the men and women who are to compose that nucleus from which radiates civilization must have security, leisure, economic freedom, and liberty to think, feel and experiment. If the community wants civilization it must pay for it. It must support a leisured class as it supports schools and universities, museums and picture galleries. This implies inequality—inequality as a means to good. On inequality all civilizations have stood.

At this point Bell broke with Arnold and the Victorian mode of thought in general. Arnold claimed the necessity of a special group, an educated nucleus, but he did not couch this in terms of the unavoidable inequality of society. He believed equality and democracy to be two unquestionable ends of society. He regarded their achievement to be inevitable, even if his statements often seemed to pay only lip-service to these ideals. Arnold was unequipped as a social analyst to work out their full implications or to find a way to organize society so that they would become a reality.

Bell challenged these two principles of equality and democracy. In a manner similar to T. S. Eliot, he aggressively stated his case: 'If you feel that such inequality is intolerable, have the courage to admit that you can dispense with civilization. . . .'[54] The intellectual shock of the First World War, he claimed, had rendered the principles problematical. Despotism now had to be reconsidered as a possible means to a desirable end; democracy, justice and liberty had to be judged in terms of their being valuable means. On the basis of these premises, he concluded that:[55]

> All else being equal, I should prefer a civilization based on

> liberty and justice: partly because it seems to me the existence of slaves may be damaging to that very élite from which civilization springs; partly because slaves too deeply degraded become incapable of receiving the least tincture of what the élite has to give. A sensitive and intelligent man cannot fail to be aware of the social conditions in which he lives, and the recognition of the fact that society depends for its existence on unwilling slavery will produce on him one of two effects: a sense of discomfort, or callousness.

Bell's conclusion is disturbing. His concerns were expressed solely in terms of the sensibility of the élite, with absolutely no qualms about the degradation that the remainder of the society may be suffering. The conditions and the quality of life of the general population only arose as matters for consideration in so far as they may disturb or cause distress to the members of the élite. The Victorians had argued against oppression on the basis of the moral effect on the oppressors, but they were primarily concerned with that oppression. Bell's writing conveys the impression that if oppression and degradation were out of sight, then they would have bothered him very little.

The bankruptcy of the traditional liberal outlook, as demonstrated by Masterman's essay, is given further expression by Bell. He attempted to revivify this mode of thought by returning to its Victorian exponents, but his interpretation was jaundiced by preoccupations particular to his age. His adoption of the liberal viewpoint in its traditional form emerged as being quite specifically in the interests of his particular social group. The isolation of this group had proved unworkable and essentially empty. Bell hoped, by providing arguments for a specific social function of power and influence for that group, to legitimate its existence and provide it with a new vitality. The social formation which he sought was one of a distinctly hierarchical nature, the type of society which had, in the past, provided support to such élitist coteries as the Bloomsbury group had attempted to be.

Neither Masterman nor Bell provided a focus for their ideas of a similar nature to Arnold's concept of culture. In Arnold's work this concept had provided the basis for his criticisms of society and his social vision. The framework of his ideas contained fundamental limitations, but nevertheless it sustained a forceful moral critique of English society. The absence of such a concept or focus in the social analyses of liberal thinkers in the period 1890 to 1920 indicated their total uncertainty as to their relationship as intellectuals to the society.

# 5 F. R. Leavis

Controversies about F. R. Leavis and his work have created long-term schisms within universities in a number of countries. Yet the enmity between the different factions has focused on Leavis's literary judgments of particular works and his general approach to literary criticism. Disputes over these issues have obscured the fundamental ideological stance in Leavis's work and represented the conflict between him and other literary intellectuals as existing largely at the level of literary criticism. The absence of any developed discussion of Leavis's social and educational ideas reveals the extent to which literary intellectuals have avoided the fundamental issues underlying Leavis's ideas on literary criticism. Their silence on this matter suggests a reluctance to reflect on their own social and educational assumptions.[1]

Leavis began publishing works in the 1930s, his first book being *Culture and Environment* (1933) written in conjunction with Denys Thompson. Until the demise of *Scrutiny* in 1953, much of his work was published in article form first in that journal which he and other literary people, including his wife Q. D. Leavis, had set up at Cambridge. His work always included essays of literary criticism and essays on social and educational issues. The combination of these interests, he claimed, stems from the belief basic to his work that literature cannot be separated from life; he advocated Matthew Arnold's dictum that literature is a 'criticism of life'.

In Leavis's writings the sense of historical continuity with the literary figures of the past that appeared to sustain Arnold has gone. Leavis's ideas bear the marks of his self-conscious return to Arnold and by the 1960s and early 1970s his writings were marred increasingly by a sense of frustration and desperation. Eagleton explains this temper of Leavis's writings, which always pervaded his works to some extent, in terms of the petty bourgeois framework from within which he operated. Speaking of Leavis, and more generally of his followers who wrote for the journal *Scrutiny*, Eagleton diagnoses their central preoccupations as being of an élitist nature, committed to a framework of overarching authority. Revealing their petty bourgeois character, the members of this group reject at once 'the democratic "anarchy", it discerns below it and the ineffectualness of the actual authority posed above it'.[2]

Eagleton is not so much concerned with the petty bourgeois origins of this movement, as with the framework of their central preoccupations. He avoids the reductionist approach to ideas which discusses their formation in terms of the social origins of the writer or thinker, but he does not attend sufficiently to the changes in the structure of English society which were undermining the traditional view of the literary intellectual as articulated by Arnold. Eagleton refers fleetingly to changes in the professionalization of English literary studies, but such developments need to be analysed in terms of broader changes.

In the inter-war period in England the universities were under increasing pressure for the specialization and professionalism of its products. The move towards the requirement that English literature lecturers be academically qualified in that area is an example of the universities' submission to these pressures.[3] As part of these changes, the literary intellectuals' position of strength in the cultural field has been under challenge since the second half of the nineteenth century; by the 1930s science could well claim to hold a position of predominance. Such changes in the traditional institutions which had provided support for the literary intellectuals' conception of their special role in the nineteenth century were accompanied by the burgeoning of new institutions in the twentieth century. New cultural forms such as radio, film, and the mass-circulation newspapers undermined the old forms, leaving all intellectuals vulnerable to the increasing pressure of the mass market and the new expectations being placed on the artist and the intellectual.

The threat to the social and cultural preserve of the literary intellectual was represented by Leavis and his followers as existing only at this cultural level. But these developments were only part of more fundamental transitions in English society, a prominent example being the initial emergence of the modern welfare state. The pressures of the mass market and the expectations of professionalism and specialization articulated at the cultural level the fundamental changes in the material base of society. Leavis's revoking of Arnold's concept of culture was a response by a certain group of intellectuals to these changes.

**Mass civilization**

Throughout his life Leavis made a concerted attack on what he believed to be the evils of mass society. He coined the term 'technological-Benthamite' to symbolize a number of his key criticisms of this society. It emphasizes the preoccupation with technical advances and utilitarian solutions which he found so distasteful. Like Arnold, Leavis found America to epitomize so many of the aspects of modern industrial society which he despised and distrusted; America is the archetypal example of a 'technological-Benthamite' society. Of particular concern for Leavis was the question of the lowering of standards in mass society, in areas such as the quality of life and aesthetic taste. One of the most significant changes in society has been the advent of mass production that accompanied the development of the machine. Mass production involves standardization and 'levelling down' outside the realm of mere material goods:[4]

> Now, if the worst effects of mass-production and standardization were represented by Woolworth's there would be no need to despair. But there are effects that touch the life of the community more seriously. When we consider, for instance, the processes of mass-production and standardization in the form represented by the Press, it becomes obviously of sinister significance that they should be accompanied by a process of levelling-down.

Leavis found films and mass advertising to be equally insidious aspects of this process of 'levelling-down'. Leavis continued to be suspicious and antagonistic towards films throughout his life. He refused to consider them as an art form even though such a high level of creative activity has been channelled into film making over the years. He believed them to involve a surrender to cheap emotional thrills under conditions of hypnotic receptivity. Similarly, advertising relies on the deliberate exploitation of the cheap response, indicating an unprecedented use of applied psychology by institutions in our society, an entirely new factor in history.

As a symbol of many of the things wrong with the mass society, Leavis often referred to *Middletown*, a study of a town in Illinois, America, which was carried out by the Lynds in the 1930s. Life in *Middletown* is centred around the machine, particularly the car, where personal communication on a community level has been reduced to a minimum and the mass media dominate the lives and values of the majority of people in the town. As such, Leavis's reaction to *Middletown* was a part of his attack on America, or

Americanization. Like Arnold, Leavis did not blame America for the process of what he, too, referred to as Americanization: 'American conditions are the conditions of modern civilization, even if the "drift" has gone further on the other side of the Atlantic than on this'.[5] America exhibits the taste for bathos, the loss of the 'organic community', the fragmentation of modern life more dramatically than other Western countries as yet. Instead of the community, rural or urban, Leavis complained, we have now almost universally, suburbanism. People live in agglomerations united only by contiguity and systems of transport, gas, water and electricity.

Leavis's attack on Americanization and his concept of the organic community were laments for an old social order. This form of society, he claimed, was destroyed by the preoccupation with progress characteristic of modern industrial society. The easy optimism, cultivated in particular by advertising, has promoted this belief and destroyed the integrated, personalized way of life of the organic community. The quality of life and traditional culture characteristic of this type of society is irretrievably lost. Any attempt, Leavis declared, to save that culture is essentially a substitute:[6]

> What we have lost is the organic community with the living culture it embodied. Folk-songs, folk-dances, Cotswold cottages and handicraft products are signs and expressions of something more: an art of life, a way of living, ordered and patterned, involving social arts, codes of intercourse and a responsive adjustment, growing out of immemorial experience, to the natural environment and the rhythm of the year.

Leavis was writing in the romantic vein which had become prevalent in the work of many nineteenth-century writers, such as Ruskin and Morris. As Williams points out, Leavis's vision also had more immediate roots in the ideas of D. H. Lawrence.[7] Yet Leavis denied the view that he and Thompson were nostalgic for the past in their examination of the organic community in *Culture and Environment*. They could see no melancholy pleasure in recalling the past, he replied, nor were they so deluded as to think that it could be recaptured. Their only interest, Leavis insisted, was to emphasize what was gone and to draw attention to the nature of human problems associated with this loss.[8]

In discussing the nature of the organic community and its collapse, Leavis refused to examine the question of the economic basis of such a society. In so doing he masked the extent to which the previous order in English society, as Williams points out, was as much characterized by 'the penury, the petty tyranny, the disease and mortality, the ignorance and frustrated intelligence which were also among its ingredients', as any adaptation to the natural environment or social integration.[9] If the organic community is anything more than a literary myth, then an analysis of its form will need to examine how both these aspects of its quality of life for all members of its population stem from its economic and material base.

The main advantage of Leavis's concept of the organic community was that it enabled him to provide a concrete image of the quality of life he envisaged as essential to our society. He employed this image in juxtaposition to the discussion with progress of modern industrial society to point out the way in which this idea is used to cultivate optimism and free spending. Such optimism, Leavis argued, postpones any attempt to see things as they really are, or to set them right:[10]

> A progress measured by a Standard of Living, a rise in which involves a decline in contentment, is, it would seem, a very special kind of Progress. The nature of the standard obviously needs to be examined. It becomes plain that a Standard of Living that is to be taken seriously by anyone besides advertisers, and perhaps economists, must take account of quality of living as well as of material goods and services.

Leavis's protest against the idea of progress and associated concept of the standard of living demonstrates the particular strengths of his critique of modern industrial society. His analysis was far less cogent than Arnold's, but at times when he attacked the dehumanization, materialism and consumer orientation of this society, Leavis's profound effect on people such as Raymond Williams can be understood. Williams did not accept the political implications of Leavis's social writings, but Leavis did provide for him the basis for a cultural critique of society when he could turn to very little in the tradition of English thought.[11]

The idea of the organic community in Leavis's work needs to be examined in relationship to his argument for a system of élites. The idea of a past form of society in which everyone had an accepted function dictated by a 'natural order' establishes a mythical version of the desirable (but lost) form of society. The only way to restore some semblance of this society, he could then go on to say, is through a system of élites or oligarchic structures, on the basis of which the social function of at least certain groups will be restored. The organic society couched in terms of a golden age legitimates this hierarchical vision of society in which the literary intellectuals have a specific and powerful function to fulfil.

Leavis was quite explicitly élitist in his ideas of how society should be structured, without being so defiant towards the idea of democracy as Eliot was to become. For Leavis the problem was to reconcile democracy with the maintenance of high standards. He adopted the stance that he would not be distressed by accusations of being undemocratic if democracy was equated with the lowering of standards in such areas as education. Yet he insisted that the democratic principle was fundamental to our well being; it means, said Leavis, the arrangements and habits which save us from the plight of Russia. He called on his readers 'to challenge with insistent explicitness the righteous confusions and betrayals that recommend themselves with the words ''democratic'' and ''democracy'''.[12]

The confusion, which Leavis increasingly sought to combat in his later writings, was associated with his general preconception about the compatibility of the existence of élites and democracy. Oligarchies, he contended, are everywhere and they are inevitable:[13]

> executive authority and power and the final processes of decision can't *but* be vested in the few.

But, he goes on:

> It doesn't follow that 'oligarchies' don't need to be kept aware that they are subject to criticism, check and control.

To check and control the oligarchies and élites, Leavis maintained, a strong educated nucleus is needed in the society.

Leavis was sensitive to accusations that he might appear to be primarily concerned with promoting his own social group and their particular realm of activity. He threw the argument back at any potential critics. Such a system of élites, he asserted, is fundamental to the well-being of the society. The term 'élitism' is brandished by progressive intellectuals, because of an unconscious desire to promote their own power as an élite. He went on:[14]

> The word 'élitism' is a product of ignorance, prejudice and unintelligence. It is a stupid word, but not for that the less effective in its progressivist-political use, appealing as it does to jealousy and kindred impulses and motives. It is stupid, and perniciously so, because there must always be élites, and, mobilizing and directing the ignorance, prejudice and unintelligence, it aims at destroying the only adequate control for 'élites' there could be.

Leavis defined two types of élites as essential to the functioning of democracy. The first type of élite is directly connected with political power. They hold specific responsibility for the actual leadership and ruling of society. The second élite is constituted by the specially educated class who are responsible for checking and controlling the first élite. The latter group will guarantee that the democratic formation of society is not accompanied by a lowering of standards.

Leavis depicted the separation of élites as a necessity in mass society, though not an ideal situation. Both he and his wife lamented the disintegration of the governing classes which they saw as attendant on the development of this type of society. Q. D. Leavis in her book *Fiction and the Reading Public* (1932) stressed the way in which the character of governing and professional classes had radically altered. The people with power no longer represented intellectual authority and culture.[15]

Yet, it is not clear when this situation, which represented the ideal for the Leavises, ever existed. They clearly had in mind a similar arrangement to Coleridge's description of the operation of the clerisy, but even early in the nineteenth century there was no such unity of élites. Coleridge wanted to clarify the divisions that already existed between the élites, separating those responsible for the general cultivation from the other two 'estates' which he believed make up the society: the landowners, and the merchants and manufacturers. The Leavises had to rely on an image of society of some centuries past, clearly revealing their predilection for a social form of a feudal nature.

Q. D. Leavis pushed the analysis of the disintegration of society further, claiming that the fragmentation of the governing class had pervaded all classes. There was no separation between the life of the cultivated and the life of the generality in Elizabethan times, she argued, as there is today. In this earlier period the general public were not catered for by a mass low-quality literature or a mass press. The general reading public today has become lazy and passive, responding only on a purely shallow level; the high-quality novels do not reach them.[16] Q. D. Leavis's comparison of the past and the present is based on scant evidence, and a number of writers have criticized her severely for this aspect of her work. Her claim for the integration of all people and the existence of a shared cultural life in Elizabethan times can be effectively demolished by reference to detailed studies of the activities and pastimes of different groups in the society.[17]

The description of the society of the past and the idea of the organic community symbolized for Leavis and his followers all that society today lacks. Their hopes for changing society, to reinvest its cultural life with some of the advantages of the past, were pinned on the actions of the conscious minority, the cultured few, not on any schemes for the restructuring or reorganization of society.

Leavis crystallized this position in the 1930s in opposition to the socialist and Marxist ideas which held considerable sway in the intellectual circles of the time. He was bitterly opposed to Marxism both for its revolutionary base and for what he diagnosed as its attempt to crush the human spirit. In 1943 he wrote:[18]

> It was a romantic and irresponsible vision that, in the Marxising days, acclaimed a human triumph that was to emerge out of catastrophe, and it is a philistine obtuseness that (whatever it may call itself) sees a human triumph in any Utopian consummation of the process of the capitalist era. The problem is to avoid both a breakdown of the machinery and its triumph—a final surrender to it of the human spirit.

Not only did Leavis stridently oppose Marxism, but he also applauded his own refusal to submit to the popular cry in the 1930s to 'declare oneself'. In the first volume of *Scrutiny*, Leavis outlined where supporters of this journal stood on Marxism and on political issues in general. *Scrutiny*, he declared, cannot be identified with any social, political or economic creed or platform. By 1940 he seemed to have abandoned or forgotten his previous policy. In 'A Retrospect of a Decade' published in *Scrutiny*, he announced that *Scrutiny* was explicitly anti-Marxist. Not to be communist in the 1930s, he continued, took courage, but *Scrutiny* supporters were specifically opposed to the economic determinism of Marxism. Such a stance does not appear to be as apolitical as the earlier claims for *Scrutiny* would seem to require.

Leavis criticized Marxism on a number of different levels. He particularly rejected the Marxist approach to literature as a serious threat to the humane tradition. Of Trotsky's book *Literature and Revolution* (1924), he alleged that a Marxist does not understand that human culture is a 'delicate organic growth'. No one could 'contemplate fifty years of revolutionary warfare' once they realized this fundamental feature of culture. Leavis purported to agree with the Marxist position that culture should not be a possession of the bourgeoisie. He departed from Trotsky and others, he claimed, because they saw the problem too simply in terms of the saving of the essential elements of the culture that exists to be imparted to the masses. Rather, Leavis contended, these essential elements must be extended into 'an autonomous culture, a culture independent of any economic, technical or social system, as none has been before'.[19] In rejecting the social roots of culture, Leavis appears almost to have believed that culture should be independent of people.

Leavis objected to the chicness and dogma of the Marxism of English intellectuals in the 1930s. The call to line up on one side or the other, to 'declare onself', suggested that there was very little thinking going on. Marxism, he claimed, provided too easy a salvation and means of explanation for the young intelligentsia. Leavis prided himself on having resisted any of the popular dogmas of his day; to align oneself with any particular alternative, he insisted, was to accept a path which is uncourageous and antithetical to thought.

Commenting on the attitude of *Scrutiny* in general to Marxism, Trodd summarizes both weak and strong aspects of its position. *Scrutiny* insisted that the wrong questions and answers were being given by the fashionable left even when they had identified the problems correctly. It chose scepticism and detachment at a time of great emotionalism in the intellectual circles. But, says Trodd, *Scrutiny* did not treat the serious core of Marxist thinking with sufficient respect; its attitudes were as casual, as light-weight 'as the thinkings of the Leftist public school-boys themselves'.[20] These comments could be applied particularly to Leavis. His refusal to declare his allegiance to any political platform in the face of great social pressure does appear admirable. Yet he revealed a very limited knowledge of Marx, so much so that we must doubt that his opposition to Marxism was as non-political and non-doctrinaire as he claimed. To refuse to declare one's allegiance to specific, public standpoints, does not signify an absence of bias.

## The minority culture

Leavis claimed to be employing the same concept of culture as Arnold, but this does not emerge clearly from his writings. Leavis appeared far more preoccupied with the role of literary criticism in society and his concept of culture was focused on promoting that cause.

Leavis perceived his position in the defining and formulating of a concept of culture as being far more difficult than Arnold's. Arnold was easily able to overcome these problems, Leavis argued, whereas today when we say 'culture' has always been in the minority's keeping, we are asked what do we mean by 'culture'. We may refer readers to *Culture and Anarchy*, but we know that this will not be satisfactory, that something more is required.[21] Leavis was distorting the differences between himself and Arnold, for he did not acknowledge Arnold's own problems. In the preface to *Culture and Anarchy* Arnold had to deny the accusations of some of his critics that he meant a knowledge of Greek and Latin when he spoke of 'culture'. The meaning of the term 'culture' has never been without some ambiguity in the English language, as Williams has documented. Leavis would have been on stronger grounds if he had claimed that Arnold's use of the term 'culture' was not unusual in his time. The literary tradition of which Arnold was part had established a general way of speaking about culture or associated notions, enabling Arnold to assume a certain understanding with confidence. In Leavis's case, he was reinstating the concept as developed by Arnold, after about forty years of its absence from English social and literary thought. During that time other concepts of culture had become prominent, in particular the anthropological notion of the whole way of life of a people.

Leavis represented his concept of culture as relying directly on Arnold's work, but his actual statements on culture tend to belie the strength of this connection. Discussing the importance of culture, he claimed:[22]

> In any period it is upon a very small minority that the discerning appreciation of art and literature depends: it is (apart from cases of the simple and familiar) only a few who are capable of unprompted, first-hand judgement.

Leavis made two major alterations to the concept of culture. The 'discerning appreciation of art and literature' was now equated with culture, rather than it being the pursuit of harmonious perfection by means of such appreciation. Culture, as Leavis described it, was no longer a process; it had become identified with the objects which previously provided its basis. But perhaps more fundamentally, culture had become the property of a minority. Arnold at least espoused a commitment to the idea that culture should be attainable by all, whereas Leavis quite explicitly asserted the élitist basis of culture. As with his opposition to Marxist approaches to literature and the arts, Leavis discarded Arnold's notion of culture as being social. Leavis rejected any claim that culture is always dependent on society for its well-being; in the organic society the traditional culture flourished, but it can be sustained today by the active co-operation of the élite of society, the cultured few.

Leavis confined the idea of culture to the arts and literature, denying the value of the study of other fields of knowledge within the framework of this concept. He made particular reference to the classics, philosophy and science, and argued that these are valuable in certain ways, but not to the same extent as objects of culture. Literary study is paramount because:[23]

> It trains, in a way no other discipline can, intelligence and sensibility together, cultivating a sensitiveness and precision of response and a delicate integrity of intelligence—intelligence that integrates as well as analyses and must have pertinacity and staying power as well as delicacy.

Leavis explained the relationship between traditional culture and the literary tradition as being not identical, but that their relation is such that we could not expect one to survive without the other. The centre of culture is language, for through language our spiritual, moral and emotional tradition is largely conveyed. Literature retains what is the best of this tradition:[24]

> For if language tends to be debased . . . instead of invigorated by contemporary use, then it is to literature alone, where its subtlest and finest use is preserved, that we can look with any hope of keeping in touch with our spiritual tradition—with the 'picked experience of ages'.

'The picked experience of ages' introduced a further aspect to Leavis's concept of culture. He used a similar notion when he discussed the relationship between the traditional culture and the literary tradition in one of his earliest essays. He suggested that 'it would seem romantic to expect that an adequate idea will issue out of amnesia—out of a divorce from the relevant experience of the race.'[25] These phrases 'the picked experience of ages' and 'the relevant experience of the race', bear some resemblance to Arnold's statement of 'the best which has been thought and said'. Once again the difference between their concepts of culture is demonstrated by Leavis's identification of culture with that which Arnold believed to be only the means of culture.

Leavis denied that he identified culture with literary appreciation, or 'literary culture'. Yet, it is easy to understand how such a misapprehension could arise, for he claimed both that culture is only attainable through literary studies, and that the minority which he conceived as being the sole possessor of culture is essentially a literary minority:[26]

> To revive or replace a decayed tradition is a desperate undertaking; the attempt may seem futile. . . . The more immediate conclusions would seem to bear upon education. . . . Something in the nature of luck is needed; the luck, let us say, that provides a centre of stimulus and a focus of energy at some university. All that falls under the head of 'English' there becomes, then, in spite of Mr H. G. Wells, of supreme importance.

Leavis proposed that the English School provide this centre of stimulus and focus of energy in the university. It would be the strong humane core within the specialist studies of the university. As he envisaged it, the School would become the nucleus of consciousness and human responsibility for the society in general. Leavis was careful to explain that his vision of the English School was not an argument for a centre of authority for the society composed solely of literary critics. He was convinced that the English School could function as a spiritual community for the rest of society and that English literature in this context, as a living reality, could be 'a real and potent force in our time'. The role of the university in which such a school existed, the 'real university', would be 'to make provision for keeping alive, potent and developing that full human consciousness of ends and values and human nature that comes to us (or should) out of the long creative continuity of our culture'.[27]

In these claims for the English School and the university, Leavis defined a positive social function for English literature. Culture was represented as an ameliorating force in society. At other times Leavis was more ambivalent about the role of culture or the cultured minority in mass society. 'Civilization' and 'culture' have become antithetical terms, he claimed, and the power and sense of authority have been divorced from culture. Leavis fluctuated between pessimism and optimism about the role of the cultured few, or more particularly, the literary critic, throughout his work. His confidence in this area would not have been helped by his own difficulties in finding official acceptance at Cambridge. For example, in 1952, at 64 years of age, he still had not been appointed to a readership at Cambridge. In this year he wrote of the literary critic's faith that he can influence contemporary affairs:[28]

> Where contemporary cultural conditions give no ground for such a faith—where there is no such public, and literature, in the critic's sense, is not a power in contemporary life—then for a critic to encourage himself with talk of the important role that the 'skilled reader' plays in a 'muddled mass-society' by reason of his superior understanding of 'contemporary social processes' is irresponsible trifling or solemn self-deception.

In Arnold's time, Leavis believed, there was a large and immensely influential educated class, so that Arnold had an educated public to whom he would address himself. Leavis sought to compensate for his greater sense of isolation by creating a coterie of students around him at Cambridge, and he attempted to establish the basis for what he believed an English School of a university should be in the journal *Scrutiny*. But without a substantial and influential educated public, Leavis complained, literary studies could have no prominent role in the society. It was easier, or seemingly more justifiable, to talk of the role of the literary mind in mass society in Arnold's time than today: 'the centre—Arnold's "centre of intelligent and urbane spirit", which, in spite of his plaints, we can see by comparison to have existed in his day—has vanished'.[29]

Whether or not Leavis's and Arnold's situations were as different as Leavis claimed them to be, the important point is that he represented himself to be more cut off, more isolated, from an understanding public. Leavis depicted his position as the culmination of a process begun by the Industrial Revolution. Before this time, he argued, the popular culture and the literary culture were integrated: Bunyan, Marvel and Dryden each exhibited in their work their sense of unity with the popular culture. Leavis contradicted the claims that he made about culture in his opposition to Marxism. In other work, he adopted the position that the quality of art, of culture, produced in each age does depend on the state of the society, and more particularly, on its relationship to the cultural life of the general population. Leavis hovered between the two positions. He wanted to attribute to the literary tradition and its keepers an autonomy from the rest of society; but he did not seek the isolation of the aesthetic movement, he wanted to assert a social function or role for art. Images of the past provided a basis for his vision of the role of the artist in a society. Leavis harked back to Shakespeare, whose poetic use of language displays the advantage of living in touch with the popular. Dickens was the last writer in whom Leavis found any of these qualities.[30]

In the eighteenth century, Leavis claimed, the sophisticated culture was cut off from the traditional culture of the people. Nevertheless, the position of the literary intellectual even in this period was more congenial than it is today. In the eighteenth century, he asserted, there was less to read and the society enjoyed a homogeneous, a real, culture:[31]

> So Johnson could defer to the ultimate authority of the Common Reader. For the Common Reader represented, not the great heart of the people, but the competent, the cultivated, in general; and these represented the cultural tradition and the standards of taste it informed.

Today, Leavis concluded, there is no Common Reader; the tradition is dead.

Leavis called on the university to take up its responsibility to society to establish an intelligent, responsible, educated public. Without such a public, said Leavis, any attempt to revivify the traditional culture of our society will be unsuccessful. The difference between Arnold and Leavis becomes marked; it is a difference of tone. Leavis's conception of the English School was in many ways similar to Arnold's notion of academy, based on what he believed the French Academy to be. Arnold dismissed his idea of the academy as being impracticable in English society because of the nature of that society and its traditions. Leavis was more desperate; he refused to contemplate that it may be too late for the university to assume the role he ascribed to it. It is this note of desperation in Leavis's writings and lectures that is most striking; and it became increasingly shrill in his work over the years. Arnold, on the other hand, maintained a certain confidence throughout his life that literary intellectuals and their products had a recognized place in society. Ironically, Leavis's lack of confidence was expressed in his handling of the concept of culture; even Leavis was not clear what ultimately he believed culture to be.

Despite his protestations to the contrary, literary criticism formed the main basis for Leavis's concept of culture. He set out quite clearly the work of the literary critic:[32]

> In dealing with individual poets the role of the critic is, or should (I think) be, to work as much as possible in terms of particular analysis—analysis of poems and passages, and to say nothing that cannot be related immediately to judgements about producible tests.

Wellek criticized Leavis's refusal to defend his idea about literary criticism more abstractly and systematically.[33] But Leavis replied that philosophic tendencies might blur the focus, blunt the edge and misdirect the attention of the literary critic. Leavis stressed the primacy of the poem or literary work and the need for the critic to enter into it, to grasp it in its concrete fullness.[34]

Anderson shows that Leavis's unwillingness to develop a theoretical framework for his literary criticism had deeper implications than have been recognized by Wellek. Leavis's insistence on empiricism rests on an epistemology, Anderson argues, which he was neither aware of nor capable of defending. The epistemology formed the basis of Leavis's literary criticism because of the very ethos of English thinking. The central idea of this epistemology, Anderson suggests:[35]

> demands one crucial precondition: a shared, stable system of beliefs and values. Without this, no loyal exchange and report is possible. If the basic formation and outlook of readers diverges, their experience will be incommensurable. Leavis's whole method presupposes, in fact, a morally and culturally unified audience. In its absence, his epistemology disintegrates.

This analysis would explain, at least in part, the way in which those who have agreed with Leavis have become disciples or followers: they have had to be initiated and to accept the faith. But more importantly, it reveals the central paradox of Leavis's position. As

Anderson says, nothing was less obvious or to be taken for granted in Leavis's day than a stable system of beliefs. Yet, a general acceptance of his approach to literary criticism depends upon such a system of beliefs. Leavis contended that an English School based on his approach to literary criticism would re-establish such a shared system of beliefs. But there is no such set of beliefs to build on, nor has there ever been. Leavis provided no evidence for a shared culture in the past, even if the organic society with its integrated communities did exist. The rift between the upper and lower classes remained; Leavis's shared culture was a fantasy.

Eagleton adds to these criticisms of Leavis's empiricism. He focuses on the *Scrutiny* approach more generally and its claim to be combating ideology through empiricism. Eagleton characterizes such a claim as a 'confession of mere incapacity', an ideological failure of a critique to break through to a theoretical discourse and its potential for more subversive judgments. The mystificatory impact of *Scrutiny*'s claims for empiricism lies in its attempt to represent experience as if it was not 'ideology's homeland'.[36] Experience is the way in which we live our lives which, according to the definition employed by Eagleton, is precisely what ideology is. Experience is not separate from ideology, nor something which ideology is imposed on to give us theoretical statements; rather what we experience as real is dependent on how we see the world.

Leavis's concept of collaborative exchange was founded on the same myths as his notion of the activity of literary criticism. The work of art is not really 'there' in any objective sense; it is only by a collaborative exchange, said Leavis, that we can establish it as an object for ourselves. He explained:[37]

> What, of its very nature, the critical activity aims at, in fact, is an exchange, a collaborative exchange, a corrective and creative interplay of judgements. For though my judgement asks to be confirmed and appeals for agreement that the thing is *so*; the response I expect at best will be of the form 'Yes, but', the 'but' standing for qualifications, corrections, shifts of emphasis, additions, refinements. The process of personal judgement from its very outset, of course, is in subtle ways essentially collaborative, as my thinking is—as any use of the language in which one thinks and expresses one's thoughts *must* be. But the functioning of criticism demands a fully overt kind of collaboration.

Leavis claimed that his literary criticism was expressed in an interrogative form: as the question 'This is so, is it not?' But despite the apparent openness of this approach, Leavis always dictated the scope of the question and any critical remarks made in turn.

Leavis believed that such an exchange would establish a shared system of beliefs and values but, as in the case of his epistemology, this involved a problem of circularity. The very possibility of collaborative exchange rests on the assumption of a basic, shared system of beliefs and values. Yet the values which have to be assumed are those which Leavis dictated, not those of some past common culture, nor empirically found, as he would have liked to suggest.

As Buckley points out, the main thrust of Leavis's criticism in *The Great Tradition* and in his other work was that the literary values which he saw as central to the English tradition are moral values. They are moral values, Leavis claimed, made literary through the exercise of the author's sensibility and expressed in the particular. Buckley summarizes Leavis's position:[38]

> the impulse to artistic creation reaches satisfying artistic results only when it is the correlative of a deep ethical preoccupation: the imagination, in great writers, is moral; the form of a great work is a moulding of deeply felt ethical concerns into a pattern.

Leavis ascribed a universal character to literature which took on a religious significance. He became more and more preoccupied with this feature of literature, an important element, says Buckley, in Leavis's increasing championship of D. H. Lawrence. Lawrence's examination of human issues took place, as it were, in a religious dimension.

Anderson sees this claim for the ethical significance of literature and indeed, Leavis's whole concern that literature be the humane centre of consciousness for the society, as the particular preoccupation of Leavis.[39] Anderson neglects the tradition in which Leavis was working. Literature, and in particular poetry, had been seen in English thought since the eighteenth century as fundamental in the sustaining of moral values. Matthew Arnold had adopted this belief as the basis for his literary criticism, an intellectual activity which he was largely responsible for establishing as a respectable discipline in England. Leavis was working within an already established tradition of literary criticism. It was not as Anderson suggests that, as philosophy became technical in English thought, literary criticism became ethical. Rather, Leavis had been attempting to re-establish a tradition of thought in the intellectual circles of his time which was flourishing in the mid-nineteenth century.

**The English School**

The main task of education in Leavis's view was to restore and maintain a continuity with our cultural tradition. Universities would be the prime movers in this process. They should be more than just symbols of a cultural tradition; they should be of such a force, capable, by reason of their prestige and their part in the life of the country, of exercising an enormous influence.[40]

This position was adopted as the basis of the *Scrutiny* approach to education. In its second volume a short report was given of a meeting held at Cambridge in May 1933. As a result of the discussion at the meeting, a number of statements were made. A key point was:[41]

> that at a time when the process of civilization tends more and more to be mechanical and blind, it becomes vitally necessary to energize consciously and systematically for the continuity of the cultural consciousness; to assert the humane values; to insist that an adequate realization of human ends is not easily achieved, and that, unrelated to it, practical and political action is likely to be worse than useless. If one asks in what ways one can propose, with any hope, to give effect to this conclusion, there is no reasonable answer but 'education'.

Education, for Leavis and his fellow 'Scrutineers', was a vitally important way of asserting humane values in the mass society.

Literary criticism was given a central role for two reasons. First, it was argued, it trains the intelligence and sensibility in a way that no other discipline can, and second, literature represents what is best in our cultural tradition. Leavis was careful to point out that literary criticism was not to be carried out as an isolated study. On the contrary, one of the virtues of literary studies, he assured us, is that they constantly lead outside themselves. In his essay 'A Sketch for an "English School"', Leavis outlined how this policy should be put into practice.

The breadth of Leavis's educational interest is illustrated by the work which he co-authored with Denys Thompson, *Culture and Environment*. They outlined their terms of reference in the following manner:[42]

> An education that conceives seriously its function in the modern world will, then train awareness (a) of the general process of civilization indicated above, and (b) of the immediate environment, physical and intellectual—the ways in which it tends to affect taste, habit, preconception, attitude to life and quality of living. For we are committed to more consciousness; that way, if any, lies salvation.

From this standpoint, Leavis and Thompson recommended a course of study of the cultural environment for students in schools, university and adult education courses. The headings for each topic give some idea of the scope of study they were proposing: advertising; types of appeal; the place of advertising in a modern economy; mass-production; standardization; 'levelling down'; the supply of reading matter; progress and the standard of living; the use of leisure; tradition; the organic community; the loss of the organic community; substitute living; and education. Questions were posed for each topic, references often given, such as works by Sturt and Stuart Chase, and passages provided for critical analysis.

As a proposal for education written in 1933, *Culture and Environment* was remarkable. The idea that children should study topics which are not incorporated in notions of the traditional disciplines still has not received full endorsement by educational authorities. In addition, the basic assumption that children should be sensitized to their society and the way in which it affects them is only beginning to be considered to be important in the schools. There is one fundamental problem with the approach adopted by Leavis and Thompson. In a number of sections, they asked questions along the lines: what kind of person would respond to this type of writing, or advertisement. This approach was taken even further when students were asked about a number of particular passages, whether they did not feel embarrassed, ashamed, when they read them. Such a style of questioning encourages snobbery, a feeling of superiority, rather than an attempt to understand why the passages are so appealing and effective as a means of advertising.

Leavis adopted what appeared initially to be a progressive approach to university teaching. He claimed that he did not like the word 'teaching' because there should be collaborative effort between teachers and students, rather than an authoritative telling. The teacher should not have to hold back his subtlest insights with first-year and second-year students. He should be able to test these out on them. A teacher should be one who gains great pleasure or profit in discussing literature with intelligent young students.[43]

In these ideas, Leavis employed his notion of collaborative exchange, which he outlined as the basis for literary criticism. It seems impressive that he believed students to be equal partners (or at least nearly equal) in this exchange. But, Leavis was, in fact, far from putting a progressive position (as he himself would have most enthusiastically agreed). Leavis was adamant that no one should be reading English at university who has not a bent for literary study and is not 'positively intelligent'. He wanted only those who can benefit from 'teaching' at the top level.

The élitism, which Leavis quite explicitly exhibited about his English School, was not extended, he claimed, to higher education in general. Raymond Williams, he said, made a drastic mistake when he accused him of being opposed to the extension of higher education; Williams made the mistake of identifying higher education and the university. Leavis asserted that he was actually in favour of extending higher education; but the more higher education is extended, he stressed, the more important it is to have a centre which maintains standards. And the only place where this can occur is 'the university properly conceived'.[44]

Leavis was preoccupied with the education of the élite. Although *Culture and Environment* was intended for a wider population, since that time he was concerned chiefly with how to improve the education of the select few. He opposed all such developments in education as the Open University and the conversion of the colleges of advanced technology into universities, which attempted to make universities more democratic. For, he claimed, democracy needs élites, and the only way to provide these is by restricting entrance into university.

High on Leavis's list of grievances with the modern university was the emphasis placed on science. This is an issue which he took up in the famous debate with the scientist-turned-novelist, C. P. Snow. In 1959 Snow delivered an address called 'The Two Cultures' for the Richmond Lecture series. Although this lecture received some public notice, it was not until 1962, when Leavis decided to challenge the assumptions of the lecture, that it became controversial. The debate then continued hotly for some time into the 1960s. Much of Leavis's vitriolic remarks were personal attacks on Snow as a novelist and an intellectual. These seem both unwarranted and unfair play in an academic debate. Leaving these aside, a number of interesting problems arise.

A point of key importance to Leavis's thought was the relative value of science and literature. In his initial lecture Snow argued that the intellectual life of the Western world was increasingly being split into two polar groups. The scientists lacked contact with the traditional group, and as a result their imaginative understanding is less than it could be. They were self-impoverished. But the literary intellectuals were impoverished too, possibly more so because they were vain about it. They liked to pretend that the traditional culture is the whole of 'culture', as though the explanation of the natural order was of no interest in its own value or its consequences.[45] Snow concluded that the gap between the two cultures must be closed in order that they might enrich each other. Literary men should realize that science satisfies our curiosity about the natural world, as well as providing important advancements for humanity.

Scientific intellectuals need to be trained humanely as well as scientifically, in order to solve the world's problems of war and starvation.

Leavis replied to Snow by arguing that science is only important as a means to an end. There is a prior human achievement of collaborative creation, a more basic work of the mind of man—the traditional culture with which literature provides us the only link. In these terms no scientific work can be equated with a literary work; Rutherford cannot be equated to Shakespeare. Literature attempts to answer the great questions for mankind: 'What for—what ultimately for? What, ultimately, do men live by? These questions are in and of the creative drive that produces great art in Conrad and Lawrence. . . .'[46] Leavis confined the significance of science to its value as a specialist study. It does not exist on the same level as English literature, whose study should be the centre of the university.

Arnold was more charitable to science. The notions of specialization had not seeped into his ideas, so that as science began to assert itself, Arnold simply accommodated it as being included in the study of the 'best which has been thought and said'. He did not give the issue a great deal of thought. Leavis, on the other hand, quite explicitly claimed that scientific endeavour cannot be included as part of our traditional culture. Culture as 'the picked experience of the race' is the collected wisdom about fundamental problems of human existence. These questions are ones which, according to Leavis, cannot be answered scientifically. In the intellectual field of the twentieth century, science has become an increasing threat to intellectuals from the humanities area. Science is now valued more by the general society than literature; its methods are held up as examples to all disciplines (all of which have, at one time or another, attempted to emulate the scientific method). If Leavis was to argue that literary studies had a special role in the society, then it is understandable that he sought to show where science was inadequate. He tried to mark out an area of vital importance to the well-being of society which is the property of the literary intellectual and which excludes the scientist. Ironically, by relegating science to the area of specialist studies, Leavis condoned one aspect of the modern university which was undermining the very notions about education he sought to reinstate.

Leavis was aware of the dilemma. He resigned himself to the increasing emphasis on specialization in the university; it is inevitable, he said. The idea of liberal culture has been defeated and dissipated by mass civilization. The problem now, he claimed, is to discover how to train a kind of central intelligence by or through which the specialists can somehow be brought into relation. The English School, he believed, should provide the strong humane centre for the specialist studies. The university, then, properly conceived, would produce 'educated men' with various stresses, various tendencies towards specialization, in touch with a humane centre.[47]

To provide an example of what this humane centre of the university should be like, Leavis and his wife set up the journal *Scrutiny*. They hoped it would provide something of the intellectual community which Cambridge, in their opinion, was failing to do.[48] Leavis published a retrospect in the index volume of *Scrutiny* which came out after its demise. In it he argued that *Scrutiny*'s relationship with Cambridge was very important. The core of the contributors, he said, particularly in the earlier years, were young graduates of Cambridge. They were generally at the research stage and frequenters of what he called 'the house at which the idea of *Scrutiny* was conceived'. Explaining the relationship between *Scrutiny* and Cambridge further, Leavis said:[49]

> The relation with 'Cambridge English' was close and essential, though institutionally uncountenanced, and known not to enjoy official favour. It represented a realized part of our conception of *Scrutiny*; here we had the active association of the concern for the critical function with the concern for the University as a humane centre. For the nucleus actually at Cambridge, work for *Scrutiny* was inseparable from their studies and teaching in (however unofficially) the English School and from their research.

Leavis believed that the un-institutional nature of *Scrutiny* was essential to its being. He claimed that *Scrutiny* could not be repeated because, for one thing, its contributors were free-lancers, 'outlaws'. It could hardly be expected that an enterprise such as *Scrutiny* could continue to rely on outlaws in that position.

Leavis's attitude to Cambridge was far more hostile than these statements might convey. He believed that he had been persecuted by Cambridge and in fact, by the academic world in general. Steiner examines Leavis's bitter statements on the establishment both in Cambridge and the English society at large. He sees them as a necessary but in some ways unfortunate concomitant to Leavis's absolute intransigence in the face of the intellectual cheapness, the unctuous pseudo-culture and sheer indifference to values of his age:[50]

> He has had to define, and in significant measure, create for himself, 'the Enemy'. Like a fabled, heraldic monster, the Enemy has many heads. . . . The enemy represents cosiness,

> frivolity, mundane cliques, the uses of culture for mutual adulation or warmth. He incarnates 'the currency values of Metropolitan literary society and the associated University milieux'. . . . The enemy is the Establishment of the mind. His brow is middle and his tone is suave.

There was a certain reality, Steiner argues, behind Leavis's dragon. Leavis suffered under the bland claw of coterie culture, but in some ways his isolation was self-imposed. He concludes that Leavis's melodramatic image of his own life and role eventually bent or corroded his critical judgment. Steiner instances the debate with C. P. Snow as a case in which his judgment suffered.

Evidence for Steiner's criticism can be seen in Leavis's writings. The tone of his criticism of society became increasingly hysterical throughout the years. Statements in early essays such as 'Mass Civilization and Minority Culture' (1943) were far more carefully thought out and stated than, for example, his collection of essays published in *Nor Shall My Sword* (1972). Similarly, in his literary criticism, Leavis's devotion to D. H. Lawrence in later years exhibited none of the fine sense of judgment of his early years, which made even his critics give him some begrudging respect.

But judgments of Leavis's work should not be made simply in terms of an increased hysteria; his emotionalism should be examined in the context of changes in the society. When Leavis started writing, the world which he valued was not as greatly under challenge as it is now. Leavis could still feel some affinity with the Victorians in the 1930s.[51] Although Leavis was accepted, and in many places greatly honoured in the later years of his life, it was no longer possible as a literary intellectual to be at all confident that the voice of culture would be heard. It is understandable, then, that Leavis experienced increasing frustration. His influence in certain universities throughout English-speaking countries has been prodigious. But his ideas, in the main, have not spread beyond the English departments, though there are no doubt many examples of teachers in the schools greatly influenced by Leavis, working in an isolated manner for the promulgation of his ideas.

Yet, in small ways, the journal *Scrutiny* has been important. It has shown that a journal with strong views about the university could find a public. It stood against an establishment which was basically hostile, and it sustained a critique of society, culture and education, which although at times was incoherent and fundamentally reactionary, is admirable for its sincerity and seriousness. A valuable summing up of what *Scrutiny* meant for its readers is given by Dawson. He asks:[52]

> where, but to *Scrutiny*, a student in the hectic and crowded

> post-war years (for all their vague but exhilarating atmosphere of promise) could have gone, not merely for reassurance, but for clarification, for education in fact? How else (and I know that I speak here not only for myself, not only for students of literature) were we to make sense of the opportunities suddenly and bewilderingly opened up for us? We were certainly not disciples; our radical and democratic sentiments had nothing to do with Dr Leavis. We were merely grateful that in those confused times the idea of a university was being preserved.

*Scrutiny* provided a place in which that collaborative exchange, which Leavis held to be so important to literary criticism, could be carried out (within certain limits). It also provided a means by which the ideas of Leavis and others on educational and social issues could be disseminated. The fact that it was a journal which catered explicitly for a minority led inevitably to its failure. It could only disseminate its ideas amongst those already converted.

# 6 Leavis's contemporaries

Analyses of the intellectual movements of the 1930s tend to focus on the drive towards political commitment and the left-wing preoccupations of many intellectuals in this period. No account yet exists which provides an adequate understanding of this movement amongst English intellectuals, nor of the short-term nature of this political commitment for many of them. Wood, in his analysis of British communism in the 1930s, claims that many of the young intellectuals turned to this mode of thought because of the disintegration of liberalism as a dynamic faith in modern industrial society.[1] Communism offered a positive vision to a generation of thinkers who had been brought up in the 1920s, a time of social depression and revulsion from political action. It was a time when intellectuals in England looked for a vision of society.

Whatever the roots of this ideological ferment amongst intellectuals, it indicates one fundamental feature of the state of English society. Though there was no marked political instability during this period, despite the severe economic depression, the hegemonic dominance of the ruling class was uncertain. Amongst the intellectuals this class was unable to command direct allegiance from a significant number of people from various fields. Communism was one of the most popular alternatives that attracted intellectuals in this time of ideological instability.[2] In May 1936 the Left Book Club was formed, and within a year its membership reached 50,000. Similarly, escapist movements were popular. And amongst literary intellectuals, a number turned to the romantic tradition of the nineteenth century to express their disquiet about society. The writers D. H. Lawrence, T. S. Eliot, Bertrand Russell, Christopher Caudwell, George Orwell and R. H. Tawney represent a number of the major perspectives amongst intellectuals at this time concerned with questions about quality of life in English society.

### D. H. Lawrence

Lawrence is best known for his novels and poems, but he also wrote a considerable number of essays on society and education. He was particularly interested in education, stemming from his experience as a teacher early in life. Lawrence, like H. G. Wells, came from a working-class background, a fact which was very important to Lawrence and had some significant repercussions in his ideas.

One of the major problems for Lawrence was to reconcile the claims of the individual to the demands of society. He argued that the freedom of the individual is essential to forming a new world of man, the true 'Democracy'. In referring to the freedom of the individual, Lawrence envisaged different requirements than may otherwise be assumed. He was not primarily interested in freedom to do as one likes, as was, for example, Spencer. Lawrence was talking about conditions under which the 'spontaneous self' may flourish:[3]

> All discussion and idealizing of the possession of property, whether individual or group or State possession, amounts now to no more than a fatal betrayal of the spontaneous self. All settlement of the property question must arise spontaneously out of the new impulse in man, to free himself from the extraneous load of possession, and walk naked and light.

Lawrence was considering something beyond the freedom of the individual to do as he likes. He described the conditions necessary for the individual to throw off the shackles which bind him, but are, to a certain extent, self-imposed. For example, an individual's desire for possessions ties him to material reality so that he no longer trusts his own desires and impulses. But these shackles are not ones which man would naturally acquire. They are ones which the industrial society, Lawrence argued, forces on him as being desirable.

Williams interprets Lawrence's argument about property or possessions to be very close to the socialism of someone like Morris.[4] Such a judgment seems mistaken on two counts, the first one being that Williams interprets Lawrence's ideas in the very way Lawrence was seeking to avoid. Lawrence criticized all the 'ism' approaches to the question of property, as Williams himself notes. Modern democracy, socialism, conservatism, bolshevism, liberalism, republicanism, communism, are all alike, said Lawrence: they idealize the possession of property. Lawrence suggested that we should not try to work out how best to organize the possession of property at all. Rather we should let the best way of doing this, once we have lost personal interest in the issue, evolve by itself.[5] To argue that Lawrence may be seen as a socialist on this question is to miss his central point. The second mistake which Williams makes in his interpretation of Lawrence, in this instance, is to look for a possible connection between Lawrence and Morris, rather than examining the more fruitful and valid connection between Ruskin and Lawrence, as evinced in Aldington's biography of Lawrence.[6] It was through his commitment to Ruskin that Lawrence absorbed many of the traditions to which Williams refers.

Exemplifying the affinity between Ruskin's and Lawrence's ideas was the vision of a hierarchical society which they shared. Lawrence believed that society should be stratified, forming a number of distinctive levels and that each of these levels should not attempt to perform the function of the other. Rather, each level should be consummated in the next, rising, said Lawrence, as a volcano to an apex:[7]

> The true democracy is that in which a people gradually cumulate, from the vast base of the populace upwards through the zones of life and understanding to the summit where the great man, or the most perfect utterer, is alone. The false democracy is that wherein every issue, even the highest, is dragged down to the lowest issue, the myriad multiple lowest human issue: today, the wage.

The populace, Lawrence argued, will never know by itself what it is to do. It will find its sole expression only through the rising of classes above it. By the recognition of the necessity of classes, too, men will be left to live according to their true natures. Those who are comparatively 'non-mental', Lawrence argued, can form a 'passionate proletariat'; and those who work well as clerks will be free to do so without humiliation. Such a stratified society will provide an organic system, as opposed to a mechanical differentiation between men.

The belief in 'the organic society', which had already gained some popularity in the nineteenth century and was an important element in Ruskin's thought, was given particular emphasis by Lawrence. Lawrence used the notion of the organic society not only to criticize the social disintegration which he believed industrialization to have brought, he also used it to suggest the ideal of 'to each class its function'. Through this ideal he opposed the formation of classes around the division of labour, by the process of material production, and sought to assert the possibility of a stratified society whose divisions were based on what he saw as being an organic basis.

Williams characterizes this concern with an organic relation between class and function as being the essence of the grievance with industrial society shared by Coleridge, Carlyle, Arnold, Ruskin, and later, Eliot.[8] Such a grievance is certainly central to these writers, but a further concern needs to be considered in conjunction with this issue. These writers can be seen to be at least as much disturbed by the lack of a consistent relationship between their own particular minority group and its function: the question of the social role of the intellectual. Each of the writers sought to place the intellectuals presiding over all other members of society or in some way as the leaders in the hierarchical structure of social relations.

Concomitant to Lawrence's belief in the organic society was his rejection of the individualism which he saw as consequent upon industrialism. He hungered for the sense of community which he believed industrialism and its ugly materialism had destroyed.[9] As Williams points out, such claims demonstrate Lawrence's involvement in the romantic tradition of the English literary intellectual, but the peculiar devotion and preoccupation with these concerns need to be understood as part of a strongly felt personal longing for Lawrence. Throughout his life Lawrence sought to establish a community of like-minded souls; all attempts failed abysmally, apparently through personality clashes.[10] Williams's analysis of Lawrence as an exile needs to be examined bearing in mind his inability to maintain friendships with anyone, though it would be fruitless to attempt to designate to what extent Lawrence's exile stemmed from his personality rather than simply from his social situation as a literary intellectual.

In his vision of society, Lawrence stressed that equality should not be a guiding principle. He was vehemently opposed to any attempts to create an egalitarian base for society. He believed that support for the principle of equality undermines the more important principle of the uniqueness of each individual:[11]

> Men are palpably unequal in *every* sense except the mathematical sense. Every man counts one; and this is the root of all equality: here, in a pure intellectual abstraction.

The democratic ideal of equality works on the notion of the average man, said Lawrence, and this is an attempt to drag all men down, to deny the essential uniqueness of each. You cannot, Lawrence claimed, average such things as spiritual and mystical needs:[12]

> This is all your Man-in-the-street amounts to: this tailor's

> dummy of an average. He is the image and effigy of all your equality. Men are not equal, and never were, and never will be, save by the arbitrary determination of some ridiculous human Ideal . . . and the Average Man just represents what all men need and desire, physically, functionally, materially and socially. *Materially* need: that's the point. The Average Man is the standard of material need in the human being.

Lawrence challenged any use of standards or ideals. Such talk, he argued, prevents men from striving to fulfil themselves, to develop according to their own true nature. He rejected the ideal of perfection so important in the nineteenth century, as a concern to ensure that 'everybody strives to look and to be as much as possible an impersonal, non-individual, abstracted unit, a standard'.[13]

To Arnold the ideal of perfection represented a way of avoiding and even combating the standardization effects of mass society. It was something which all men could strive for and a goal which provided a basis for preoccupations other than those of self-interest. Lawrence, on the other hand, argued that the ideal itself reeked of standardization. A standard or ideal does not recognize the extent to which all living people are separate and single, distinguished by nature from everyone else. Lawrence opposed the whole notion of having ideals, and instead emphasized the living, spontaneous individuality of every man and woman. For Arnold something outside the individual would counteract the self-interest and materialism of mass society; for Lawrence there was only the individual.

Lawrence's stance on this issue had implications for his perception of the role of the intellectual. He scorned any attempt to introduce 'culture' into the schools:[14]

> Away with all smatterings. Away with the imbecile pretence of culture in the elementary schools. Remember the back streets, remember that the souls of the working people are only rendered neurasthenic by your false culture. We want to keep the young populace robust and sufficiently nonchalant. Teach a boy to read, to write, and to do simple sums, and you have opened the door of all culture to him, if he wants to go through.

Unlike Arnold, Lawrence did not believe that the creative products of intellectuals have direct value to the general populace. The intellectual, particularly the novelist, could act as a mentor and moral guide, but only to a small section of the community. For these selected few, the novelist would provide the essential insights and reference to them would allow them to see to what extent they were alive or 'dead men in life'. The novelist, he declared, is supreme:[15]

> And being a novelist, I consider myself superior to the saint, the scientist, the philosopher, and the poet, who are all great masters of different bits of man alive, but never get the whole hog.

Yet, not everyone will learn through such reading and consultation of the works of intellectuals and novelists in particular. The working class, or as Lawrence expressed it, the group in the population who are comparatively 'non-mental', should be left to live according to their instincts and passions.[16] These members of society should be given as little education as possible because it only succeeds, Lawrence claimed, in severing them from their instincts and feelings. Indeed, he believed that education has this undesirable effect on all members of society. To counteract this process it should concentrate more on the feelings. Lawrence criticized the emphasis in education on teaching geography, history and other subjects related to an industrial society as being 'all France without Paris, *Hamlet* without the Prince, and bricks without straw'. We learn nothing about our own individuality, nothing about ourselves.[17]

Lawrence believed this to be a fundamental problem in industrial society: man has lost touch with his basic self, his innermost feelings. Not only has he lost touch, he does not even allow that these feelings exist. This was a central theme in Lawrence's novels: in *Women in Love* (1920), for instance, Gerald is tormented by his inability to feel, to respond, so that he cannot let himself go or know what his emotions are. Lawrence argued that we now have to educate ourselves in feelings:[18]

> If we can't hear the cries far down in our own forests of dark veins, we can look in the real novels, and there listen-in. Not listen to the didactic statements of the author, but to the low, calling cries of the characters, as they wander in the dark woods of their destiny.

Lawrence argued that our mental consciousness is a double-edged blessing: it interferes with our spontaneous, instinctive consciousness. But to ignore our mental consciousness would be dangerous. If it is not educated it may lead men into dangerous experiments and explorings, which other animals, through instinctive consciousness, would not pursue. Lawrence advocated the education of both our mental consciousness and our spontaneous feelings, so that there may be a perfect correspondence between the two. Educators, said Lawrence, will be the 'priests of life'. They will be responsible for developing spontaneous individuality in every man and woman.[19]

On a more practical level, Lawrence proposed that elementary education be kept to a bare minimum. His suggested programme consisted of three hours in the morning of the 3Rs, and three hours in the afternoon of swimming, games and gymnastic work. The latter, Lawrence argued, is important because we should learn to discipline our bodies. The 3Rs are all that is necessary to teach a child in his early years. If he wants to go on with more intellectual education, then these would be sufficient basis. Lawrence was quick to add that he was not in favour of a minimal amount of schooling because of some idealized view of the child. The child is not born naturally good, he claimed; it is totally unformed in one direction or the other:[20]

> Instead of worshipping the child, and seeing in it a divine emission which time will stale, we ought to realize that here is a new little clue to a human being, laid soft and vulnerable on the face of the earth. Here is our responsibility, to see that this unformed thing shall come to its own final form and fullness, both physical and mental.

## T. S. Eliot

Eliot had a totally different conception of the child and the nature of man. In accord with his conversion to Anglo Catholicism, he believed that man is born evil. After a period of great torment and depression, Eliot was baptized in 1927. His conversion played a significant role in the development of his poetry and his ideas about society. His poetry is often referred to as epitomizing the ethos of the 1920s and 1930s; it expressed the disillusionment with the idea of material progress that had so fired the Victorians, and anxiety about the life of the individual in industrial society. Eliot's 'The Wasteland' (1922), in particular, is seen as the symbol of his age. In his poem he expressed his view of modern existence as meaningless, a life-in-death:[21]

> After the torchlight red on sweaty faces
> After the frosty silence in the gardens
> After the agony in stony places
> The shouting and the crying
> Prison and palace and reverberation
> Of thunder of spring over distant mountains
> He who was living is now dead
> We who were living are now dying
> With a little patience

Eliot looked to the establishment of a community to counteract the evils of modern industrial society. His vision was similar to

Lawrence's and to the ideas of an organic society, but he was concerned that this society should be grounded in the idea of a Christian society. Membership of a community, Eliot argued, should be determined on a geographical basis, so that generations may grow up in the one place providing the basis for a social unity. All members of the community would have direct personal relationships. This would be guaranteed by the smallness of the community but would be strengthened by the requirement of a shared code of beliefs, the beliefs of orthodox Christianity. Whether or not individual members were fully conscious of the extent to which their shared beliefs were distinctively Christian and religious, they would nevertheless act in accord with this social code of behaviour. The traditional way of life of the community would not need to be imposed by law and nor would it be the result of arbitrary individual beliefs.[22]

The idea of community in Eliot's writings is synonymous with that of the organic society that arises throughout the romantic literary tradition. In essence this concept denotes a society that is well-integrated, in which all members fit quite naturally and harmoniously. The idea of the organic society sometimes also includes the condition that members can be broken up into groups (or classes) and that each of these groups has a definite and important function to fulfil in that society.

Eliot employed the term 'community' for another purpose when he described a need for what he called a 'community of Christians'. A notion similar to Coleridge's clerisy, it called for the formation of a body of consciously and thoughtfully practising Christians, especially those of intellectual and spiritual superiority. Eliot acknowledged the similarity between his concept of community of Christians and Coleridge's clerisy, but he claimed that his idea was at once wider and more restricted. The community of Christians, unlike Coleridge's clerisy, would not include all of the teaching body; but it would include some of the clergy and some intellectuals.[23]

Eliot became defensive when he talked of intellectuals. Discussing the constituting elements of the community of Christians, he remarked that it would include 'those who are ordinarily spoken of, not always with flattering intention, as "intellectuals"'.[24] Such a comment signifies the distinct change in tone which had occurred since Arnold's writings. Harking back to the literary intellectual's tradition of which Coleridge and Arnold were part, Eliot felt on uneasy ground. To be an intellectual within an artistic field, no longer carried with it certain clear assumptions of a place and role in the society. Instead the literary intellectual was a possible object of derision.

Eliot paid considerable attention to clarifying the composition of the élite or community of Christians. He argued that it would not be a caste-like group:[25]

> It will be their identity of belief and aspiration, their background of a common system of education and a common culture, which will enable them to influence and be influenced by each other, and collectively to form the conscious mind and the conscience of the nation.

But his ideas about how such an 'identity of belief and aspiration' was to be achieved changed between writing his first major essay oriented to an analysis of society *The Idea of a Christian Society* (1939) and his second major essay *Notes Towards the Definition of Culture* (1948). In the latter Eliot was adamant that 'identity of belief and aspiration' could not exist in any other way than through a concurrence of social background, in particular family background. By this time Eliot had turned to a notion of a class-based élite. He denied that this meant that he identified the élite with the upper class, for he was quick to acknowledge that a large part of the upper classes had always been conspicuously lacking in the desirable culture. Nevertheless, to a great extent, members of the élite, Eliot argued, should be drawn from the dominant class of the period.[26]

Identity of class background was essential to Eliot in order that members of the élite should communicate with each other properly:[27]

> In an élite composed of individuals who find their way into it solely for their individual pre-eminence, the differences of background will be so great, that they will be united only by their common interests, and separated by everything else. An élite must therefore be attached to *some* class, whether higher or lower: but so long as there are classes at all it is likely to be the dominant class that attracts this élite to itself.

Eliot was strongly opposed to any idea of a meritocratic system in which those judged most capable rose to the top of the hierarchical structure of society. He was convinced that only the family can transmit the necessary values and beliefs to be shared by members of the élite. In rejecting any ideas of a meritocratic system he queried the use of criteria to select members for this type of élite. Any choice of criteria would have an oppressive effect on novelty, he maintained, and new works of genius would encounter great opposition simply because they would inevitably challenge these criteria. Eliot dismissed all suggestions that the class-based élite system would deny opportunities to creative talents amongst the largest proportion of the population. He merely claimed to doubt that there had been or was likely to be any undiscovered Shakespeares or Miltons in the world.

Bottomore demolishes Eliot's argument that common family background is the fundamental factor in the cohesion of an élite by referring to the number of other social institutions in the past which have been responsible for this task. Religious associations, philosophical schools and academies, he argues, have been at least as important as the family in transmitting culture to the members of the upper class. Eliot did not acknowledge the dominant role of education and religious institutions in maintaining the cohesion of the dominant classes even up to the end of the nineteenth century.[28]

Yet within his own terms, Eliot did have grounds for concern at the disintegration of élites based on a common social background. As Bourdieu points out, 'the sharing of a common culture, whether this involves verbal patterns or artistic experience and objects of admiration, is probably one of the surest foundations of the deep underlying fellow-feeling that unites the members of the governing classes. . . .'[29] An education which concentrated purely on the preparation of people for specific occupational activities might not provide the basis for social unity amongst a specific group in society. But as Bourdieu has shown throughout his work, this situation has not yet arrived; education continues to play a dominant though thoroughly disguised role in the society in the maintenance of hierarchical structures based on the class divisions of society.

Eliot's anxiety about the social basis of élites has to be interpreted, then, as more a concern with the reinstatement of the class basis of élites of the past than a simple desire to have a class-based élite. The hierarchical division of society continues, but the dominant class has changed over the centuries. Eliot essentially developed a feudal vision of society in which the dominant class resembled none of the existing fractions of the middle class, but instead echoed the aristocracy of pre-capitalist society. In his opposition to the disintegration and materialism of mass society, Eliot sought to return to a society based quite directly on an image of society in which a feudal aristocracy once again would take responsibility for the moral and social welfare of its people.

Austin diagnoses Eliot as being fundamentally authoritarian. One wonders, he asks, what would happen to all free thinkers in Eliot's society. Eliot disguised his authoritarianism with his concern for religion and spirituality, but Austin declares Eliot's vision as conformist and repressive. He can find no possible attraction in Eliot's conception of society except perhaps for some members of the community of Christians.[30] Indeed, with an obsession for order, Eliot carried the notion of a consistent relation between class and function to extremes and, as an artist, he seemed bent on forming a society in which creativity would be stifled. His belief in the necessity of a hierarchical society demonstrated a distinct lack of concern for anyone but those at the top of the hierarchy (a claim which cannot be made of Lawrence, for example, at all).

But it is vital that we do not dismiss Eliot as having only limited appeal. Historically this has not been the case. Amongst educationalists he has gained considerable attention, particularly amongst those involved in the 'Black Papers' movement of the 1960s and 1970s. Amongst intellectuals who sense a threat to their cultural preserve, Eliot offers a coherent image of society in which the role of the intellectual is central. He provided a specific formulation of the problems and weaknesses of education with recommendations about how to counteract these. His appeal rests not only on the specificity of that analysis but on its compactness.

In his ideas about education and culture, Eliot ignored questions about the prospects for any group except those at the top of the hierarchy. Like Lawrence, he believed that only a small section of the population should receive an intellectual education. Education in a secular society has an added responsibility, he claimed: to help preserve the classes and select the élite. But Eliot was critical of the rising preoccupation with education as a tool for the promotion of certain social changes. One of the prime faults in education, according to his diagnosis, was that its relationship to knowledge was being forgotten. No agreement could be found as to there being any body of knowledge which an educated person should acquire at a particular stage in his life. He suggested that:[31]

> What we remark especially about the educational thought of the last few years, is the enthusiasm with which education has been taken up as an instrument for the realisation of social ideals. It would be a pity if we overlooked the possibilities of education as a means of acquiring *wisdom*; if we belittled the acquisition of knowledge for the satisfaction of curiosity, without any further motive than the desire to know; and if we lost our respect for learning.

Emphasizing knowledge and wisdom, Eliot developed a fairly traditional notion of education, though he did not elaborate sufficiently on his ideas about education in a practical sense, to know what form he envisaged this taking. Nor did he make it clear what sort of education he proposed for the rest of the population who had not been lucky enough to be born with the right sort of family background. It is not until Bantock takes up Eliot's ideas on society and education, and fills in the obvious gap left by him on the question of the education of the masses, that we have any suggestion of a system of popular education which may be developed on the basis of Eliot's ideas.

Eliot adopted an aggressive stance on his claim that our traditional culture should be confined to the members of a class-based élite. He insisted that his arguments stemmed from the only legitimate usage of the term 'culture':[32]

> What I try to say is this: here are what I believe to be essential conditions for the growth and for the survival of culture. If they conflict with any passionate faith of the reader—if, for instance, he finds it shocking that culture and equalitarianism should conflict, if it seems monstrous to him that anyone should have 'advantages of birth'—I do not ask him to change his faith, I merely ask him to stop paying lip-service to culture.

In this passage, Eliot carried out a brilliant, but somewhat dishonest, *coup de grâce* for his whole argument about culture and élites. Williams provides an excellent analysis of the passage:[33]

> From *try to say* and *what I believe to be* there is an abrupt movement to something very different: the assertion, backed by the emotive devices of *passionate, shocking, monstrous,* and *lip-service*, that if we do not agree with Eliot's conditions we stand self-convicted of indifference to culture. This, to say the least, is not proved; and in this jump from the academy to the correspondence column, which Eliot is far too able and experienced a writer not to know that he is making, there is evidence of other impulses behind this work than the patient effort towards definition; evidence, one might say, of the common determination to rationalize one's prejudices.

This analysis can be applied to much of Eliot's social criticism, which often appeared largely an attempt to rationalize Eliot's two major value-positions which increasingly dominated his outlook on life: conservatism and Anglo Catholicism.

Eliot sought to return to a concept of culture similar to that employed by Arnold. He emphasized the sense in which culture is 'a whole way of life', an element in this term which did not always clearly emerge in Arnold's work. As Williams points out, this sense of culture as a whole way of life has gained prominence in the twentieth-century anthropology and sociology, but it had its origins in the literary tradition of Carlyle and Coleridge.[34] Eliot criticized the tendency to assume that the minority culture is the only culture in our society and that 'the humbler part of society' only has 'culture in so far as it participates in this superior and more conscious culture'. Any attempt to force this culture on the general population will only adulterate and cheapen it: 'For it is an essential condition of the preservation of the quality of the culture of the minority, that it should continue to be a minority culture'.[35]

Eliot was by no means advocating cultural relativism in his claims to recognize the existence and validity of other cultures in our society. The minority culture is without doubt in his mind the 'superior' culture, as were other classes the 'humbler' sectors of society. Eliot's position is quite distinct from Hoggart's, for example, who does actually exhibit and give reasons for respecting the cultural differences in our society. Eliot's discussion of the existence of other cultures was mere gesturing. He did not give adequate thought to what it meant to speak of culture as a whole way of life, as he very clearly demonstrated in his attempt to identify features of such a culture:[36]

> It includes all the characteristic activities and interests of a people: Derby Day, Henley Regatta, Cowes, the twelfth of August, a cup final, the dog races, the pin table, the dart board, Wensleydale cheese, boiled cabbage cut into sections, beetroot in vinegar, nineteenth-century Gothic churches and the music of Elgar.

As Williams points out, this description is nothing more than some of the leisure activities of English life. The passage is amusing, but ultimately a trick. Eliot added nothing to the definition of culture, but instead confused his audience so that they believe his analysis of society has some sociological basis.

Though Williams points out the way in which Eliot played with the sense of culture as a way of life, he too was trapped. Williams believes that Eliot, through his insistence on culture as 'a whole way of life', valuably criticized orthodox theories of the diffusion of culture. He commends Eliot for recognizing that culture cannot be limited to that which is transmitted through a formal system of education.[37] Yet Williams does not recognize the extent to which the relationship between the minority culture and the ruling class (as analysed by Eliot) forms part of the very basis of the cultural domination by that class. As Bourdieu points out, the educational system only transmits the minority culture to that group who already has the cultural tools, or 'cultural capital', to be able to use it; and yet this process is not acknowledged by the educational system or the society. The failure of the majority of the population to acquire or even appreciate the minority culture is attributed to their intellectual inadequacy. In this manner the hierarchical structure or class divisions of society are legitimated through the ideological use of terms such as 'intelligence', 'brains', or 'IQ'.[38]

Far more central to Russell's social and political writings was the question of how to reconcile the ideal of the liberty of the individual with the need for social order. He recognized the need for some form of governmental control, but lamented the extent of its use in English society at that time.[45] Writing at a time when the state was intervening increasingly in the welfare of the population, Russell was apprehensive that individual initiative was to be crushed. Not only were there changes at this level, but conjointly, the rise of large corporations signified a major shift in the capitalist social formation. Russell, with allegiances to the *laissez-faire* liberalism of the nineteenth century, sensed a threat to the individualism of earlier capitalist forms.

Russell offered four proposals for the reconciliation of the individual with his role as citizen. First, we need to eliminate war, for by so doing we would eliminate the conflict between private and public morals. In war, man is allowed to murder and steal; whereas in private life he is forbidden such activities. Second, we need to eliminate superstition. When men are not full of fear of the unknown, they will not feel threatened by the unusual. Third, we need to eliminate too great a love of uniformity. And finally, we should be aware of the danger of the administrator. His expertise does not require intimate familiarity with the purposes of the work he organizes. Such a situation can lead to too great a love of classification and statistics. Education, said Russell, has suffered in this manner.[46]

On a governmental level, Russell hoped to reconcile the claims of the individual and the citizen still further. He wished to limit the power of the government to three spheres: security, justice and conservation. Otherwise the main aim of the government should be to promote non-governmental initiatives. A certain amount of control is necessary, Russell argued, but the powers of the state should be relegated as much as possible to various bodies—geographical, industrial and cultural.[47]

Russell advocated the formation of a 'World Government' whose prime function should be to prevent wars. Russell opposed all notions of nationalism and patriotism as being of a possessive or negative nature. Much of the fervour which merges as a love of one's country is based rather on hatred of other countries. A world government whose powers were limited to the prevention of war and responsibility for the creation of a spirit of internationalism was the only force which Russell could conceive as being able to change these possessive and negative feelings so dominant in modern society.

Russell did not trouble with the concrete problems of the actual workings of such a government, beyond laying down the simple guidelines that a government's domain is the regulation of our possessive impulses, whereas the creative impulses, although they may be encouraged by the government, are the domain of individuals and groups. Despite his dabbling at various times with the ideas of the social democrats and guild socialism, Russell never departed very far from his background of aristocratic liberalism and its affinity with nineteenth-century *laissez-faire* individualism. In a letter to a friend he revealed his underlying sentiment in all political considerations: 'I don't like the spirit of socialism—I think freedom is the basis of everything.'[48]

Russell devoted himself to this concern, rather than to the development of a coherent theory of society. He particularly warned of the tendency in democracy for 'tyranny of the herd': [49]

> Democracy as a sentiment has two sides. When it says 'I am as good as you', it is wholesome; but when it says 'You are no better than I am', it becomes oppressive and an obstacle to the development of exceptional merit. To put the matter more accurately: democracy is good when it inspires self-respect, and bad when it inspires persecution of exceptional individuals by the herd.

America exemplified the trends which Russell wished to forestall in England. Unlike many others, he did not find America more materialistic than any other country, but he found the emphasis on popular opinion disturbing. He was convinced that such an emphasis would lead to uniformity, and mediocrity, threatening civilization. In America the tyranny of the herd allows no room for eccentricity 'and unusual opinions bring social penalities upon those who hold them'.[50]

These issues particularly concerned Russell in his wish to obtain the freedom for intellectuals to pursue their essential function, as he perceived it, in society. The pursuit of truth and new ideas could not be undertaken unless the infringement of the multitude on his endeavour was eliminated. The multitude, Russell claimed, have neither the talent nor the knowledge to be engaged in any way in the fulfilment of this task. The intellectual must be allowed full autonomy to achieve a certain amount of detachment or political scepticism.

Russell was particularly committed to questions of how to change society. He was not sanguine about the chances of any significant change for some time to come, for he believed that 'there is no obvious means of altering education and the Press until our political system is altered'.[51] His scepticism extended to education as a social institution because in this form he believed it to be generally a reactionary force in society. He argued that education as a social institution supports the government when it is conservative and opposes it when it is progressive. Yet he valued education in the non-institutional sense as a means for the development of the individual and the promotion of the pursuit of truth. He believed that the best type of education tends to be one which is hostile to the status quo rather than one which is friendly to it. In this type of education both intelligence and sympathy will tend to be less repressed. In contrast, the first thing the average educator at the present time is trying to do, said Russell, is to kill the imagination as being 'a lawless thing'.[52]

Russell's interest in education was heightened when it came near the time when he would be sending his own two children to school. Park describes Russell's decision:[53]

> Russell found himself questioning the narrow curriculum, the formal and impersonal methodology, and the rigorous and uncompromising examination system, all of which flourished in the English elementary schools of 1925. Because of these conditions, the Russells decided not to send their children to one of these schools, choosing instead to develop their own school.

Russell and his second wife, Dora, set up a school at Beacon Hill in 1927. It has been described as one of the schools of the New Education movement, but the ideas in this movement are so diverse and confusing that it is simpler to look at Beacon Hill by itself.[54] In his educational ideas Russell attempted to combine both Freudian and Watsonian influences. He avoided confronting the violent conflicts which the employing of these two approaches together would seem inevitably to involve, by having no coherent theory of education. As in his political thought, Russell combined ideas based on his own experiences with ideas drawn from his particular background of aristocratic liberalism. He agreed with others in the New Education movement that attendance at lessons should be voluntary, as much as possible. Compulsion in education, he claimed, destroys originality and intellectual interest. But he placed quite specific limits on this freedom, disagreeing with the stress on total freedom which educators such as A. S. Neill advocated. Freedom in the schools should not be an absolute principle; children should be taught discipline, according to Russell.

Russell expounded this belief with particular reference to the nature of the 'herd' created in the school. There are two types of herd which the child has to cope with, Russell claimed: the great herd of the whole society, and, more important to the child, the small herd or school fellows. In establishing a school the character of the herd thereby created must be the first concern of the educator. No matter how kindly and tolerant he might be, Russell warned, if the educator permits the school herd to be cruel and intolerant, the children will suffer greatly. Russell suggested that such a painful environment was likely to exist in some modern schools where the doctrine of non-interference was carried to extremes.

Russell further departed from the ideas of many of those in the New Education movement on the question of curriculum. He believed, as he said, 'with a dying few', that knowledge is desirable on its own account.[55] Russell designed his curriculum around the disciplines of knowledge, ensuring that the content of the children's education should be of a traditional nature. The only concession he made in this area to current ideas about education was to draw up a separate programme for each child.

In discussing education, Russell employed a notion of culture, but it appears to have been a rather idiosyncratic usage of the term. He warned that the trend in schools was away from the promotion of culture: [56]

> the elements in current education which are concerned with individual culture are, in the main, products of tradition, and are likely to be more and more replaced by education in citizenship. Education in citizenship, if it is wise, can retain what was best in individual culture. But if it is in any way short sighted it will stunt the individual in order to make him a convenient tool of government.

Just what Russell meant by the term 'individual culture' is difficult to discern. In this passage he seems to be using it in the sense of 'cultivation of the growth of the individual'. On another occasion he seemed to use it in the sense of tradition: he suggested that a consciousness of 'Western culture' is one way to create a unity between countries, transcending national boundaries.[57] On yet another occasion, he seemed to employ something of the sense of Arnold's concept of culture, but he added his own particular flavour:[58]

> The narrowness of the traditional conception of culture has a great deal to do with the disrepute into which culture has fallen with the general public. Genuine culture consists in being a citizen of the universe, not only of one or two arbitrary fragments of space-time; it helps men to understand human society as a whole, to estimate wisely the ends that communities should pursue, and to see the present in its relation to past and future. Genuine culture is therefore of great value to those who are to wield power, to whom it is at least as useful as detailed information. The way to make men useful is to make them wise, and an essential part of wisdom is a comprehensive mind.

Russell's usage of 'culture' was precisely of the type which Eliot criticized. Russell used the term very much as he wanted to, without any real reference to traditional usage. There was some resemblance to Arnold's concept, but on the whole it was distinctly his own. Russell was using 'culture' to cover the things intellectual of which he approved. By using the term in this manner, he made it little more than a term of approbation. This is not to denigrate what Russell was saying; it is merely to point out that his use of 'culture' was somewhat confused and had very little to do with the concept as it has been discussed so far in this study.

Russell, then, was concerned with the problem of excellence in mass society, but he was mainly interested in intellectual pursuits other than in artistic fields. He regretted the loss of social function of the artist, yet the main thrust of his work was towards the promotion of the pursuit of knowledge of a scientific kind. Education is the prime means by which he believed this promotion could be carried out. Russell recognized that his experiment at Beacon Hill had only limited implications for education. The school was possible to organize in the way it was, because of the smallness of the pupil intake—it never exceeded about twenty-five. However, the state, said Russell, is still necessary to finance education, if it is to be provided for the masses. Matters of finance and organization make it impossible to approach anything like the ideal of a tutorial system.

Despite the fineness of his thinking, the humanity of his concerns, there is a disappointing sense of limitation in Russell's social and political thought. His aristocratic liberal background pervaded all his thought and, above all, his commitment to traditional intellectual pursuits dominated his ideas both about society and education. More than any of the other thinkers examined, Russell's desire was to set the intellectual at the top of the hierarchical structure of society. He provided very little discussion of how the rest of society was to be formed or the way in which the members of society, not part of the élites, were to lead their lives.

## Christopher Caudwell

Caudwell was one of the generation of communists who arose in the 1930s, an intellectual movement which was essentially pro-soviet Russia and Marxist-Stalinist in doctrine. Caudwell did not live long enough to see the rapid disillusionment with and rejection of communism in England. He went to Spain, as did many young English intellectuals, to fight in the civil war which lasted from 1936 to 1939. Caudwell joined the resistance forces in December 1936 and was killed in February 1937.

Before his early death, Caudwell wrote a number of books and articles whose significance lies not in any subtlety of thought, but in their attempt to establish a Marxist aesthetic, an area of thought notably neglected by English intellectuals until the 1960s. In a series of essays entitled *Studies in a Dying Culture* (1936), Caudwell vehemently attacked what he referred to as the 'bourgeois illusions' of English culture. Our culture is seriously ill, he claimed, because we do not recognize that it is based on a central illusion: that man is necessarily free:[59]

> It would be fine if freedom were as easy as this, that man was naturally free. But it is not true. Freedom is the product, not of the instincts, but of social relations themselves. Freedom is secreted in the relation of man to man.

We are not, said Caudwell, suffering from disillusionment as Freud, Jung, D. H. Lawrence and T. S. Eliot have claimed. These men have been victims of the central illusion of bourgeois culture which has prevented them from wishing for anything better than the freedom of the individual. Thinkers like Lawrence have been unable to escape from the essential selfishness which is the pattern of bourgeois culture. The liberty which the bourgeoisie seek, Caudwell continued, relies on the non-liberty of the proletariat. Indeed, bourgeois social relations depend on the existence of both freedom and unfreedom for their continuance. The bourgeoisie could not enjoy his idleness without the labour of the worker, nor the worker remain in a bourgeois relationship without the coercive guidance and leadership of the bourgeois.

Caudwell did not reject the necessity of freedom; he claimed that he was a communist because he believed in freedom. Man attains freedom, he claimed, by co-operation with his fellows. If we believe, as did Russell, that freedom of the individual is the essential goal of human effort, then civilization should be abandoned and we should return to the woods. In a world in which communism prevails Caudwell suggested that all would 'participate in ruling and active intellectuals, no longer divorced from being, learn from the conscious worker just as much as the workers demand guidance from thought'.[60]

Such a system, Caudwell declared, would close the gap that exists at present between thought and action, whose separation leaves thought immobilized or racing like a machine out of control. Thought, he argued, guides action, but also learns how to guide from action. In a bourgeois society, thought is divorced from action by the division of members of society into classes. Thought or consciousness is established as the right of one class: 'Consciousness becomes a privilege which is not actively created but which is "given" by birth or chance.' The distortion characteristic of the ideology of that class stems from their assumption of these rights, and in turn this distortion is inevitably reproduced in 'the ideology of that society's whole culture'.[61]

Caudwell argued that the ideology of the society's whole culture is the ideology of the ruling class. His claims in many ways adumbrated the general basis of the theory of hegemony being developed by Gramsci, but Caudwell had no knowledge of this work, as Yurick points out, nor of any other contemporary movements in Marxist thought amongst continental intellectuals.[62] Caudwell's thought reveals the constraints of his limited English background. In particular, he failed to develop a theoretical basis for his thoughts. By way of contrast, similar ideas to Caudwell's were often expounded by his continental counterparts, but they enlarged upon them and incorporated them into theories of society or social change. Such was the case, for example, with Caudwell's claims about the relationship between the ideology of the ruling class and the dominant ideology of society. Gramsci's notion of hegemony was developed at about the same time, but it is an integral and focal point in a complex discussion about society, whose theoretical ramifications are extensive. Similarly, the fundamental connection asserted by Caudwell between thought and action has also been explored by continental intellectuals such as Jean Paul Sartre, and developed into a theory of praxis.

Caudwell, it seems, despite his awareness of certain basic assumptions underlying the English intellectual tradition such as the supreme importance attached to the notion of the individual and his freedom, was unable to escape the English approach to social thought. His ideas, occasionally insightful, rested on a crude doctrine of Stalinist-Marxism, for he was unable to develop his own theory of society or revolutionary change. Consequently, when Williams in the 1950s set out to establish his cultural critique of society, Caudwell's work could offer him only shallow insights rather than a developed Marxist cultural analysis.

## George Orwell

Orwell claimed that it was not until 1936–7 that he became certain of his political commitment to socialism, the end result of a culmination of a variety of experiences: schooling at Eton, imperialism in Burma, poverty, and, as a consequence, a deep sympathy for the working class, and then finally the Spanish Civil War.[63] Yet, despite his involvement with the socialist cause, Orwell should not be classified simply as a socialist. He was very critical of socialists (as distinct from socialism) and, particularly in his later novels *Animal Farm* (1945) and *1984* (1949), contributed some of the most damaging criticism of the socialist movement to come out of England. Moreover, to add to the difficulty of understanding Orwell's position, it has been suggested by some authors that Orwell was essentially conservative in outlook. Sandison, for example, argues that despite a kind of romantic socialism, Orwell's thinking was steeped in the English Protestant tradition. Orwell eventually resolved this central paradox in his work, Sandison claims, in favour of conservatism.[64]

It is this apparent central paradox in Orwell's work which makes him so fascinating to study. As a writer he was fundamentally attracted to the humanist tradition traced through other writers and artists in this work. And as an intellectual in the 1930s he was confronted with the call 'to declare oneself'. Leavis had claimed that the writer, the artist, should defy this call, yet he himself was unable to resist entering the political debate, to declare himself against Marxism. Orwell took the opposite path and turned quite openly to embrace socialism, making it necessary for him to reconcile the two commitments he had chosen. Williams analyses this as a conflict in Orwell's thought and claims that in Orwell the humane tradition 'disintegrates into a caustic dust'.[65] This seems an unduly pessimistic view of Orwell's work. Despite an air of bitterness in much of his work, Orwell was always interested in effecting some sort of compromise between the two commitments.

The main way in which Orwell attempted to make this compromise was to adopt a detached stance from both commitments, criticizing in particular other supporters of these commitments. One of Orwell's major condemnations of socialists was their insincerity on the issue of class distinctions. All revolutionary opinion draws its strength from the 'secret conviction that nothing can be changed', for very few people seriously want to abolish all class distinctions. If we were to be truly honest, Orwell argued, then we would accept that class distinctions cannot be eliminated and would try to develop socialism despite this restriction. He believed that class distinctions are too hard to escape because of the fundamental nature of class. Class is more than just a question of money; it also consists of traditions, attitudes, speech and manners. Middle-class revolutionaries should particularly face up to this problem, Orwell claimed. One of their great difficulties is that they still want to remain middle class, to keep their manners, and so on.[66]

In *The Road to Wigan Pier* (1937) Orwell was most belligerent about middle-class revolutionaries. He accused them of having no idea about what the working class are really like. He was severe with people like Beatrice Webb whom he called 'slum-visitor socialists', who only want reform not revolution. These people have no true feelings about the working class, he claimed, and fear any proper contact with them:[67]

> The truth is that to many people calling themselves Socialists, revolution does not mean a movement of the masses with which they hope to associate themselves; it means a set of reforms which 'we', the clever ones, are going to impose upon 'them', the Lower Orders.

Yet even in his account of living amongst miners and visiting their mines which formed the basis of *The Road to Wigan Pier*, Orwell himself was unable to provide a fully sensitive portrayal of working-class life. As Gross points out, the miners themselves as Orwell described them remain types rather than individuals.[68] Orwell seems to have been unable to go beyond his mixed feelings of guilt and admiration towards the miners. His description of the miners and their lives is fascinating, but ultimately frustrating in its limitations.

Gross analyses Orwell's work as being underpinned by a strong vein of social masochism as revealed particularly in his works *Down and Out in Paris and London* (1933), *A Clergyman's Daughter* (1935), *Keep the Aspidistra Flying* (1954), and *The Road to Wigan Pier* (1937). The conclusion to the last book is, Gross believes, significant and particularly striking for Orwell's social masochism. In the conclusion, Orwell described what may happen after the socialist struggle, finishing with the statement:[69]

> And then perhaps this misery of class-prejudice will fade away, and we of the sinking middle class . . . may sink without further struggles into the working class where we belong, and probably when we get there it will not be so dreadful as we feared, for, after all, we have nothing to lose but our aitches.

Gross claims that the talk of 'sinking' into the working class suggests less a manifesto than social masochism.[70]

Gross has missed the essentially facetious tone in the passage from Orwell. Orwell is sending up the middle-class disdain of working-class speech. The ridiculous image of what will be the outcome of the sinking down shows clearly that Orwell was not at all worried. It is only the middle class who abhor the dropping of aitches in our speech, and only someone concerned with such trivialities who will see the process of the disappearance of class, as a 'sinking down'. Orwell believed that class distinctions would eventually disappear, but he also was certain that they are so deeply entrenched that it is impossible, for the present, to get rid of them. Consequently, he suggested that what socialists must do is to try to persuade different classes to act together, for the moment without being asked to drop their class differences. Orwell argued that once this principle is accepted socialism will have a better chance.

Orwell saw two still further fundamental problems for the successful introduction of socialism in England. If its claims are to reach a wider audience, he argued, then it must dispel its image as being the property of cranks; and second, it must lose its current association with an over-emphasis on machines and technical progress. Orwell did not denigrate the need for technical progress; on the contrary, he believed it to be inevitable. He mocked anyone who desired a return to the past, to the past of the individual craftsman. Nevertheless, he also recognized that technical progress must be tempered by the needs of creativity and humanity, two qualities in English society being usurped by the uncritical acceptance of this process. Summing up his position, he declared that:[71]

> The job of the Socialist is to get it out again. Justice and Liberty! *Those* are the words that have got to ring like a bugle across the world. For a long time past, certainly for the last ten years, the devil has had all the best tunes. We have reached a stage when the very word 'Socialism' calls up, on the one hand, a picture of aeroplanes, tractors, and huge glittering factories of glass and concrete; on the other, a picture of vegetarians with wilting beards, of Bolshevik commissars (half gangster, half gramophone), of earnest ladies in sandals, shock-headed Marxists chewing polysyllables, escaped Quakers, birth-control fanatics and Labour Party backstairs-crawlers. Socialism, at least in this island, does not smell any longer of revolution and the overthrow of tyrants; it smells of crankishness, machine-worship, and the stupid cult of Russia. Unless you can remove that smell, and very rapidly, Fascism may win.

Orwell's ideas indicate a significant change in the socialist thought prevailing in England between the 1880s and 1930s. Morris in the 1880s and 90s developed a socialist theory strongly flavoured by a romantic medievalism, in his preoccupation with craft guilds and utopian communities. By the time Orwell was writing, socialist thought had largely discarded these visions and had become far more 'hard-headed'. Machine civilization was largely recognized as being irreversible. Orwell's position was one of resignation, rather than positive acclaim for technology; he recommended only continued vigilance, so that technical progress should not undermine our humanity any further.

Orwell's actual commitment to socialism also appears at times to have been one of resignation. Writing in the two or three years before the war he declared that the only real choice anyone had at that time was between socialism and fascism. And fascism, he claimed, is at its very best, socialism with the virtues left out. But despite any initial reluctance there may have been on Orwell's part, he argued powerfully for his commitment to socialism. He described its necessity as 'elementary commonsense' that everyone does his fair share of the work and gets his fair share of the provisions.[72]

Orwell found the claims for socialism to have a certain undeniable force; but he also found the claims of socialists totally lacking this force. This was one of his major struggles. He found the pressure to conform which this group exerted exasperating. It conflicted strongly with the ideal of intellectual liberty which he held as a writer. He compared his age unfavourably with the Victorian period in England when intellectuals did not suffer the same pressure from their peers to conform to the political orthodoxy of the time. A modern literary intellectual, he claimed, is disadvantaged by 'living among clear-cut political ideologies and of usually knowing at a glance what thoughts are heretical'.[73]

Orwell was romanticizing the position of the Victorian literary intellectual. At that time too a dominant orthodoxy could be said to have existed: middle-class liberalism. Any ideas which departed markedly from this standpoint, such as Marxism, received no serious, general hearing among intellectual circles in England. Orwell made the mistake of assuming that the absence of explicit pressure to conform indicated freedom of thought. This aspect of his thought signals a fundamental lacuna in his discussions of society. Orwell did not develop any systematic concept of ideology or culture. He used the terms but with no acknowledgment of any complex theoretical questions' being involved in this area.

Orwell became increasingly strident in his criticism of socialism (or socialists), a process which Williams described as a retreat to be understood as a condition of his exile.[74] Williams attempts to make some rather uncertain distinctions between the vagrant and the exile to explain the tensions in Orwell's work. But the vague psychologism of this explanation remains undeveloped and hence unsatisfactory. Williams does not provide any specific definition of the social and personal dimensions of these terms. Moreover, as Gross points out, Williams's use of these concepts blurs the fact that Orwell, in his criticism of socialism, was responding to social realities, not just private frustrations.[75]

Orwell discussed these realities, as he perceived them, in the essay 'Writers and Leviathan' (1948). He accused the left of accumulating 'in our minds a whole series of unadmitted contradictions, as a result of successive bumps against reality.'[76] The first bump, he claimed, was the Russian Revolution: socialists could not recognize that socialism did not exist in Russia. The second was the rise of fascism. The events which occurred with this development shook the pacifism and internationalism of the left. Third, the left was in power when Orwell was writing (1948), and obliged to take responsibility and make decisions.

Orwell's analysis provides some valuable insights into the socialism which gained widespread support in the 1930s and then disappeared again so quickly. His criticism of socialism should be seen in the light of this analysis. While supporting socialism, he was most concerned to point out the inconsistencies that were prevalent in much of socialist writing and discussion in his time. Such a stand cannot be accused of conservatism. There seems, in fact, to be very little evidence for Sandison's claim that Orwell eventually opted for a conservative outlook. As Gross points out, the essays which Orwell wrote in the last three years of his life clearly show that he did not sink into any sort of misanthropic despair.[77] In his essay, 'Lear, Tolstoy and the Fool' (1947) he reconfirmed the principle which had been the basis of his socialism: live for others.

The fundamental tension underlying all of Orwell's work was the conflict of commitment to politics and to writing. In his later writings, he maintained that it is necessary to keep the two commitments separate. A writer cannot lock himself in an ivory tower: it is both impossible and undesirable; but he cannot yield himself to a political group. To Orwell acceptance of any political discipline appeared to be incompatible with literary integrity. The only solution he could envisage was to keep his work as a writer separate from his work as a politically committed person.

In accord with this stance, Orwell not only flayed his contemporary socialists for their shortcomings, but he also expressed strong distaste for the literary world of the time. He painted a sordid picture of this world:[78]

> The modern English literary world, at any rate the highbrow section of it, is a sort of poisonous jungle where only weeds can flourish. . . . In the highbrow world you 'get on', if you 'get on' at all, not so much by your literary ability as by being the life and soul of cocktail parties and kissing the bums of verminous little lions.

Orwell's distrust of his fellow writers and his commitment to the fundamental restructuring of society meant that the concept of culture of the romantic literary tradition could have no appeal for him. He could not envisage a particular role for the literary intellectuals as an ameliorating force in society. As an alternative to the vision of this literary tradition and to the prevalent socialist ideas, Orwell advocated a humanized socialism. The fundamental principles underlying his socialism were that there should be plenty of provisions in the world for everybody; we must all co-operate to ensure that everyone does his fair shaire of work, and that everyone gets his fair share of provisions.

Yet, Orwell was drawn towards a similar set of questions in his discussion of contemporary society as those posed by the literary tradition. He sought to determine the developing implications of mechanical progress for the creative or aesthetic features of the life of the individual members of society. To counteract some of the disadvantages of mechanical progress for this aspect of the quality of life, Orwell proclaimed the virtues of bringing art to the people, a position which he perceived as defying both contemporary socialists and the English literary tradition. The former, Orwell claimed, held that no conscious act will effect a closer connection between art and popular culture; such a relationship is dependent on major changes in the society. The latter view, he suggested, held that art and popular culture's estrangement was irretrievable, the result of the mere going astray of tradition at some point or other.

Unlike Leavis, for example, Orwell believed the people, the mass, can be led to an appreciation of poetry, particularly through the modern cultural technologies such as the radio and the cinema. Orwell pointed out that the current usages made of these two technologies could not be identified with their full range of uses. The cultural institutions based on the modern technologies, he argued, are controlled by the state or big companies who desire the status quo to remain and prefer people not to think. The stranglehold maintained by these institutions beguile us into conflating present use with the potentiality of broadcasting and cinema, for example.

The main hope for the artist and the intellectual, Orwell suggested, is contained within the very trends in society which at present make things seem so bleak for him. The increasing totalitarianism in society means that more and more the channels of production are under the control of bureaucrats. Their aim is to destroy the artist, or at least castrate him. The mitigating process taking place within this trend is, Orwell believed:[79]

> that the huge bureaucratic machines of which we are all part are beginning to work creakily because of their mere size and their constant growth. The tendency of the modern state is to wipe out the freedom of the intellect, and yet at the same time every state, especially under the pressure of war, finds itself more and more in need of an intelligentsia to do its publicity for it.

In some ways Orwell's prediction was right; he analysed one of the contradictions of capitalism. Yet at the same time, he did not recognize the complexity or the resilience of the capitalist system. The intellectual has been increasingly called upon in modern industrial society, but as an expert or technocrat. In these roles the traditional ideals of the intellectual of the necessity of the freedom and autonomy of the intellect are not so much discarded, as never raised as relevant issues, so that they provide no threat to the system. Orwell, on the other hand, was preoccupied with these ideals; his continual wrestling with the problem of how to adopt a critically detached position on all issues was an attempt to pursue the traditional role of the intellectual.

The centrality of this concern to Orwell's writing demonstrates that even though his solutions to society's problems differed, often, markedly from the romantic literary tradition, he worked very much on the same terrain as these intellectuals. Though neither culture nor education were dominant issues for him, Orwell was nevertheless taunted by the same questions of the role of the literary intellectual, the future of aesthetic or creative activities in the society, and the quality of life in modern society. These issues signal the essential lines of Orwell's problematic.

## R. H. Tawney

Tawney was not one of the new breed or new generation of socialists of the 1930s. He had been writing on socialism for some time and three of his major books dealing with questions about socialist principles came out in the 1920s.[80] He was a well-known academic, economic historian, but he had a continual interest in education. Soon after leaving Oxford he joined the Workers' Education Association (WEA) as a tutor. Here he consolidated his concern and respect for the working man and became an important advocate of an education in which class distinctions did not operate. Tawney argued that the first task of a society such as the WEA should be to lay to rest the illusion that culture is the property of one class: 'the educated'. The WEA, he claimed, fought against the restricted view of education inherent in this illusion, to show that higher education, like elementary education, should be provided for all. Education as the means by which we are initiated into the common heritage of civilization, from elementary through to university level, should be readily available to all no matter what their occupation was likely to be.

Tawney was reluctant to become involved in theoretical discussions of the nature of education (he found the literature on this topic impossible to read), but he did outline briefly what he saw it as being and why it was important:[81]

> Education, as I see it, though it is much else as well, is partly, at least, the process by which we transcend the barriers of our isolated personalities, and become partners in a universe of interests which we share with our fellow-men, living and dead alike. No one can be fully at home in the world unless, through some acquaintance with literature and art, the history of society and the revelations of science, he has seen enough of the triumphs and tragedies of mankind to realize the heights to which human nature can rise and the depths to which it can sink.

In more social terms Tawney spoke of education as promoting fellowship. As Terrill points out, this notion of fellowship was central to Tawney's ideas about society.[82] The individual's self-fulfilment cannot be acquired through the extreme individualism of the nineteenth century; it must be sought in social relations.

Such is the principle behind Tawney's egalitarianism. Equality, he claimed, is not a question of emphasizing the individual's 'rights', but of promoting what men share together. All social institutions, such as the system of public health and education, or the organization of industry in our society should be planned, he argued, 'to emphasize and strengthen, not the class differences which divide, but the common humanity which unites, them'.[83] Tawney used this principle as the basis for his humanistic socialism, stressing its importance in distinguishing the means and ends of socialism. It is often forgotten in talking of socialism, he claimed, that a new basis of organization in society which distributes economic power more equitably, is only the means towards socialism. It must also be ascertained, he continued, the extent to which this new social organization will be more favourable than the old to 'a spirit of humanity and freedom in social relations'.[84] In contrast, Orwell was primarily concerned with the individual's right to freedom under socialism, and in particular the intellectual's freedom. Both Tawney and Caudwell, on the other hand, opposed the idea of the equality of *individuals*, as they rejected the idea of the *individual's* rights.

Tawney argued that the individual's rights were only conditional on the function which he performs in the community. Men must regard themselves, he said, not as the owners of rights, but as trustees for the discharge of functions and the 'instruments of a social purpose'.[85] The idea of function is a very important one in society, he claims: in a 'functional society' even the humblest and most laborious craftsman would be honoured. In English society, organized on the basis of class divisions rather than function, reverence of honour is only given to wealth. This society is what Tawney called an Acquisitive Society. In such societies, whose whole tendency and preoccupation is to promote the acquisition of wealth, no consideration is given to the attempt to 'secure the fulfilment of tasks undertaken for the public service.' Acquisitive Societies, Tawney predicted, would justify their social organization in terms of the formula 'the greatest happiness for the greatest number'. But happiness, Tawney objected, 'is individual and to make happiness the object of society is to resolve society itself into the ambitions of numberless individuals, each directed towards the attainment of some personal purpose.'[86]

Tawney analysed the preoccupation with wealth in modern society as self-defeating, because the very principle which makes wealth meaningful has been discarded. Without the idea of function which sets a limit to the acquisition of riches, to be rich can only be seen as meritorious in itself; it can have no other significance or value. The result has been, on the social scale, that the division between social classes has been deepened so that there is not one society but two, which dwell together in uneasy juxtaposition, worlds apart in ideals and economic interests. Tawney characterized this division simply as being between: 'the society of those who live by labour, whatever their craft or profession, and the society of those who live on it'.[87]

In describing the class divisions in society in these terms, Tawney was self-consciously echoing Disraeli's depiction of England in the nineteenth century as 'two nations'. Tawney was attempting to compel his readers to realize the fact that England was still as much a class society as it was in the nineteenth century. He was battling against the hegemonic force of the middle class which represented the society as now being all one people, one nation. Tawney stressed the importance of recognizing the existence of class divisions in society in order that we can begin to fight this ultimate and unforgivable wrong. The trouble is, he suggested, we fail to recognize that terrible inequalities still exist in society today, perpetuating the division of class. Tawney compared his own time with Matthew Arnold's observation on English society of the mid-Victorian period as preserving inequality almost as if it was a religion:[88]

> Institutions which have died as creeds, sometimes continue, nevertheless, to survive as habits. If the cult of inequality as a principle and an ideal has declined with the decline of the aristocratic society of which it was the accompaniment, it is less certain, perhaps, that the loss of its sentimental credentials has

so far impaired its practical influence as to empty Arnold's words of all their significance.

Tawney was influenced considerably by Arnold and Ruskin, sharing with them the search for moral solutions to the problems of society as he saw them. Tawney wanted economic equality for all members of society, equality that is not only of pecuniary incomes, but of environment, of access to education and the means of civilization, of security and independence, and of social consideration and respect. But he also believed that the community, to be a community at all, must be based on the sharing of a common culture.

By using such a concept Tawney anticipated the way in which Williams was to attempt to reconcile anomalies in the concept of culture. But Tawney's idea was firmly based on his beliefs in Christianity; what is shared is the belief in Christianity and the moral values based on this belief. Tawney was always a religious man and this formed a very important part of his socialism. He explained the connection as stemming from the fundamental support which Christianity gave to the principles of socialism. Christianity, he declared, affirms 'that all men are the children of God, it insists that the rights of all men are equal. . .'.[89] Tawney drew strength from these beliefs, to combat the preoccupation with human appetites which he diagnosed as undermining the social, economic and industrial institutions of society.

In turning to Christianity as providing a set of immutable beliefs and values, Tawney was involved in a search similar to that of the literary intellectuals of the romantic tradition. The concept of culture represented something which goes beyond or higher than the individual man. As such it rejects the extreme individualism or materialism of modern industrial society. But the concept of culture in Tawney's time no longer carried these connotations. Leavis attempted to re-establish them, but was not, on the whole, successful. Tawney sought to find the same sort of principles in Christianity. His ideas in this realm were more coherent than Leavis's, but their impact was similarly confined to a particular audience as were Leavis's. Tawney's influence has been significant, but largely for intellectuals of left-wing inclination and the specific group of working men whom he taught in WEA classes.

Despite his concern for the generation of a common culture, it is apparent that in many ways Tawney's vision bears greater resemblance to Eliot's idea of the Christian society than to Williams's concept of a common culture. Williams believes that a common culture can be established by co-operation between members of the society. Tawney also stressed co-operation, but this was on the basis of a set of immutable beliefs and values. Yet, in sympathies and basic orientation, Tawney had little affinity with Eliot. Eliot's vision of society was hierarchical, strictly based on class divisions; Tawney was above all concerned with fellowship and the equality of men. Eliot was preoccupied with standards of excellence in mass society; Tawney argued that the position which Eliot represented was based on a sham criterion of excellence:[90]

> Culture may be fastidious, but fastidiousness is not culture; and though vulgarity is an enemy to 'reasonableness and a sense of values', it is less deadly an enemy than gentility and complacency. A cloistered and secluded refinement, intolerant of the heat and dust of creative effort, is the note, not of civilization, but of the epochs which have despaired of it.

Finally, Eliot wrote chiefly about the upper classes, the élite of society; Tawney was primarily concerned with the working class. Terrill remarks that Tawney had a great respect for the working class, more so than many 'quasi-Marxist' English writers today.[91] Though a great deal of his work and his writing was devoted to the working class, Tawney was not uncritical of them or the working-class movement in England. This movement, he claimed, stood for the ideal of social justice and solidarity, but sometimes this was forgotten and its ends were seen purely in terms of a different distribution of economic power. Capitalism, Tawney observed, was as much maintained by the poor who admire the rich and the poor who would like to be capitalists, as by the capitalists themselves. Tawney's respect and love for the working-class men whom he met and worked with is comparable with William Morris's attitude to the working class. But, Tawney's awareness of the working class's contribution to their own oppression was a significant advance in the English socialist critique of society.

Tawney forms part of the same romantic tradition as Morris because of the focus of his concerns on a moral critique of the quality of life in modern industrial society. Both saw the problem in terms of capitalism treating men as means rather than as ends. So, too, did they each display an interest in opening up the society's traditional culture to working men for their appreciation and participation, rather than thrusting it on them in any way. The most obvious difference between Tawney and Morris is that the former displayed very little interest in art. When Tawney spoke of culture or of education, he did at times mention literature and art. But these were not major preoccupations. He was a historian, so that the problem of the artist in modern industrial society did not have the same emotional significance for him as it did for his mentors, Arnold and Ruskin; while their approach to social problems as a moral critique of society had had a considerable impact on his thought, their particular battle for the artist did not seem to concern him. Nor did he show any particular apprehension about his own intellectual domain of historical studies.

# 7 Raymond Williams

In the 1950s affluence held a hegemonic grasp over the general population in England. By the second half of this decade consumerism dominated the concerns of the majority of the English people, and the cold war served to dispel any suggestion of possible alternatives to such capitalistic preoccupations by establishing, as Anderson remarks, 'a powerful negative identification of socialism with the political order of the Soviet Union under Stalin'.[1] The Labour Party, after its initial post-war success, became the battleground for arguments between left and right about the fundamental principles of its socialism, debates which were to be crucial for the 1960s when, according to commentators such as Nairn, the Labour Party would become a formidable buttress of the capitalist state.[2]

Developments such as these have formed the background to the activities and writings of the New Left in the 1950s and 60s. Anderson analyses this intellectual formation as a 'conjunctural' movement that arose out of a response to the two international crises of October–November, 1956 in Hungary and Suez.[3] These intellectuals were essentially concerned with a moral critique of industrial capitalism and were committed to a humanistic socialism. Their movement reached its peak with the Campaign for Nuclear Disarmament (C.N.D.), but ironically this involvement demonstrated the fundamental weakness of their stance. This protest campaign focused on issues of morality without attempting to develop a rigorous theory of English capitalism. As critics of their society, the New Left failed to move beyond attacking that society on its own terms.

Central to this failure of the New Left was their revival of the moral critique of English society developed by the humanist literary tradition. They accepted the fundamental problematic of this tradition which confined their analysis to questions of the quality of life in English society. These questions need to be asked, but in the context of a complex analysis of the structural bases of that society. In academic circles, a number of Marxists in the 1970s have been concerned to rectify this weakness and acrimonious debates have often arisen as to whether they have gone too far in attempting to break out of the past limitations of Marxist cultural analyses.

Raymond Williams was at various times associated with the New Left. His work over the last twenty years needs to be examined in the light of the development of this movement, the central Marxist debates in England, and the socio-political context of that period. He also stresses the centrality of his Welsh working-class background to the evolution of his ideas. He has been a Fellow of Jesus College, Cambridge, since 1961, where he is now Professor in Drama. Though he has written a number of books which focus specifically on English literature, the main thrust of his work is in the area of cultural theory. Throughout his writing he devotes considerable attention to a critique of society and an analysis of the true nature of a democratic society.

**Democracy and the masses**

Williams argues that the idea of the masses is a conscious creation of the élites of society. The idea does have some basis in the way in which society is organized, but in the main it is simply a convenient way of looking at people. It is particularly convenient if the predominant interest in a large number of people is to manipulate or persuade them. Whereas in fact, says Williams, there are no masses; masses are only other people. All we actually see 'is other people, many others, people unknown to us'. The idea of the masses reflects the hierarchical organization of society. The majority of people, or the masses, are ruled, governed, instructed, and entertained by an élite or élites, who may or may not be selected on a hereditary basis.[4]

In addition, says Williams, the idea of the masses or mass society repeats in a new way the idea of the market. The masses influence society not by participating in decision-making, but by placing demands on, and expressing preferences about, the market. The pattern of demands provides opportunities for the élites to study the masses in order to manipulate their desires and needs. The idea of the masses, Williams believes, serves as an ideology for a certain sector of society: 'those who . . . [seek] to control the new system and to profit by it'.[5]

Eagleton, in his critique of Williams's work, lists this analysis of the notion of the masses as one of the central confusions in Williams's thought. Eagleton argues that Williams failed to perceive that the massing together of people was not just a condition of their oppression, but also, because of the contradictions of capitalism, a condition of their emancipation. Eagleton highlights Williams's confusion by substituting the word 'classes' for 'masses' to show that Williams's claim that 'masses' is only a way of seeing people would serve to perpetuate the divisions in society by refusing to see them. Eagleton accuses Williams of shortchanging the people he set out to defend by trading 'a theoretical instrument of revolutionary struggle' for 'liberal humanitarianism'.[6]

In a later work, *Keywords* (1976), Williams appears to have been aware of this type of criticism. In his discussion of the concept of the 'masses' in this context he acknowledges that there is an alternative use of the term in the revolutionary tradition where the masses are the subject of political action, rather than the object. Because this book is entirely concerned with an enquiry into a specific body of words or vocabulary in the English language, Williams does not enlighten us as to whether this recognition of a more revolutionary use of the term 'masses' coincides with a change in his theoretical position in any way.

Williams's discussion of the notion of the masses in his early work demonstrates both the fundamental strength and weakness of his thought. Williams was heavily influenced by Leavis, but he was able to break with that literary tradition while continuing to draw strength from its critique of society and its social vision. It provided him with intellectual roots, but he rejected its hierarchical conception of society. At the same time Williams did not confront the fundamental ideological preconceptions of this tradition, so that he was often caught within its problematic. In examining his early work and the shift in his ideas in the late 1960s this tension needs to be explored.

Williams repudiates Leavis's analysis of mass culture as inferior and threatening to high culture. Williams suggests that mass culture should not be regarded as the culture of the 'ordinary man', but rather as the culture of the disinherited. He blames those who have sought artificially to isolate the great tradition for continuing this disinheritance; they have a significant responsibility for the destructive elements in mass culture. The only alternative, Williams claims, is a democratic culture which rests on two basic rights: 'the right to transmit and the right to receive'. These rights could only be tampered with by a majority decision which had been arrived at after open and adequate public discussion.[7]

Underlying all Williams's writing about the nature of a truly democratic society is his fundamental belief in the possibility of open communication through which all members of society will be able to have a real share in decision-making. He draws a sharp distinction between this type of political structure and the consensual politics which exists in most capitalist societies today. The latter do not permit the ruling élites to impose their will on society by coercion; democracy has become instead a structure which needs to be negotiated and manoeuvred. Around each issue for which a decision has to be made and action taken, politicians build a coalition of interests and seek especially to woo powerful sections of the society. It is this form of democracy that Williams sets out to criticize.

Democracy, Williams believes, should take a quite different form:[8]

> If man is essentially a learning, creating and communicating being, the only social organization adequate to his nature is a participating democracy, in which all of us, as unique individuals, learn, communicate and control. Any lesser, restrictive system is simply wasteful of our true resources; in wasting individuals, by shutting them out from effective participation, it is damaging our true common process.

As Miller points out, Williams views society as fundamentally a system of communication.[9] In a democracy the system of communication should be open; people should have free access to both transmitting and receiving ideas. In the struggle for democracy in the nineteenth century, Williams claims, dissenting minorities had comparative access to places where opinions were formed, the cheap printing press, the hustings, the soapbox, the chapel, the public hall. Now the channels for communication of ideas have changed radically and public access to them has been reduced drastically. Television, the national press, the monolithic political parties, are all institutions to which there is very little access by ordinary members of the public. Space has to be bought in a newspaper or on television for minorities to express their views.

Williams hopes to promote a sense of community through the establishment of an effective system of open communication. He attributes the strength of his belief in the necessity for such a sense of community for true democracy to his experiences as a child amongst the Welsh rural working class. In rural, working-class villages, particularly the mining villages of Wales, Williams claims, there was a certain amount of local and practical democracy, but, more significantly, each man had a sense of self-respect, a belief in his own importance and place in the community. But Williams is adamant that in using this term 'community' he is not nostalgic for his own childhood experience of society, nor is he preoccupied with reproducing some past state of society.[10]

Williams condemns those who seek to set against the disturbance and disorder of the present, an ordered and happier past. In particular he rejects the notion of an organic society as based on an historical myth which cannot be substantiated. In his work *The Country and the City* (1973) he traces the belief in a past glorious age, in which men existed in an organic community, back to classical writings. The ideal society always just ceased to exist before the particular author describing it lived. The notion of an organic society, as developed by English writers in the nineteenth and twentieth centuries, desires a return to a feudal order of social relations. Williams criticizes this yearning as myopic:[11]

> It is authentic and moving yet it is in other ways unreal. Its ideal of local paternal care, and of national legislation to protect certain recent forms of ownership and labour, seems to draw almost equally on a rejection of the arbitrariness of feudalism, a deeply felt rejection of the new arbitrariness of money, and an attempted stabilisation of a transitory order, in which small men are to be protected against enclosures but also against the idleness of their labourers. Thus a moral order is abstracted from the feudal inheritance and break-up, and seeks to impose itself ideally on conditions which are inherently unstable.

Apart from pointing out that the idea of the organic society idealizes the past, Williams makes a further criticism of quite a different order. He argues that it is a myth which serves to obscure the real nature of our present crisis. The concept of the organic society perpetuates the illusion that it is not capitalism which is the basis of our problems, but the more obvious, more isolatable, system of urban industrialism. This criticism is significant for a wide range of ideas and standpoints prevalent in our society. First, it shows the limited basis upon which the concept of an organic society has operated. It has failed to go beyond the more evident features of the dehumanization of modern society, to basic economic causes. Williams's criticism demonstrates the impossibility of trying to alter the life style of urban industrialism, while leaving the economic system intact. Second, Williams's criticism has implications for the wide range of views generally subsumed under the term 'counter culture'. Although he does not examine this phenomenon, it would seem that many of the ideas underlying the counter culture are based on similar myths about 'natural' or 'organic' society. Nor is any rigorous economic analysis evident in these ideas. The life style of urban society is attacked, industrialism is vilified, but the root causes in the economic structure of capitalism are not sought.

In attacking capitalism and any solutions to the problems of modern society which leave this system fundamentally intact, Williams is also quick to point out that he does not automatically regard some form of socialism or communism as a desirable alternative. Historically, he argues, socialism or communism may be the enemies of capitalism, but in detail and often in principle, they continue and intensify some of the fundamental processes of dehumanization of country and city. The claims of socialism have frequently been limited to political and economic spheres, ignoring the human order. Socialism in this manner has committed one of its gravest errors by limiting itself frequently to the terms of its opponents. Williams goes on:[12]

> If socialism accepts the distinction of 'work' from 'life', which has then to be written off as 'leisure' and 'personal interests'; if it sees politics as 'government', rather than as the process of common decision and administration; if it continues to see education as training for a system, and art as grace after meals (while perhaps proposing more training and a rather longer grace); if it is limited in these ways, it is simply a late form of capitalist politics, or just the more efficient organization of human beings around a system of industrial production. The moral decline of socialism is in exact relation to its series of compromises with older images of society and to its failure to sustain and clarify the sense of an alternative human order.

Yet, perhaps Williams in his early work overcompensated for these weaknesses of the socialist doctrine in his concern to humanize it, for he was frequently criticized for that very omission of which he accuses the supporters of the idea of the organic society. He seems to have ignored the political and economic context of the issues he discusses, not only when he is examining socialism but in other important areas. For example, E. P. Thompson criticized *Culture and Society* for wresting the meanings of the intellectuals studied out of their social context;[13] Hoare claims that Williams ignores the concrete, political and cultural structure of Britain in his ideas about education;[14] and Smith implies a bias towards anti-industrialism in Williams's examination of English social and cultural thought, which fails to confront the social and political advances attendant on the Industrial Revolution.[15]

Anderson claims that this failure was characteristic of the New Left in general. They were unable to offer any structural analysis of British society, but tended instead to rely on a simplistic rhetoric in which 'common people', 'ordinary men and women', were opposed to the 'interests' of 'the establishment', and so on. Its most valuable work Anderson believes to be in the moral critique of capitalism, which became increasingly concerned with cultural problems. Such an interest was obviously vital to the members and audience of the New Left, which consisted largely of teachers, writers and students. It produced 'a serious socialist programme for the transformation of the system of communications', but this achievement, says Anderson, is ironically tied to the 'specific situation of British intellectuals'. Their social criticism was undertaken from a position of inextricable involvement in the official politics of their country. Anderson instances the impact of the New Left's critique on the Pilkington Report, published in 1960, as testimony to the extent of their involvement. The characteristic position of English intellectuals limited their concerns to specific problems in the society and steered them away from the development of a sophisticated theory of English capitalism.[16]

These comments by Anderson are particularly pertinent to a later work of the New Left intellectuals, *May Day Manifesto, 1968,* which Williams edited. Its analysis of social problems is fragmented, as is its programme for social reform. It is firmly entrenched in the English predilection for piecemeal changes of society, rather than considerations of more fundamental change. The programmes for change which it offers are within the already existing institutional structures. Violent revolution, it is argued, is only relevant when the struggle is against authoritarian or military regimes.

Similarly, Williams advocated the necessity of piecemeal reform to bring about the advent of a socialist society, and the changes he recommended are limited to remaining within the existing institutions and their organization in society. For example, when making proposals for the creation of a participatory democracy, he did not query the existence of any of the institutions of society, nor their structure, only their quality:[17]

> First, in education, we can find new ways of developing the capacity for personal and independent response and choice. Second, in amendment of institutions, and in legislation, we can make sure that our cultural organization is, in real ways, responsible to the society of which it is so important a part. Third, in new social construction, we can propose and try to get agreement for radical changes in institutions, to make them adequate to the needs of a growing society.

Furthermore, in his article 'Towards a Socialist Society' (1965)

Williams does not seem to consider it necessary to confront the possibility of revolution as a means of radical change.

Williams describes the reformism of his early work as 'a strong and active reformism of the majority of the British Labour Movement'.[18] He sees himself as breaking with that reformism in 1966 when the Labour Party came to power with a large majority and quickly showed itself to be 'an actual and necessary agency of the mutation of capitalism by the representative incorporation of the working class'. He continues to hold a reformist position but it is one which is centrally concerned with the transformation of the social order. On a practical level it turns to specific reform as the most accessible means of political mobilization, holding that these reforms must be not only worthwhile in themselves, but necessary stages in the transformation of the dominant order.

This transformation in William's idea has had repercussions for the development of his cultural theory. He explains his failure in his early work to provide a satisfactory examination of the social and political background to his cultural analysis as being largely the result of a mistaken belief that 'in other areas of theory and therefore in other parts of the social process, Marxism *already possessed* adequate principles, procedures and positions. . . .'[19] The absence of these considerations in his work, he claims, resulted from his presumption that he could take many of these principles for granted. But such an explanation does not acknowledge the extent to which his work was confined within the terrain of the ideological field of the literary intellectual tradition. His inheritance from this tradition of thought enabled him to ignore the broader context of cultural analysis and to believe that the 'other areas of theory' could be dealt with by separate analyses.

**Culture**

One of the central questions that needs to be asked in an examination of Williams's analysis of culture is the extent to which he has broken with the problematic of the romantic literary tradition. His essay 'Base and Superstructure in Marxist Cultural Theory' (1973) is often referred to as indicating such a transformation in his thought, but he himself dates the major transformation as being the political disillusionment of 1966. The nature of this transformation needs to be analysed and in particular the extent to which it constitutes a break with the literary intellectuals' tradition needs to be assessed.

In his early work on culture Williams is concerned with two different types of analyses: first, an analysis of previous usage of the word, and second, the development of his own definition, based on its historical usage, but attempting to reconcile inconsistencies and contradictions which he had analysed in the historical discussion. His study *Culture and Society* evolved from being a narrowly defined analysis of the concept of culture to being a more widely set frame of reference, in which the context of the term's usage and development is examined. Williams argues that the concept represents two different though related responses in the changing society:[20]

> In summary, I wish to show the emergence of *culture* as an abstraction and an absolute: an emergence which, in a very complex way, merges two general responses—first, the recognition of the practical separation of certain moral and intellectual activities from the driven impetus of a new kind of society; second, the emphasis of these activities, as a court of human appeal, to be set over the processes of practical social judgement and yet to offer itself as a mitigating and rallying alternative.

Williams traces the development of the concept of culture in the English language from the beginning of the Industrial Revolution in Britain. He distinguishes a number of different usages and levels of meaning which have gained prominence at certain times. His study displays considerable scholarship and a fine sensitivity to his material. At the end of this study, Williams attempts to define his own concept of culture, a project which he continues in his next book *The Long Revolution* (1962). Williams believes that to develop a satisfactory concept of culture, an attempt should be made to envelop all the ways in which the term has been used. He argues that the variation of meanings for the term 'culture' should not be seen as a disadvantage, but as a genuine complexity corresponding to real elements in experience. Each definition of the word has a significant reference and the relationships between all of them should be the focus of our attention. He claims that there are three main significant usages of the concept of culture:[21]

> We need to distinguish three levels of culture, even in its most general definition. There is the lived culture of a particular time and place, only fully accessible to those living in that time and place. There is the recorded culture, of every kind, from art to the most everyday facts: the culture of a period. There is also, as the factor connecting lived culture and period cultures, the culture of the selective tradition.

It is necessary to grasp the meanings of 'culture' at the three levels, and the fundamental relation between the meanings, says Williams, before we can reach a satisfactory understanding of the term. We will then be in a position to reconcile culture as 'creative activity' and culture as 'a whole way of life'.

In an attempt to explain the relationship between the different levels of culture, Williams turns to a discussion of creative activity and the nature of reality. This work lacks theoretical depth. Williams exhibits very little knowledge of other work in the area, and he appears to rely rather heavily on those authors to whom he does make reference. For example, Williams refers to the work of Professor J. Z. Young on man's perception of reality, but his application of Young's ideas is disjointed, and the discussion and analysis of it limited. The central thrust of his argument concerning reality as a social phenomenon is to show that art forms part of our attempt to categorize and communicate experience. As an individual creative act, he says, art is part of the general process which creates conventions and institutions, through which the ways of seeing, 'the meanings that are valued by the community are shared and made active'.[22]

But such an analysis does not enable us to grapple with the peculiar significance of 'the arts' in our society. In assuming that one definition of culture can be produced through the collapsing of the three levels of meaning in the term, Williams obscures the very basis for the existence of these three concepts. His mistake is to believe that a concept will always be coherent and consistent once fully analysed. Gellner points out that this assumption is quite common amongst anthropologists and sociologists.[23] The danger lies in being unable to recognize the way in which a concept, such as the concept of culture, forms part of an ideological language. For example, in attempting to reconcile the different levels of meaning for the term 'culture', Williams fails to confront the fact that Eliot appears to have undertaken a similar task and yet provided totally different conclusions about culture, education and the structure of society.

Furthermore, in his attempt to find the foundations for a single definition of the term 'culture', Williams denies the importance of the class structure of society to the discussion of any such concept. This is particularly striking when he analyses the concept of culture as selective tradition, which refers to the arts and those artistic products which have continued to be appreciated through the ages. Williams introduces the term 'minority culture' for which he analyses two meanings. On the one hand, it can refer to the work of great artists and thinkers, as well as the work of lesser figures who help to sustain the activity. On the other hand, it can also mean the work of these figures as received and used by a particular social minority. The distinction is between art as produced, and art as consumed. But, Williams argues, the work of great artists and thinkers has never been deliberately confined by them to their own company. He suggests that: 'We must always be careful to distinguish the great works of the past from the social minority which at a particular place and time itself identifies with them.'[24]

John Berger's work suggests that such a connection is, on the contrary, fundamental to the understanding of our 'selective tradition' or culture. In *Ways of Seeing* (1972) he provides a compelling argument for the view that the history of oil painting needs to be understood in terms of its relation with the rise of capitalism and its expression of the way of seeing the world of the ruling class. Berger does not deny that some artists have broken free of the norms of the artistic tradition, but he points out that the tradition quickly closes around them, incorporating certain innovations and continuing as if no challenge had occurred. Our 'selective tradition' or minority culture is constituted by works of art which have both broken with the tradition they are now considered part of, as well as those that were created firmly within the principles of that tradition. Williams does not deal adequately with these issues.

Williams appears to have undertaken the task of reconciling the different levels of meaning in the term 'culture' as much on the basis of his own social background, as from any theoretical impetus. He came from a Welsh rural village where his father worked as a railway signalman, a background of great personal significance as he has shown particularly in his novels *Border Country* (1964) and *Second Generation* (1964). After being educated in the village school, he went to study at Trinity College, Cambridge on a scholarship. Williams wrestles with two fundamental commitments on the basis of this background: a commitment to the working class and its tradition; and a commitment to high culture and the value of education.

Through his notion of a common culture Williams seeks to resolve the tension between these two fundamental commitments. He holds the ideal that a common culture would help to purge society of its divisions and inequalities. We have no basis for effective communication between all members of our community, he says, because of the inequalities of many kinds which still divide us. Without a common culture, the genuinely common experience, our society will not survive much longer. But its growth is dependent on the necessary, or 'natural' conditions arising. Nobody, Williams claims, can inherit a common culture, it has to be made and re-made by the people themselves; it cannot be achieved in any final sense.

Williams defines the common culture in these terms:[25]

> The struggle with which that process confronts us now is, I believe, the struggle to create public meanings which are authentic forums: to create a society whose values are at once commonly created and criticised, and where the discussions and exclusions of class may be replaced by the reality of common and equal membership. That, still, is the idea of a common culture, and it is increasingly, in developed societies, the detailed practice of revolution.

In arguing for an egalitarian society as the basis for the common culture, Williams is sensitive to the confusion which now surrounds the word 'equality'. He stresses that he does not desire human beings to be made equal in all ways. On the contrary, he sees inequality in many respects as being both inevitable and desirable. The only equality which he wishes to strive for is equality of being, for its obverse, inequality of being, he claims, in practice rejects, depersonalizes, and degrades other human beings. Just exactly what Williams means by equality is not clear. His exposition of the principle suffers from the usual vagueness which surrounds the discussion of this word. The only indications which he gives are negative: cruelty, exploitation, the crippling of human energy, depersonalization, ways of treating men which divide them from each other, and so on, are all part of what should not be, if equality of being is to exist in society. It is not clear from Williams's discussion of equality whether he envisages anything more positive than the elimination of these features of inequality of being. Nor is it clear how they can be eliminated.

Williams opposes the idea of the manufacture of an artificial working-class culture on the basis of his argument that any culture arises as a natural growth out of specific social conditions. But he spends some time commenting on those aspects of the existing working-class culture which he finds most laudable. In particular, he admires what he believes to be the basic collective idea of social relationships that underlies the working-class culture and the institutions, manners, habits of thought, and intention which proceed from this. In contrast, the bourgeois culture is basically individualistic and its institutions, manners, habits of thought, and intentions reflect that.

Williams explains how he sees the working-class collective idea being reflected in its institutions and way of life:[26]

> The working class, because of its position, has not, since the Industrial Revolution, produced a culture in the narrower sense. The culture which it has produced, and which it is important to recognize, is the collective democratic institution, whether in the trade unions, the cooperative movement, or a political party.

> Working-class culture, in the stage through which it has been passing, is primarily social (in that it has created institutions) rather than individual (in particular intellectual or imaginative work). When it is considered in context, it can be seen as a very remarkable creative achievement.

On the basis of these ideas of co-operation and brotherhood the British working-class movement, says Williams, has developed a moral critique of society, in particular of its selfish individualism. Throughout the history of the movement, he claims, this theme has dominated their concerns, modified only occasionally by the developed language of Marxism with its emphasis on class and power. Williams believes this to be both the fundamental strength and the fundamental weakness of the British working-class movement. On the one hand, it has been responsible for an essentially undivided mass party, which is capable of parliamentary power and has a continually surprising endurance and resilience. On the other hand, trying to operate as a brotherly and co-operative institution in an individualistic economy has meant that frequently the movement, under pressure, has opted for the preservation of its own institutions rather than widespread societal change.

Williams traces two sources which have directed the moral critique as developed by the British working-class movement. At the level of local organization Puritanism has taught it self-reliance and endurance, both of which have given it great strength, but it has also been restricted by the restraint and limitations of human needs, which the movement inherited from the same tradition. The other influence, equally important but decidedly non-Puritan, stems from the work of Cobbett, Ruskin and Morris whose essential doctrine, according to Williams, is 'the claim to life, against the distortion of humanity by the priorities and disciplines of industrial capitalism'.[27]

Williams interprets the C.N.D. movement and the New Left of England as inheritors of this moral critique developed within the working-class tradition. Both movements, he claims, challenge the governing ideology of the established labour movement with its attachment to utilitarianism and paternalism, by their concern with questions of morality and humanity.

Williams assumes that the moral critique developed by the working-class movement is paralleled by the moral critique of the humanist literary tradition. This assumption over-simplifies and confuses the way in which the two traditions have developed. Both traditions are concerned to criticize the individualistic basis of capitalism, its depersonalization and lack of community, but their perspectives are fundamentally different. One of the central aims of the working-class movement is to establish the sense of community, which does not exist in mass society. Writers in this tradition have wanted to go forward, for society to change in positive ways, even if their rhetoric has sometimes included images of past societies which were believed to have had a sense of community. The literary intellectuals, on the other hand, want to re-establish the type of society in which they had an important function, and where they had a sense of community based on the compactness of their audience and the intellectual field. Mass society, because of its social organization and its technical advances, has destroyed the sense of community which is believed to have existed prior to the Industrial Revolution. The literary intellectuals' vision is then essentially backward-looking.

The similarity between the two traditions lies as much in their Englishness as in any other factor. Both turn to a moral critique of society because of its particularistic approach, which is characteristic of the English style of social thought. Structural analysis or discussion of changing society in any fundamental way are not considered. As such, these two traditions are part of the liberal humanist ideology that dominates English thought.

The point at which the two traditions intersect is in the work of particular individuals, who, like Williams, have for one reason or another commitments to both traditions. When the traditions do intersect, democratic ideas come to the fore, but culture as an ameliorating force recedes into the background or disappears entirely. For example, William Morris first formed his ideas in the tradition of Carlyle, Arnold, Ruskin, but increasingly throughout his life he became committed to the working classes and the idea of democracy. The idea of culture, thus, plays no signifcant role in his thought. Leavis, on the other hand, forms an allegiance only to the literary tradition, and is correspondingly less interested in democracy than in culture. Finally, Williams, like Morris, is committed to both traditions; democracy, therefore, plays a dominant role in his thought, whereas his concept of culture has lost the force and the sense of vision which it had in Arnold's writings.

The point which seems to have escaped Williams is the essentially undemocratic nature of the moral critique as expressed by the word 'culture', developed by literary intellectuals. A commitment to the idea of democracy is simulated where it forms a basic presupposition of the intellectual climate of the time. But it would appear that the idea of democracy has never been so deeply ingrained in English thought that it has become an integrated part of the social thought of diverse groups within the society. The literary intellectuals could contribute a powerful critique of their society without necessarily being fundamentally committed to the democratic formation of that society.

In this context the weakness of Williams's definition of culture becomes particularly interesting. He does not convey the same sense of a strong social vision as did his nineteenth-century counterparts within the humanist literary tradition. Nor can he endorse their view that culture is an ameliorating force in society. Yet at the same time he claims that we will not survive without a common culture. Intellectually, he is unable to explore the possibility that the culture is in some way totally dependent on the structure of society. He must attribute it some positive influence; just as he steers away from the view that education may always be a conservative force in society. Williams's reluctance to explore or even fully confront these possibilities suggests a fundamental tension in his work: a tension between his working-class background and his success in the educational establishment of his society.

This tension is not unusual amongst modern intellectuals. Since the Second World War intellectuals in many institutions have had this varied background, a fact which has added to the crisis for many in determining the nature of the intellectual's role in society. This crisis has confronted intellectuals in the traditional fields, such as literary studies, more than in other fields because of the remnants of earlier notions about the intellectual's role in society. Socialization into an academic discipline will include a generally unconscious initiation into these tensions about the role of the intellectual; and the working-class student will experience further conflict on the basis of his different, if not opposing, commitment from his early socialization.

Williams recognizes this problem to some extent. For example, in discussing the prevalent interest in communication and communication systems he suggests that the genesis of this inquiry lies to a certain extent with the particular difficulties of intellectuals in an advanced capitalist society and with the further problems of a new generation of intellectuals with a working-class background.[28] Similarly, he suggests that English literary sociology began from the need of a radical, critical group to locate and to justify its own activity and identity.[29] But in neither case does Williams believe that these factors have any import for the inquiry. He does not consider the possibility that these features of the inquiry suggest the limits of its underlying problematic: the interest in culture and communications in the 1950s and 60s has been confined within the concern of the role of the intellectual in society. This problem has limited this area of thought from fully confronting the possibility of culture, the artist, the intellectual and their products as having no positive role in society. Similarly, no serious questioning of the liberal humanistic framework of the moral critique of English capitalism could be undertaken within this problematic. Whether or not the ultimate judgments of this intellectual formation may have been correct, the limitation of its questioning frustrates its ability to provide an answer for any opposing school of thought.

Williams's political transition during the late 1960s constitutes only a partial break from this old problematic. In the essay 'Base and Superstructure in Marxist Cultural Theory', in which he made his first fully developed public statement of his new position, he demonstrates that he is still very much preoccupied with questions of the specialness of art, or as Eagleton remarks, he continues to seek 'to preserve the primal reality of art'.[30] Williams remains fundamentally opposed to a materialist reduction of art. Though he rejects all ideological notions of literary production, he continues to seek to establish the social value of art or creative activities defined fairly broadly.

Williams's failure to move fully beyond the problematic of the humanist literary tradition limits his thought most noticeably when he confronts anti-humanist Marxist cultural theory. He criticizes modern structuralists for their rejection of the notion of the individual and their collapsing of the 'living and reciprocal relationship of the individual and the social' into 'an abstract model of determinate social structures and their "carriers"'.[31] But Williams provides no theoretical arguments to oppose this view. He simply concludes that if faced with 'either the practice or this version of the theory, it is not surprising that many people run back headlong into bourgeois-individualist concepts, forms, and institutions, which they see as their only protection'. Such a rejoinder to a major school of thought whose impact on cultural studies in England in the 1970s has been considerable is more than disappointing. It indicates that Williams is unable to confront its fundamental principles from within the confines of his own thought.

The transition in Williams's thought consists primarily of a coming to terms with Marxism. In *Culture and Society* he rejected any suggestion of being called Marxist; but by the late 1960s he was addressing himself more and more to the development of a Marxist cultural theory. He shifted his attention away from questions of cultural change to issues such as those concerned with the relationship between base and superstructure.

Indicative of this development was his attention to the concept of hegemony as derived from Gramsci. This concept describes the process by which the dominance of the ruling class is maintained through a complex interlocking of political, social and cultural forces. In times of crisis this dominance will be maintained chiefly by direct coercion, often of a specifically physical nature. But at other times the ruling class's rule is expressed predominantly through its hegemonic influence. The advantage of the concept of hegemony, says Williams, is that it emphasizes the 'lived experience' of people; rather than the imposition of a structure on their consciousness. The dominance of the ruling class is not experienced passively and nor is it static: it has to be renewed constantly if it is to be maintained.

Williams describes the concept of hegemony as including and going beyond both the concepts of culture and ideology. 'Culture' in the sense of a 'whole social process' as Williams defines it in his later work is included within the sense of 'hegemony', but this latter concept adds a further consideration through 'its insistence on relating the "whole social process" to specific distributions of power and influence'. Similarly, the concept of hegemony adds to the concept of ideology through its recognition of 'not only the conscious system of ideas and beliefs, but the whole lived social process as practically organized by specific and dominant meanings and values'.[32]

In these discussions of the concepts of culture, ideology and hegemony Williams highlights one of the most significant developments in his thought. Through the concept of hegemony Williams seeks to examine the social and political context of our culture. Analysing the different levels of meaning in the term 'culture' and the concept of culture in his early work, Williams did not recognize the extent to which he was ignoring questions of 'power and influence'. Nor did he examine issues concerned with the extent to which culture, rather than being a creative activity in our society, could form or be one of the bases for the subordination of specific groups in the society. In his later work Williams has provided valuable analyses of this problem, attempting to go beyond mechanistic accounts of ideology and cultural institutions as means of social control. Through the notion of a hegemonic process, he has stressed the extent to which the contradictions and conflicts inherent in the capitalist social formation require the constant establishment and maintenance of hegemonic influence.

Williams extends his exploration of a Marxist cultural theory through the use of a number of specific concepts. He suggests the notion of 'structures of feeling', for example, to escape the rigidity which Marx also criticized when people talk of 'ideologies' or 'world views'. These concepts convey a sense of their being fixed forms, rather than in constant flux. 'Structures of feeling' emphasizes the way in which meanings and values are actively lived and felt. This concept stems from Williams's early work; he us quite extensively in *The Long Revolution*.

More recent are his concepts of effective dominative culture and residual and emergent cultural elements. He argues that artists and intellectuals are sensitive to trends in the culture and anticipate changes or 'breaks' in the cultural patterns of our society. They express these insights in their work. But, just as importantly, their work provides a central articulation of the effective dominative culture. By 'effective dominative culture' Williams means 'the central, effective and dominant system of meanings and values, which are not merely abstract but which are organized and lived' in our society.[33] 'Residual' cultural elements are similarly 'lived' even though they are remnants from the past; they are active elements in the cultural process rather than being experienced as archaic and not part of our lived culture. 'Emergent' cultural elements, on the other hand, are quite separate from the dominant culture; they are new meanings and values, new practices which may develop, for example, with emergence and growing strength of a new class.

As part of the effective dominative culture, according to Williams, there is the selective culture which is represented as '*the* tradition', 'the significant past'. It consists of what we refer to as the traditional wisdom, knowledge and art of our society (sometimes, as in Leavis's work, also associated with terms like 'minority culture' or 'high culture'). As such the selective culture serves to perpetuate the effective dominative culture, in a process of continual making and remaking. Through this selective tradition or culture our relationship with history, society, and knowledge is defined for us. Williams argues that this process accompanies the processes of education, the processes of much wider social training within institutions like the family, and the practical definitions and organizations of work, as forces in the maintenance of hegemony in the society.

In these ideas Williams has turned to a more effective way of looking at the different levels of culture—lived culture and selective culture. He has moved away from his attempts to reconcile the different levels of meaning in the term 'culture', which was his prime concern in the concept of a common culture, to a consideration of culture in its relationship to the structure of society. In so doing he has transcended what was essentially an idealist approach to the concept of culture in his book *Culture and Society*, to a recognition of the importance of focusing on the relationship between ideas and the social structures in which they are embedded.

This transition in Williams's approach to culture is not yet fully developed. His theoretical discussions appear disjointed largely because of his reliance on the exploration of concepts as the framework for his theory, but also because he has not yet provided concrete explorations of many of these concepts. Nevertheless, his work remains significant in the field of English cultural studies, particularly in his efforts to provide a basis for understanding the constant shifts, the contradictions and conflicts in the culture and society relationship.

## Cultural institutions

Throughout his work Williams has been concerned with the educational and communications systems of English society. He has examined them both in terms of the way in which they serve to initiate members of the society into its dominant patterns of thought and its fundamental values, but he has also believed them to have the potential to form the basis for the evolution of a common culture.

Williams regards education in a similar manner to Arnold in so far as he believes it to be essential to the promotion of culture. But his attitude to culture leads to quite a different conception of the content and process of education. The outlines of his general attitude to education, throughout his writings, are succinctly expressed in the work *May Day Manifesto, 1968:*[34]

> The socialist alternative, of education as a preparation for personal life, for democratic practice and for participation in a common and equal culture, involves several practical and urgent measures. We need to abolish a private educational provision which perpetuates social division. We need to create a genuinely comprehensive system of nursery, primary and secondary education which will be more than a matter of 'efficiency' or 'streamlining' but will break through the existing, self-generating system of a class-structured inequality of expectancy and achievement. We need to shift emphasis, within what is actually taught, from the transmission of isolated academic disciplines, with marginal creative activities, to the centrality of creative self-expression and an organic inter-relation between subjects, between theory and practice.

Williams explores more concrete ideas about the potentialities of education in his book *Communications* (1962), but his major preoccupation is the analysis of how education actually operates in our society. He diagnoses a number of features of education as fundamental to its role of the perpetuation of class divisions in English society. First, he draws attention to the present basis for most school curricula with their stress on specialized and unconnected disciplines suitable mainly for the professional class; the remaining large proportion of the population receives the fall-out from these disciplines. Second, the gearing of the educational system to a narrow and restrictive conception of human intelligence confirms and perpetuates the class structure. Williams associates this approach with the liberal education of an élitist nature provided for the 'leaders', and the rigidly vocational training provided for the 'lower ranks'. Third, Williams points out that the basic organization of the educational system relies on a sorting and grading process natural to a class society. Williams denounces the idea that education can provide a ladder for people to escape their class origins. It is not enough, he argues, that some working-class boys may be able to reach Oxford or Cambridge. The hierarchical, class-based image of society is maintained by such a system, but is presented in a more palatable form by offering the hierarchy of merit as something different from the hierarchy of money or birth. The image of a ladder will never do, Williams claims, it is a product of a divided society, and will fall with it.

Williams believes that education, because of its potential in the promotion of a common culture, is fundamental in the movement away from the divided society. In his discussion of the opposing images of country and city, he shows that divisions exist on many levels in our society:[35]

> The division and opposition of city and country, industry and agriculture, in their modern forms, are the critical culmination of the division and specialisation of labour which, though it did not begin with capitalism, was developed under it to an extraordinary and transforming degree. Other forms of the same fundamental division are the separation between mental and manual labour, between administration and operation, between politics and social life. The symptoms of this division can be found at every point in what is now our common life; in the idea and practice of social classes; in conventional definitions of work and of education; in the physical distributions of settlements; and in temporal organisation of the day, the week, the year, the lifetime.

Williams suggests that we will only progress beyond these divisions and their reflection in education when we learn to think of a genuinely open culture. In education this will mean that learning will have to be regarded in a genuinely open way and as the most valuable resource we have.

Yet, even in his earlier work Williams does not perceive education as the key to social change. He warns against such a view, because it ignores the way in which the form and content of education are affected, and in some cases determined, by the systems of decision and maintenance in the society. Thinkers and artists, and the extension of education, have visibly affected social change but, Williams points out, they have been equally used by people to confirm their own patterns and beliefs. Moreover, he adds, children do not merely learn what is presented to them at school; they learn from their whole social environment. Once they leave school, they have to compare what they learnt there with the actual practices of their society.

Williams is nevertheless adamant that this view of education has never committed him to some version of a Marxist economic reductionism. He continues to criticize the way in which Marxists in the 1930s adopted the received formula of base and superstructure, which they converted very quickly to an interpretation of superstructure as a simple reflection, or ideological expression, of the base. For this reason, Williams believes that his ideas and those of the New Left gained more from the *Scrutiny* approach to education and communications. *Scrutiny*, too, was essentially looking at the effects of capitalism, as were the Marxists, but its analysis was in the end more satisfactory, he claims, because it did not resort to over-simplified formulas. The common ground between *Scrutiny* and the New Left, on the issue of education, rests on the emphasis which they each placed on a good critical education, that will examine, not only highly regarded literature, art, and so on, but also the products of mass culture. The main conflict and tension between the two lies in arguments about a minority culture versus a democratic culture.

In his earlier work Williams discusses education in terms of its vital contribution to what he believes to be the third revolution that British society will undergo. Britain has had the Industrial Revolution and the democratic revolution; now we are seeing, he claims, the beginnings of the cultural revolution, the 'long revolution':[36]

> The human energy of the long revolution springs from the conviction that men can direct their own lives, by breaking through the pressures and restrictions of older forms of society, and by discovering new common institutions.

Education may be changed to express and create the values of an educated democracy and a common culture. It is utopian, says Williams, to think that we can produce the sort of society we desire without changing our training institutions. He makes some specific recommendations for education. First, that there should be less emphasis on 'public-school speech', if we are to have a common culture. We should learn to listen to ourselves and to others with no prior assumptions of correctness. Second, creative expression should be taken up as a serious activity in the classroom, not just as light amusement as it is now. Third, direct experience and discussion of all contemporary arts at their best should be encouraged, including not just the classical forms, but jazz and the cinema, for example. Fourth, teaching about the institutions of communication should be undertaken. Finally, Williams recommends that education should be critical of all cultural work. The debt which Williams owes to Leavis and his fellow Scrutineers in their work on education can be clearly seen in these recommendations.[37]

The opposition between Williams's and Leavis's thought in this realm is highlighted by their proposals for higher education. Williams advocates 'the creation of genuinely comprehensive universities', through which the present class structure of institutions of higher education would be broken down. He believes that it would be possible to establish 'regional centres of an open kind' through the linking of colleges of technology, and education, domestic science and adult education, and the existing university departments.[38] As Williams himself points out, Leavis was committed to a minority culture and its preservation through the limitation of access to the universities; Williams is committed to a democratic culture, whose existence will depend on the opening up of all educational institutions.

This difference between Williams and Leavis is further revealed in their discussion of mass communications. Leavis was completely opposed to all new media; Williams, on the other hand, attempts to show that it is not the actual communication processes that are at fault, but only the way in which they are used. The idea of mass-communication, he claims, depends very much more on the intention of the speaker or writer, than on the particular technique employed. Williams explores this point in both his earlier and later work. In his examination of the technologies and cultural form of television, radio and the press he provides historical evidence for his claim that the contexts of these mass communications were not defined until some time after their technologies could have been developed. Indeed they need not have been *mass*-communications at all. Williams is particularly concerned to dismantle the various versions of technological determinism which prevail in discussions of the media. He emphasizes the interaction between the technology and the social context in all forms of mass-communications.

On the basis of this analysis of the weaknesses and dangers of communications, Williams examines the threat which they pose to a living culture. He believes that there is a threat, but it does not only come from mass communications, or their concomitant mass culture, it comes also from many kinds of routine thinking and routine art. The sway which these hold over us is in some ways possible because of our own laziness or insufficient strength to reject them; but also many interests are served by the insulation from reality which these formulas and routines effect. Interests such as old forms of society and those who benefit by them, old and discredited beliefs, the wish to keep people quiet and uncritical, are served by this kind of insulation.

Williams is aware, however, that it is not necessarily the case that mass culture distorts reality, and minority culture does not. The minority position of the latter can easily insulate it from reality, by adding to its works its own local habits, its own facts and feelings. At no time, then, does Williams reject those social activities which have come under the label of mass culture:[39]

> The argument against these things, and the immense profits gained by their calculated dissemination, cannot afford to be confused by the collateral point that a good living culture is various and changing, that the need for sport and entertainment is as real as the need for art, and that the public display of 'taste' as a form of social distinction, is merely vulgar.

But Williams does not completely reject all notions of standards, rather he wishes to defer any such judgment until we know more of what a majority culture would look like. Any attempt to undertake such a task at this stage, he claims, is in danger of substituting righteousness for reason; it is a preoccupation with the duty of defending a standard against the mob. Instead he advocates that we should attempt to ensure that the technical changes which have made our culture more dependent on literate forms are matched by a proportionate increase in training for literacy in its fullest sense. Education should be geared to deepen and refine the capacity for significant response so that changes can be constantly criticized and their implications understood.

Quinton Hoare commented in 1965 that Williams's proposals about education provided the only authentic socialist programme for the educational system in Britain at that time; but he also outlined a number of fundamental weaknesses in these ideas, the main one being that Williams's proposals are purely institutional, detached from political reality. For example, in Williams's work there appears to be no consideration of how his educational reforms would be implemented, nor of who would implement them. Similarly, says Hoare, he ignores the problem that in changing education it is also necessary to change educators too: consciousness and ideology throughout society will have to be challenged and modified. A socialist programme, Hoare claims, cannot consist purely of a conceptual alternative; a fusion of theory and practice, that is praxis, is needed.[40]

These criticisms apply chiefly to Williams's early work. More recently, in accord with the general transition in his thought, Williams has shifted his attention away from specific proposals for change within cultural institutions such as education. The main focus of his work in this area is now concerned with issues of social control rather than social change. Education is mentioned far less in his work and he now refers to it largely in the context of the legitimizing and selective socializing process of formal institutions. 'Education', he argues, 'transmits necessary knowledge and skills, but always by a particular selection from the whole available range, and with intrinsic attitudes, both to learning and social relations, which are in practice virtually inextricable.' The institutions of education, family, churches, and the major communications systems of modern society, all act, with varying degrees of explicitness, as a means of incorporation, the foundation of the hegemonic process in a class society.[41]

Williams's work in the field of cultural studies has always been stimulating and has provided the impetus for much of the activity going on in that realm in England today. His later work has in many ways been a response to some of the trends in those studies and debates, as well as a dialogue with continental writers with whom he now has broad contacts. His excursions into the field of pure theory remain at a fairly embryonic stage at this time and would benefit greatly from further exploration at a more concrete level. Such a move would be valuable not only in the refinement of his notions of structure of feeling, emergent cultural forms, and so on, but also in the further clarification of his ideas about cultural institutions, such as the media and education.

# 8 Williams's contemporaries

A number of intellectual trends since the Second World War have challenged the humanist literary tradition represented by the concept of culture. For example, the positivistic methods of the science of the twentieth century were beginning to insinuate themselves into all realms of intellectual endeavour, challenging the traditional methods and activities of intellectuals, including the areas of literary and historical studies. At a different level, the romantic concept of the primacy of the individual was beginning to gain great popularity in various ways, particularly in the form of progressive ideas in educational thought. In the 1960s these ideas began to be used as the basis of major innovations in the type of education offered in both state and independent schools. As a mode of thought progressive ideas about education challenged the belief in culture and its commitment to supra-personal values. And finally, the anthropological or relativistic concept of culture became more prevalent in academic debates and in lay discussions than the literary tradition's concept. The reasons for this shift are in part connected with the changing emphasis on the individual and in part connected with the rise of anthropology and sociology as academic disciplines; but they are obviously far more complex than this and would require detailed study.

Despite these trends, a number of intellectuals continued the humanist literary tradition in the 1950s and 60s. They can be split fairly clearly into two ideological groups: either they have been preoccupied with questions of the possibility of the evolution of a common culture, or they have turned to élitist ideas about education and the perpetuation of traditional values and attitudes.

**Richard Hoggart**

In a conversation between Hoggart and Williams recorded in the *New Left Review* (1960), they remarked on the extraordinary coincidence that they both published their first important books, which expressed similar concerns and interests, at approximately the same time (in 1957–8), never having met each other. Yet this coincidence has significant implications which neither Hoggart nor Williams acknowledges here. It illustrates dramatically the fragmentation of the literary intellectuals' world which has become increasingly a problem for those who aspire to a traditional conception of their role. Culture as an ideal in the mid-nineteenth century expressed a conviction about that role, as well as a confidence in the centrality of intellectuals and their craft to society and the importance of their voice. The fragmentation of the intellectual world has been part of the changes which have shifted their position in the society and undermined their confidence about their role and its significance in the society. The unity of the intellectual world, which was supported by personal ties as well as intellectual ones, helped to sustain that confidence in the nineteenth century. After the Second World War the vestiges of that unity, which had continued during the first half of the twentieth century, largely disappeared.

In their attempts to develop a notion of a common culture both Hoggart and Williams reveal one of the consequences of the fragmentation of the intellectual world. Through the formation of a common culture they seek unity with 'the people', the 'masses', rather than with other intellectuals as a select group (while still maintaining the specialness of their craft); 'culture' in Arnold's sense, expressed the intellectuals' confidence in their unique role in society and the necessity of unity with each other as intellectuals.

Hoggart works within a very similar problematic to Williams. One of his key concerns, in his best-known book, *The Uses of Literacy* (1969), and in his later works, focuses on the relationship between art and society. He claims that art is important to the individual and the society for it acts as a civilizing agent:[1]

> I don't think it's true to say that the arts necessarily make you act better; I think that's a misunderstanding. It would be pleasant to say that if you read good books you will become a 'gooder man'. I don't think so; that's up to your own conscience. What you can say I think is that appreciating the arts, pondering on them, taking them to yourself, submitting to them, can nourish your imagination and your imagination can, if you wish, nourish your conscience. So that it can, as it were,

> make you more available to act better, if you so will it; but the will must be yours.

In addition to the increased potential for sensitivity and moral awareness, Hoggart believes that art is fundamental to the humanity of a society. A country without great art, he proclaims, would be nothing more than a 'thriving collection of earthworms'.[2] He believes his own realm of intellectual endeavour to be of vital importance: 'literature' is a 'criticism of life', he declares, echoing Arnold and Leavis, and as such, it is morally educative. It can make us sense the inter-relations and demands of human experience more fully.[3]

But Hoggart also stresses constantly that such increased sensitivity does not necessarily cause us to act differently, to be more moral. This warning provides clear support for Steiner's claim that it became impossible for literary intellectuals after the Second World War to suggest that there are direct benefits to be accrued by society from the prevalence of good literature and good art.[4] This war provided stark evidence to show that qualities of aesthetic feeling can exist in the same individual alongside barbaric, politically sadistic behaviour. But Hoggart's stance needs also to be analysed in the context of the changing position of the literary intellectuals in society. The problematic nature of their role in modern society confronts Hoggart constantly, not only as an academic, but through his membership of a number of influential councils and committees.

Through his work on the Pilkington Report, Hoggart appears to have been particularly perturbed by the difficulties of defining a satisfactory role for art and its intellectuals in society. He was a member of the committee which was set up in 1960 'to consider the future of the broadcasting services in the United Kingdom. . .', under the chairmanship of Sir Henry Pilkington.[5] The report, says Hoggart, was criticized as being highbrow, authoritarian, socialist and priggish. He analyses the reasons for the difficulties encountered by such a report:[6]

> In the weeks after the Report came out, I often remembered Auden's line about the lack today of any 'sane affirmative speech.' There is not even a moderately precise vocabulary for discussing the cultural questions raised by the study of broadcasting. There is no adequate terminology, no adequate sense of the history and process of this kind of cultural change, and no adequate language for discussing the popular arts.

His complaint echoes Leavis's prediction of the total incomprehension that would greet his usage of the term 'culture' if it was not carefully explained. Not only is the relationship between art and society uncertain, but no adequate language exists to discuss that relationship, making any attempt to do so open to complete misinterpretation.

The problem of an adequate language is a problem of shared meanings and values. In Arnold's time his audience could be assumed to be sustained by a homogeneous educational and social background and would thereby share a common set of values and attitudes. As the intellectual's audience widens, this homogeneity begins to break down and misunderstandings arise where taken-for-granted assumptions about specific issues no longer exist. This is a particular threat which mass society poses for the intellectual: fragmentation of his audience.

Hoggart perceives the main problem for the artist today as being the temptation to take up a defensive stance completely outside of society. Such action can only be self-destroying, he claims, because it will not be 'nourished by a considered criticism of the society'.[7] Nor will the artist be sustained by that very phenomenon which is essential to its existence: a sense of fellow feeling with other individuals, a sense of community. We cannot speak of art without recognizing the importance of this concept of fellow feeling to art, according to Hoggart, for this above all defines the social relevance of art: 'the arts, we like to say . . . are a way of speaking to each other'. The arts thereby become fundamental to society as a way of founding a shared culture and a sense of 'common humanity'.[8]

Hoggart does not suggest that in seeking to build up a sense of common humanity amongst all members of society we should attempt to restore some past state of society or a forgotten folk culture. On the contrary, he argues that:[9]

> So my own working hypotheses are: that, given better conditions, more people are capable of more than we usually imagine; that, since we no longer live in closed societies with high, dense, local textures, no unself-conscious folk-culture is possible; that, since we are all under a centralized pressure towards what I called mindless togetherness, we must commit ourselves to the increase of individual knowledge and self-consciousness, to greater self-awareness (in which is naturally included the development of the imaginative life). We all seek this for our own children; why should we seek less for the children of other people?

Hoggart advocates the centrality of education in the pursuit of these goals. He defines its main purpose as being to encourage individuals in the attainment of a fuller, more self-deciding life. Education should be concerned with the transmission of culture,

Hoggart argues, but not culture narrowly conceived as being something one can grasp by acquiring certain 'manners', but rather it is associated 'with the growth of the responsive and responsible imagination'.[10]

It is never clear throughout Hoggart's writings what he means by 'culture'. His work tends to suffer from a lack of academic rigour at times, so that he does not attempt to provide a definition or explanation of such complex terms. His reference to 'culture' when speaking of education bears some resemblance to Leavis's concept of culture, but he does not indicate any connection with prior usages of the term. Yet Hoggart depends heavily on his reference to the connection between culture and education to clarify the potential of education for society and its members.

Hoggart contrasts his way of perceiving education with prevalent technocratic and meritocratic ideas about its function. He does not believe that education should be regarded as simply a matter of training students to fit their country's economic need, nor does he favour the meritocratic model of education. The latter, he argues, does not lead us towards greater equality (as it is claimed to do) at all. The basic trends in education, at the moment, are not towards equality, but continue a fundamental stratification of the society. Though scholarships may help a boy of any class to acquire an education suited to his abilities, says Hoggart, all we are doing is replacing the old gradings of birth in our society, for 'a new grading, a new hierarchy, a new stratification by function'.[11]

Hoggart's remarks are particularly apposite for those exponents of the meritocratic model of education who claim that the grammar schools, contrary to appearance, help redress the inequalities of society. Szamuily, one of the *Black Papers* writers, claims that in the past the grammar schools have served to redress the balance with 'no little success'.[12] As Hoggart points out, all they have in fact done is served to establish a new set of inequalities. Hoggart, indeed, seems to stand for everything conservatives such as the *Black Papers* writers oppose: he is egalitarian; he opposes meritocratic ideas; he is more concerned with the working class than an intellectual élite; he proclaims the merit of certain aspects of modern popular culture; and he does not believe that the spreading of culture means the lowering of its standard of quality.

Hoggart claims that questions of standards in a mass society are thrown up, in conjunction with the whole issue of the relations we assume between class and culture, by what he interprets to be the 'condition of England' question:[13]

> Of all the changes in British society today surely the most evident—since it increases the clamour of persuasion,

> overcrowds the roads and resorts, determines the general programming of mass communications, puts extreme pressure on higher education—is the 'entry into society' (to borrow a phrase from a sociologist) of whole classes of people who were previously too poor to be able to make themselves felt. Now they have some money and often even some sense of security; they are making their own choices more, rather than following the economically determined customs of their class; and their horizons are lengthening. Other people are having to move over to make room for them.

The greatly increased demand for cultural objects in a mass society, for education and so on, which Hoggart outlines, poses once again the particular problem which has haunted literary intellectuals over the previous century. The issue is phrased in terms of whether the spreading of culture (in the sense of the arts) leads to its dilution. Hoggart characterizes the main danger of mass communications in a technological society as being the process by which, more and more, a great many things, including culture, are made into objects of consumption. At one level, says Hoggart, this development can lead to a dilution and a thinning out, but to take this view is to look at the problem too narrowly. Relying on a concept of culture as a process of training of 'the intellectual and imaginative life', he declares that if we ensure 'that what is done is well done, then I cannot see how the fact that ten people have had this opportunity instead of only one in itself makes the slightest difference' to the training or its quality.[14]

Hoggart does not totally condemn mass culture. He suggests rather that we should stop talking about 'mass culture' and start looking at it in terms of new categories such as 'synthetic culture' or 'processed culture'. These labels draw attention to the features of the 'culture' produced by the mass media which Hoggart deplores for their undesirable intellectual and moral consequences:[15]

> Most mass-entertainments are in the end what D. H. Lawrence described as 'anti-life'. They are full of a corrupt brightness, of improper appeals and moral evasions. To recall instances: they tend towards a view of the world in which progress is conceived as a seeking of material possessions, equality as a moral levelling, and freedom as the ground for endless irresponsible pleasure.

By way of contrast, says Hoggart, good art whether it be highbrow or popular, still embodies its moral sense in all specific details: it will encourage its audience 'to arrive at a wisdom derived from an inner, felt discrimination in their sense of people and their attitude to experience'. He stresses the importance of holding fast to both our beliefs about the nature of good art, and the basic facts about the nature of popular publications, if we are not to lose our power to make individual decisions.[16]

These claims indicate that Hoggart operates within a similar problematic to the humanist literary tradition. He focuses on questions of the quality of our cultural life, the effects of mass society on high culture and he asserts the necessity of art for its moral and critical training of the intellect and our sensitivity in general. These concerns indicate the ideological and political limitations of Hoggart's problematic, for they are essentially a preoccupation with the role of the literary intellectual in modern society. His analysis of 'the condition of England question' thereby refers to the cultural effects of post-war affluence without going deeper into the significance of this development in terms of fundamental shifts in the structure of society. His critical analysis is couched in moral terms, as is his solution to the problems of mass society a moral solution.

Hoggart's uniqueness in this literary tradition is his preoccupation with and commitment to working-class culture. Unlike Morris who writes of the valuable aspects of the culture of the people, the masses, of previous periods, Hoggart is referring to the very recent past rather than the pre-capitalist era. He writes extensively of the working-class traditions, of the values, attitudes and activities which constituted a specific culture even during his early childhood. But what remained when he knew it in this early part of his life were only remnants, Hoggart believes, of a particularly vital culture of the people which thrived in the youth of his grandparents. His work has been seminal in the creation of an active interest in academic circles and amongst the general public in the culture of the working class or more broadly, the 'masses'.

Yet Hoggart's actual analysis of the working-class culture is seriously flawed. Though he criticizes romanticism about the working class, he himself presents overall a romantic account of them. For example, he describes a typical visit to the seaside by a group of working-class people, giving it a quaint air of jollity. Much of the description quietly sends up these trips, but the overriding impression is Hoggart's own romanticism. Concluding his account, he says:[17]

> Somewhere in the middle of the moors the men's parties all tumble out, with much horseplay and noisy jokes about bladder-capacity. The driver knows exactly what is expected of him as he steers his warm, fuggy, and singing community back

> to the town; for his part he gets a very large tip, collected during the run through the last few miles of town streets.

Such sympathetic, warm accounts of the working class of old are juxtaposed with ugly descriptions of the local milk bar, the juke-box world of the 1950s teenager:[18]

> Compared even with the pub around the corner, this is all a peculiarly thin and pallid form of dissipation, a sort of spiritual dry-rot amid the odour of boiled milk. Many of the customers—their clothes, their hair-styles, their facial expressions all indicate—are living to a large extent in a myth-world compounded of a few simple elements which they take to be those of American life.

Hoggart does not attempt to enter empathetically into the culture of these new working-class groups. He condemns it with the use of emotive devices, just as he promoted the old working-class traditions with carefully chosen words.

Despite his romanticism about the working class of earlier periods Hoggart does not desire to revive their culture. An urban folk-culture, he argues, is not possible or desirable. What, he asks, would be likely to emerge if we attempted to promote such a formation in the face of 'the new persuaders' of today; why would such a culture not 'prove to be simply a mindless, soporific, "togetherness" culture'?[19] Hoggart argues instead for the promotion of sensitivity and critical awareness through education so that we can all resist the temptations of the manipulators of modern mass communications.

### Richard Wollheim

In his essay 'Culture and Socialism' (1961) Wollheim examines a number of issues concerning the concept of culture in the context of questions about mass society. His essay was published as a Fabian tract and although it has not aroused any long-term interest, as an historical document it is invaluable, for it epitomizes a number of the fundamental characteristics of English socialist thought.

Wollheim nominates the concept of culture as central to social thought because it raises the question of 'the quality of life experienced in a socialist society'.[20] On this basis he examines the contemporary situation in Great Britain, describing the cultural conditions as being in a state of transition. In many ways the culture which has been transmitted and supported by the system of public schools and universities, the English middle-class culture, has remained unchanged for nearly a hundred years, says

Wollheim, relying on the educational funnel to retain its dominance. Despite changes in the recruitment to the educational institutions, a certain widening of the bottom of the educational funnel, the character and structure of the middle-class culture rests unchallenged. But, he argues, there is a 'new culture' which contrasts markedly with the 'old culture': the 'old culture' is primarily literary and exclusive; the 'new culture' is a leisure culture, very accepting rather than critical, ostentatious, based on high consumption, and classless.

The present situation of a compromise mainly between the middle-class culture and the 'new culture' is totally unsatisfactory in Wollheim's eyes. He undertakes to assess the various alternative proposals for society. Turning first to the vision of an integrated society and the suggestion that we should return to a traditional working-class (or folk-) culture, he attributes this view chiefly to socialist thinkers, though he does also mention Leavis and Denys Thompson. Yet such a social vision should be untenable for socialist thinkers, Wollheim argues, because there is an intimate connection between the cultural life of a people and their material conditions of existence. The old working-class culture was, in an important sense, the product of these people's downgraded existence, their exploitation and misery.

Wollheim's criticism of this view echoes Williams's analysis of the concept of the organic society. The point is indeed worth making for writers such as Leavis who romanticize the past without acknowledging the social degradation which the majority of the population suffered in earlier times. Yet the concurrence between Williams's and Wollheim's position in this instance indicates that the latter's specific attack on socialist thinkers is misdirected. Even writers like Hoggart, who tend to romanticize the old working class, cannot be accused of overlooking the conditions of existence that went with their culture. The socialist thinkers concerned with these questions of culture may wish to recapture some aspects of the old working-class life, such as its comradeship or its sense of corporateness, but they do not suggest a return to the old way of life.

Wollheim further attacks the view that he has attributed to socialist thinkers of completely disregarding the arts and their vital importance in any culture in their desire to revive the old working-class culture:[21]

> In the narrow sense of the word 'culture' there is no thriving popular culture in England. If one is seriously concerned about the painting and the music and the poetry of the socialist future, then it seems to me quite unrealistic to think that these can spring from the thin soil of English proletarian life.

Wollheim accuses those who hold this view of being fundamentally uninterested in art, art that is a full expressive activity of man, rather than simply entertainment, or a leisure activity. Yet he seems to be flaying vainly at windmills, for there are no apparent exponents of this view. He names Hoggart as one of the chief protagonists, but he offers no evidence for this claim. Hoggart is nostalgic for aspects of the traditional working-class culture, but he does not suggest that we attempt to recreate this culture. Nor could he be accused of having no interest in art beyond its value as entertainment; on the contrary, his essays display a vigorous commitment to the arts as a vital expression of man and his humanity.

Wollheim's own solution to the problem of the quality of cultural life in mass society entails accepting the present hierarchical structure of society. Access to different levels of the hierarchy is now based more on the educational ladder, he claims, than a class structure. In order to maintain our present supply of individual talent, we must continue to support a system of education formed around processes of grading and streaming. Wollheim advocates such conservatism so that we may continue to enjoy the high level of prosperity and security. Further, he adds, in the public mind increasing social mobility and educational mobility have been associated with the process of liberalizing and improving society. Any changes which could be seen as breaking that connection, he concludes, would only increase frustration and discontent amongst the general population.

Wollheim's liberal conservatism on questions of education belie his professed commitment to socialism. He argues essentially that in this instance the present system should be allowed to remain, basically unchallenged, because it is what we know; changing it would only bring about uncertainty and a result of which we cannot be sure. Similarly, when addressing himself to the question of the future of the arts under socialism, he suggests that it is not necessary for the arts to be appreciated by everyone. Once again he advocates the need for an élite, proposing that as long as there is a sub-section of society that truly understands what the artist is trying to say, he will continue to lead a valid existence.

Wollheim suggests that the belief that only an integrated society will provide the proper conditions for artistic creativity is based on a false assumption about the relationship between art and reality. The assumption is, he claims, that art mirrors reality. Once again it is not clear who is responsible for the view that Wollheim is attacking. A crude form of a socialist theory of art which claims that art mirrors reality has been espoused at times but not by the English intellectuals of the literary humanist tradition. Art is considered to be influenced to some extent by the society in which it was created, a thesis difficult to refute; but there has been general agreement amongst English intellectuals, beginning with Morris and Ruskin in the late nineteenth century, with Wollheim's belief that we cannot specify under what conditions 'great art' will flourish. Neither Williams nor Hoggart, for example, expresses the view that art can only function as a mirror for society.

Finally, Wollheim reveals his commitment as a liberal thinker rather than a socialist in his arguments in favour of a pluralist culture rather than a common culture. Basically his reason for this stance, he claims, is that he opts for the ideal of 'Liberty' rather than 'Equality' or 'Fraternity'. He provides very little more than this statement of preference in support of the idea of a plural culture. Rather he turns to attack the notion of a common culture, particularly as it is expressed by Williams. The essential weakness in this concept of culture, according to Wollheim, is that Williams commits himself to a desire for conformity that he himself would be unwilling to accept:[22]

> Williams sometimes tries to explicate his ideal [of a common culture] by means of the expression 'common meanings, common values'. But what he fails to see is that he has compressed into this expression two quite different ideals: the modest ideal of a society in which people speak the same language, and the more comprehensive ideal of a society in which people say roughly the same things. The first ideal does perhaps follow from his original conception of what culture is: the second certainly doesn't.

Wollheim's comment demonstrates the fundamental vagueness of the concept of a common culture, but there is no evidence that Williams desires conformity amongst members of society.

Wollheim further attacks the concept of a common culture on the grounds that fundamental problems will arise if any attempt is made to introduce a common culture forcefully. The basic essence of culture, he claims, lies in the fact that it cannot be imposed on anyone. Yet Williams has taken great care in order to forestall such criticisms, for he too sees this as a fundamental feature of culture. His notion of the 'long revolution' is an affirmation of this belief; a common culture, he argues, can only ensue with the process of changing the material and social conditions of society.

Despite the weakness of Wollheim's analysis of such issues, his essay provides a valuable illustration of a number of significant trends in the English literary humanist tradition. First, as an intellectual in the field of art, he attempts to employ a concept of culture to legitimate the role of art as he sees it in society. But just as Hoggart fails to provide a meaningful concept, so does Wollheim. He switches from one meaning to another, without ever clarifying the sense with which he wants to associate himself. The main way in which he refers to 'culture' is in the sense of 'the arts', and yet many of the usages which he examines (such as the notion of a pluralist culture) are based on quite different senses of the term. Second, Wollheim's essay indicates the inadequacy of the English radical tradition. He claims to be a socialist and write for a Fabian publication, yet his ideas are basically liberal conservative in orientation. Such a discrepancy has not been unusual in English social thought as was apparent when Fabianism was at its heights earlier in the century. It stemmed from the containment of the English radical tradition within a commitment to parliamentarism with its attendant assumptions of the continuance of the state and its existing institutions. Though the contradiction between Wollheim's concrete proposals and his commitment to socialism appear blatant, they could remain obscure for him because of the tensions within that tradition.

## G. H. Bantock

Bantock, a professor of education, is on the whole a rather derivative thinker, for he draws very heavily on the work of T. S. Eliot and also uses, when it suits his argument, the ideas of such diverse writers as F. R. Leavis, D. H. Lawrence, Marshall McLuhan, and H. L. Wilensky. This feature of his work contributes to a sense of its inadequacy for the problems of the last twenty years. Instead of his own careful analysis of the issues arising from, for example, the youth culture, the counter culture, or the increasing importance of the mass media in the everyday life of the whole society, Bantock uses the ideas of diverse writers to argue this case. As Hoggart points out, the trouble with this approach is that 'someone else, using a different selective frame, [could] produce a book supported by quotations from at least as large a range of authors but running in quite the opposite direction'.[23]

Bantock seeks, as did Eliot, to develop a sense of 'culture' which rests between the anthropological term which denotes the whole way of life of a society and the concept as developed by Matthew Arnold. 'Culture' becomes that which provides the fundamental texture of our lives, it provides the means by which we articulate our thoughts and make our actions meaningful. Using the term in this way, according to Bantock, eliminates any evaluative aspects of the term:[24]

> To speak of '*a* culture', then, in this usage, will be simply to refer to a number of important forms of human thought and behaviour without any distinction of value as between one manifestation and another, and to the pattern of their inter-relationship.

This definition of 'culture' has more in common with the anthropological usage of the term than with Matthew Arnold's concept. It bears a distinct similarity to one of the best-known anthropological definitions given by Tylor as early as 1891: 'culture is that complex whole which includes knowledge, belief, art, morals, laws, customs and any other capabilities or habits acquired by man as a member of a society'.[25] There is, however, a slight but important difference in Bantock's use of the term. In discussing culture and education, Bantock always includes a qualification about how these activities are pursued along the lines of: 'the unselfconscious participation of people in worthwhile activities which they pursue with discrimination and passion'. He refers to this ideal in discussions of the 'cultured person', but it is also apparent in his references to education as the transmission of culture.[26]

Bantock attempts to remain neutral to the range of activities that he sees as forming different cultures. The value-neutrality of his definition of culture is essential to his argument about the place of 'high culture', or the arts, in society. Like Eliot, he wants to restrict involvement in the arts to a select group in society, but to claim that this realm of human activity is far superior to any other, and to exclude the majority of the population from it, would be an untenable position in the democratic temper of the mid-twentieth century. To appease both his audience and his own conscience, it is necessary that Bantock claim that the 'culture' of the arts is only one realm of human thought and behaviour, which is not superior to any other realm.

Bantock does not accept that such a view leads to a relativistic theory of values. On the contrary, he challenges the relativism which he believes popular culture fosters. It teaches the common man, says Bantock, to regard himself as the ultimate authority on all matters of taste and morality. Popular culture, he argues, is cheap and tawdry, encouraging a shallow, emotionally deficient response. It appeals to thwarted desires raised to a high pitch of expectation. It is not a culture of the people, he declares, but a culture manufactured by 'clever men who thus feed rather than check the dreams of unreality'.[27]

Relativism so threatens Bantock that at times his reactions to it undermine his own definition of culture. He claims that a cultured person is one who exploits the emotional, intellectual and practical possibilities of any activity, whether it be bird-watching, horse-riding or enjoying 'high' cultural activities. Yet, he cannot accept that such an approach can be taken to popular culture activities such as rock or jazz music. He argues that:[28]

> In recent years the English quality press has increasingly contained regular critical articles on pop manifestations. Even if we allow—which is true—that some pop is clearly better than some other, one wonders if it deserves this scholarly attention except as a sociological phenomenon. After all, people like Jerome Kern and Cole Porter were producing a comparable level of music in the thirties, but no one made these pretentious claims for them. As distractions such music may be allowed a limited appeal; as a serious contribution it is a non-starter.

Yet, to say that something was not discussed and analysed on a serious level at a previous date, does not prove that that is not a legitimate activity now. Moreover, in his definition of a cultured person, Bantock claims that the attitude taken to an activity designates it as cultural, not the content of the activity. In dismissing the critical articles on 'pop manifestations' he contradicts his own definition of culture.

Indeed, if Bantock had included the serious and often intense appreciation of 'pop' culture activities prevalent today, his discussion of the culture of the people might have sounded more plausible. As it is, his outline of activities which should be regarded as providing a viable basis for a culture of the people is limited to those activities which would appeal mainly to past generations. Insufficient attention is given to the vast range of activities which form the basis of various sub-cultures in our society today. For example, Bantock argues that:[29]

> It is, it seems to me, when we come to see people, not as a mass public for the largely (though, of course, by no means exclusively) decreative media of mass communication but as pigeon fanciers, market gardeners, riders of horses, amateur singers and actors, photographers and cine enthusiasts, and so on, that the qualitative opportunities open to a modern community set the problem of mass civilization in a rather different perspective. 'Culture', in fact, is what happens when people pursue activities with passion and discrimination.

In much the same terms as Lawrence used to discuss the education of the working class, Bantock contends that the great majority of the population are historically and psychologically ill-prepared for the demands placed on them by the highly literate culture. Literature, he says, fosters an inward-looking mentality, encouraging individualism and an intense interest in privacy. As literacy has spread, the search for identity has become one of the obsessive themes of English literature. In traditional society, according to Bantock, the existence of communally accepted mythological figures defined the socially acceptable behaviour for all, establishing a comparative stability of personality; in modern society a whole new dimension of personality has been added, accompanied by 'an increasing psychic rootlessness in face of the multiplying models for conduct that a book culture provides'. The majority of the people, he claims, have traditionally lived by their emotions and hence are not equipped to cope with this rootlessness.[30]

Such a judgment about the historical contribution of literature to individualism and psychic rootlessness seems, at the least, exaggerated. Bantock provides no developed theoretical or empirical analysis which could support his claim. Nor does he justify his view that literature is a causal factor (rather than, for example, a reflection) of certain features of modern society. Similarly, he provides no evidence for the 'psychic unpreparedness' of the general population for 'high culture' except to argue, in a similar manner to Eliot, that many scholars 'retreat' into popular culture, though of tested good aptitude at school, because of 'unpropitious cultural circumstances'.[31] The assumptions behind this claim are manifold, but chiefly Bantock makes groundless connections between interest in popular culture and home background, he precludes the possibility of a deep appreciation of 'high culture' accompanying an equal appreciation of 'popular culture', and he blames any lack of full understanding of 'high culture' on home background with no evidence and no recognition that other factors may be involved.

The majority of the population, Bantock concludes, should not be initiated into the realm of the 'literate culture' or 'high culture'. In support of this view he frequently quotes Lawrence's statement from *Fantasia of the Unconscious* (1922) that: '*The great mass of humanity should never learn to read and write—never*.'[32] But neither Bantock nor Lawrence believes that this situation could ever arise because of the practical necessity for everyone to be able to read and write in order to exist in modern society. Bantock advocates that the schools confine themselves to 'the basic tools of literacy' but eliminate a great deal of 'the ordinary culture of literacy' that they attempt to provide.[33]

Bantock wants to see different types of culture being provided for children in schools. For the children of the élite 'a culture primarily linguistic', based on reading, is appropriate; for the others, 'an action-orientated culture', based on movement and images would be more accommodated to their cultural background. He completely rejects the idea of a common culture, arguing that the notion of social unity in its modern sense, at the level either of power or culture, is a mirage, a 'pipe-dream of humanity'. Varied social groupings, he says, are inevitable in a large-scale society, and differentiation on the basis of class is a natural way of recognizing differences between individuals in a society. Bantock does not believe that the class system should be rigid, but it is a useful 'rough-and-ready' way of recognizing pre-existing inequalities, intellectual, moral, ethical sensitivity, daily behaviour, and cultural orientation, though he admits that the class system will serve to reinforce these differences. He concludes that we should not be complacent about this.[34]

Egalitarianism, Bantock declares, is nothing more than well-meant sentimentality. It substitutes a considered, genuine judgment of 'the potential of particular children in relation to a specific socio-cultural environment' for 'highly abstract—one might even say, bookish—schemes of human improvement which fail to accept the complexity of human existence as it actually faces us.'[35] But, Bantock goes on, the social consequences of this egalitarianism make its well-meaningness naively dangerous. If the like-mindedness, which egalitarianism seems to favour with respect to cultural meaning, is to be introduced, it can only be done by appalling, *1984*-style, tyranny. Bantock makes the same judgment as does Wollheim in his opposition to any notion of a common culture. He fails to acknowledge the extent to which those he criticizes espouse, just as strongly as he, a belief in the fundamental importance of recognizing and promoting the human diversity of interests and abilities.

Bantock firmly rejects any idea of equality of opportunity in education:[36]

> For whatever reason, then—heredity or environment—we are ineluctably faced with a wide diversity of identifiable human achievement and, as a corollary, of potential for achievement in our schools. For if historical circumstances (to go no further) can inhibit, they can also encourage and sustain. Hence, whether on biological or historical grounds, we are likely for the foreseeable future to be faced with a reasonably identifiable group of highly talented human beings to whom justice on the Aristotelian principle demands that we pay attention.

Further, he argues, in terms of specific social returns from education, it is a wastage of talent not to provide élite education for those capable of benefiting from it. Similarly, he questions the value of the principle of a rapid assimilation of the culturally impoverished into the prestigious sections of the community for 'the rise of the merely clever in these terms to positions of social influence is a culturally doubtful manifestation'.[37]

Bantock claims that he is not totally opposed to the principle of equality of opportunity, but it is too easily taken to extremes. He clarifies the way in which he believes a system of equality and justice can be instituted in the schools, by outlining what he sees as three distinct models for equality of education:[38]

> The fault of the meritocratic model lies in its too frequent indifference to the living potential by which we are faced in order to serve the purely functional efficiency of the industrial-bureaucratic society. . . . Yet in the meritocratic school at least certain sections of the potential are reasonably catered for. The able are not neglected or despised. The fault of the egalitarian model lies even deeper—a perverse attempt to homogenise both ends of the spectrum in a mediocre common experience satisfying to neither. . . . The cultural model at least looks to satisfactions beyond the functional—and to an attempt to provide an equally appropriate but essentially differentiated school experience—differentiated in terms of cultural expectation and potential.

Bantock provides concrete proposals for the two totally different forms of education he advocates for the intellectually able and the 'less-able' child. For the former education should continue along the lines of the traditional élitist education, based on the formal discipline. For the less-able child (those who would form the lower end at the secondary modern school), the disciplines such as history and geography should be dispensed with. Instead, folk-crafts requiring no mental training, domestic education for girls and training in mechanical activities for boys, and physical education should form the core of the curriculum.

The most significant change that Bantock wants to see effected in schools is a greater concentration on the education of the emotions. This can be carried out only to a limited extent, because in Bantock's view the school is not a therapeutic institution; but it should be a vital part of the education of all children and a very necessary antidote in a world given over to 'heady restlessness' and 'insecure self-indulgences'.[39] Bantock suggests that the emotional growth of most children can be promoted in the schools through the arts and crafts whose greater part in the school curriculum would increase a child's intellectual and emotional control of the self.

In suggesting that mental health is an important part of the school's responsibility, Bantock is adamant that this should not be understood as support for progressive principles of education. He criticizes this school of thought for not drawing the proper distinction between activities such as play and learning, or between needs and interests. A great deal of confusion is created by the use of jargon, he claims. Interest is largely the creation of circumstance; the child is not born with it, which is what the progressive educationists assume. Consequently, the teacher will have to create interest in the child in the direction of our highly civilized realms of activity. Bantock defines the responsibility of the school as opening up opportunities of a rich existence for the child:[40]

> For to evoke art and literature is to adumbrate the possibility of a finer order, a more releasing discipline; the lesson of the greatest artistic creativity is transcendence, not relaxation. Not the least of the curses that romantic progressivism has bestowed on us is the belief that achievement results from the lifting of restraints rather than from their conquest, that creativity springs from a spontaneous outpouring rather than from knowledge and discipline.

Progressivism, Bantock claims, completely mistakes the nature of human creativity. It is not the result of allowing a child complete freedom to follow his particular whims; true creativity can only occur when the individual has fully mastered the set of structures, social, emotional and intellectual, which he inherits from his society. Creativity consists in transcending these forms to make an original contribution to the culture of which they are a part.

Though advocating discipline and the use of authority in education, Bantock is not fully in accord with the form in which education has been provided over the last hundred years. For example, he criticizes the development of the examination system as being closely connected with the rational and impersonal temper nurtured by bureaucracy and industrialization. A 'diploma-grabbing ethos', says Bantock, is not one in which the wider benefits of 'general culture' are likely to be fully diffused.[41]

In this respect, Bantock differs from fellow contributors to the *Black Papers* (which came out first in 1969). This group of writers operate on the basis of a number of assumptions about issues such as class differentiation and egalitarianism which are akin to those employed by Bantock. Their overriding concern in writing these papers is to oppose the prevalent progressive ideas about discipline and teacher-centred classrooms. Consequently, only a couple of writers mention the demands of culture, and their support for the traditional examinations reflect this. Bantock opposes examinations because they narrow the focus of the student's learning. The *Black Papers* generally support examinations both as a protection for students against 'unscrupulous teachers', and as a protection for the public, a guarantee of the sound training of professionals and others.[42] Writers for these papers tend to show no real concern for the qualitative aspects of learning; their preoccupation with standards is a preoccupation with past traditions or ideas about learning and knowledge, failing to recognize that traditions should be dynamic.

Similarly, the *Black Papers'* characteristic call for a return to discipline in the classroom is expressed in far more mechanical terms than is Bantock's. They object to the current *laissez-faire* approach in teaching, advocating a far more systematic 'hard process of learning' approach to the mechanics of subjects.[43] Bantock, too, wants a return to discipline, but he suggests that this can arise from the demands of the subject rather than be arbitrarily imposed. His concern with culture seems to provide a deeper, more humane basis for his ideas about education than that which is apparent in the *Black Papers*. The latter exhibit mainly a preoccupation with the structures, the traditional forms of education. Bantock wishes these to continue in so far as he believes that they provide a framework for education to promote a better quality of life.

The concept of culture in Bantock's work expresses an ideal towards which teachers and educators must always be turned, for 'it contains within itself the possibility of man's essential development and freedom'.[44] As such he expresses a similar preoccupation to Arnold with an ideal which goes beyond the individual's egoistic concerns, an ideal which provides a court of appeal by which we can judge society's activities and provide a vision for its improvement. Bantock reasserts this notion of supra-personal values in the face of intellectual movements such as progressivist educational ideas, but to interpret his particular preoccupations at this level only would be to accept his own representation of his stance. His ideas articulate the dismay of certain groups at the shifts in the society which undermine the explicit recognition of class differences. Intellectuals of traditional orientations, such as teachers of the classical disciplines, have particularly responded to ideas such as those expressed by Bantock, because their position and status in the society has depended in the past on the explicit acceptance of hierarchical structures in the society. Bantock's appeal to educationalists rests primarily on his attraction for these entrenched interests.

**R. S. Peters**

Peters works on a similar terrain to Bantock. He is a professor of philosophy of education at the London Institute of Education and has been a dominant figure in this area of discourse particularly during the 1960s. His central focus is to define the concept of education using the philosophical method of linguistic analysis. He defines education as initiation into worthwhile activities. More fully, he sets out certain criteria for something to be called education:[45]

(i) that 'education' implies the transmission of what is worth while to those who become committed to it;
(ii) that 'education' must involve knowledge and understanding and some kind of cognitive perspective, which are not inert;
(iii) that 'education' at least rules out some procedures of transmission, on the grounds that they lack wittingness and voluntariness.

The particular activities which Peters regards as being worthwhile are distinctly of an intellectual nature. Science, history, literary appreciation and poetry are serious curricula activities, he claims, in that they illuminate other areas of life and contribute much to the quality of living. In comparison, sports and games are largely a matter of 'knowing how' rather than 'knowing that'. The central distinction between history, science or literature and the activities not considered worthwhile rests, says Peters, on the 'immense amount to know' in the former areas and the way in which this knowledge 'throws light on, widens, and deepens one's view of countless other things'.[46]

Worthwhile activities, then, are those which transform our way of looking at things, a view similar to Bantock's requirement that cultural activities be undertaken with 'passion and discrimination'. Yet Bantock is critical of Peters for what he describes as an 'old fashioned' preoccupation with the rational or intellectual side of man:[47]

> Professor Peters' view of the educated man comes, today, to wear something of an old-fashioned look; though he is in most respects so much superior to what may well replace him—the Organisation Man—that one welcomes, to that extent, his resuscitation. Yet he was never an adequate figure for many in a mass society; and that he is being replaced results partly from the too restricted view of the dimensions of human personality out of which he was formed. . . .

Bantock's analysis of the difference between himself and Peters in this instance is valid, for the latter does not acknowledge any need to educate the emotions or to allow for differences between children, whatever their basis. He does not seek a different type of education for different children.

Indeed such a consideration would be antithetical to Peters's fundamental claim about the concept of education. In referring to 'education', he asserts, we mean only one thing, and according to his analysis this means the initiation into certain activities which can only be seen as worthwhile. A different type of education cannot be offered to a less able child; rather different children will progress to different levels along the same avenues of exploration and appreciation.

Education is the process of initiation of the individual into activities or modes of thought and conduct that are worthwhile. And this notion, says Peters, is shorthand for 'summarizing our notion of a form of life which is worth while enough to deserve being handed on from generation to generation'.[48] On this basis, it would be impossible to deny that it is mandatory that all children should be introduced to this particular path of exploration; it is essential to their quality of life. But equally important, there can be no question that the results of this process of education should be discussed. The educated man is one who works with precision, passion and taste at worthwhile things. To be educated is not a fixed state, Peters declares, but a continuing process of self-development: 'To be educated is not to have arrived at a destination; it is to travel with a different view.'[49]

The concept of the educated man becomes increasingly important in Peters's work as he finds the concept of education inadequate for his purposes. In his earlier works such as 'Education as Initiation' (1965), he claims that 'education' is a value-laden term: it is used only to describe processes in which a desirable state of mind develops. In his later work Peters accepts that 'education' does not always refer to activities that he necessarily condones: for example, when we talk of Spartan education, the three criteria which Peters sets out for education are not satisfied. Consequently, he suggests in one of his later essays that we employ two concepts of education: one that is not associated with value or knowledge, a descriptive term; and one associated with the ideal of the educated man.[50]

Peters argues that these concepts of education are both common usage, a position which is fundamental to his method of philosophical analysis. Peters represents a school of philosophical thought which, until the 1970s, gained a considerable following in England, particularly in the field of the philosophy of education: linguistic analysis or conceptual analysis. In Peters's terms this type of philosophy engages in 'the clarification and discussion of the concepts used and of how they have meaning, and of the procedures by means of which these questions are answered. . . .' Philosophy's task is no longer considered to be, he claims, to provide high-level directives for education or for life.[51]

This view of philosophy has been challenged by a number of writers, Ernest Gellner in his book *Words and Things* (1968) being one of the first. David Adelstein has taken Gellner's work and applied it to Peters's philosophy of education. Adelstein argues that by assuming justifications already exist in 'common sense' and 'ordinary language', Peters very subtly puts forward a typically English, pragmatic conservatism.[52] This technique is well illustrated in the switch which Peters makes from claiming that there is only one concept of education, to claiming that there are two. In his earlier analyses of the concept of education, Peters had been able to make prescriptive statements about what education should be, under the guise of claiming that this was what was conveyed by common usage of the term. In fact, there is no such consensus, as the different opinions about the nature of worthwhile activities, which Bantock and Peters exemplify, illustrate.

Once Peters had to acknowledge that 'education' does not necessarily denote worthwhile activities, he turned to the idea of the educated man. Through this term he sets down his own criteria for what education should be, though he purports to be merely clarifying how the term is ordinarily used. He claims that the main criteria to be satisfied by an 'educated' man are:[53]

(i) An educated man is one whose form of life—as exhibited in his conduct, the activities to which he is committed, his judgement and feelings—is thought to be desirable.

(ii) Whatever he is trained to do he must have knowledge, not just knack, and an understanding of principles. His form of life must also exhibit some mastery of forms of thought and awareness which are not harnessed purely to utilitarian or vocational purposes or completely confined to one mode.

(iii) His knowledge and understanding must not be inert either in the sense that they make no difference to his general view of the world, his actions within it and reactions to it *or* in the sense that they involve no concern for the standards immanent in forms of thought and awareness, as well as the ability to attain them.

But the concept of education implied by these criteria is quite alien to progressive ideas of education, for example. It would seem necessary that 'education' in the sense that it conveys a positive value judgment will have to be able to include these sorts of usages, even if Peters does not approve of them. The ideal of the educated man which Peters develops is not necessarily implicit, as he would have us believe.

Peters's conservatism is apparent in the traditional, intellectual education which he advocates. But at a deeper level this conservatism is inherent in the philosophical methods he adopts: on the one hand, it entails a conceptual conservatism and a strong distrust of intellectual innovation, a point which Gellner makes about linguistic philosophy in general;[54] and on the other hand, Adelstein points out that Peters's method is ideologically conservative in its avoidance of the idea of contradiction:[55]

> That the real social world is one in which classes and segments of classes, that is real social generalities, engage in contradictory, and therefore often conflicting, activity, is ignored by our philosophers. . . . The philosophers would insist that the conflict was due to conceptual confusions and that, if only those involved would apply a bit of conceptual analysis, they would realize that there was no contradiction after all.

Not only are Peters's statements about education strongly conservative under the pretence of being value-neutral, but they are also shallow reproductions of similar statements made, particularly by Matthew Arnold, in the nineteenth century. Adelstein expresses this view, though perhaps more strongly than would be adhered to here:[56]

> We do not find the stylistic brilliance and vigour of his English ancestors, nor their suggestiveness, nor imagination, but merely the incantation of platitudes containing supposed depth.

Leaving aside judgments on the depth or style of Peters's writing, the similarities which can be drawn between Arnold's and Peters's ideas are striking. Both Peters's concept of education and Arnold's concept of culture can be analysed as resting on the same essential criteria. They each claim that the process involves the development of a desirable state of mind and that this process is an enduring one, though it is couched in terms of a pursuit of a certain goal of perfection; and they each declare that this process involves the whole man. Though they pin these requirements on different concepts, the same judgments are made.

Arnold thought of education in much narrower terms than Peters. 'Education' was used to refer to the process that goes on in the schools and other similar institutions. Arnold was interested to reform education so that it was concerned with culture; but he did not see 'education' as necessarily implying culture. Peters's concept of education, on the other hand, is not restricted to institutions, but is a process which continues throughout a man's life. Instead of using the concept of culture as a guide to what should be going on in education as Arnold does, Peters says that the direction is implied by the concept of education itself.

Peters indicates some recognition himself of a connection between his concept of education and nineteenth-century ideas of culture:[57]

> though previously to the nineteenth century there had been the ideal of the cultivated person who was the product of elaborate training and instruction, the term 'an educated man' was not the usual one for drawing attention to this ideal. They had the concept but they did not use the word 'educated' quite with these overtones.

In Peters, then, as with Bantock, there is an apparent attempt to revive the tradition associated with the concept of culture as developed by Arnold. However, in both cases there is a lack of vigour or vitality compared to other members of the lineage. Bantock depends on the work of others to give his arguments force and Peters disguises his position by the adoption of a suspect philosophical method.

This weakness in both writers suggests the demise of the tradition within which they have tried to work, but the question remains as to why these two figures tried to revive it. The most significant common factor seems to be that they are both educationalists. They have both established a career as academics working within the field of educational theory. The lack of a literary or artistic commitment reveals itself in that the ideals of culture and education which they espouse do not emphasize the power of the artistic imagination. The main thrust of their ideas is the importance of supra-personal values over the individual, a position which is basically similar to the nineteenth-century reaction to the extreme individualism of mass society.

In the mid-twentieth century progressivism represented a resurgence of the claims of individualism. It articulated a threat both to the supra-personal values of which the intellectual has traditionally seen himself as keeper, but also to the value of intellectual work at all. Progressivism, being essentially an educational theory, was, therefore, the chief target of intellectuals working in this field. Both Bantock and Peters drew on the concept of culture and its tradition in the attempt to answer the challenge of progressivism, this being the most sustained tradition of English intellectual thought which offered an alternative vision to the extreme individualism and demands of a mass, technological society.

The intellectual tradition represented by the concept of culture has revealed openly now its ability to accommodate both radical and conservative ideologies. The tradition appears fairly unsteady, as these two perspectives vie for its possession, though both perspectives continued to share the essential concern which has sustained it for over one hundred years: the retention of the traditional cultural preserve of the intellectual.

# 9 Conclusion: cultural studies

In the 1970s interest in the concept of culture has assumed new forms in England. This work stems from the project of the cultural critics, the literary tradition of Matthew Arnold to Raymond Williams, but attempts to reformulate the fundamental questions of that project. Before briefly outlining the direction of work in this field, a retrospective glance at the literary tradition will provide a basis for elucidating the domain of these cultural studies.

### A retrospect

The concept of culture in the mid-nineteenth century formed the central motif in discussions about the nature of art and its relationship to society. Its roots lay in the romantic notions of art and the artist's role in society which had dominated literary circles in the first half of that century. Assertions of the superior reality of art and the special function of the artist in the society implied by the concept of culture were given their most forceful expression in England by the romantic poets. But in turning to this concept, writers such as Matthew Arnold rejected the temptation implicit in romanticism for the artist to withdraw, to set himself apart from society. Arnold claimed the special powers of the artistic imagination to judge the quality of life in modern industrial society.

Arnold represented the concept of culture as the guiding principle to preside over all activities of the society. Culture and its prophets exhorted every individual to act in accordance with its notion of perfection; to pursue that ideal in both its individual and social form. Modern industrial society was criticized for its lack of due regard for humane values, those values that look beyond individualistic satisfactions. Individualism and materialism prevailed, according to Arnold, crushing the most valuable qualities of the human spirit.

As a moral critique, Arnold's attack on Victorian England, particularly in his earlier work, was a powerful expression of a humanistic vision. But this vision of society which informed the critique undertaken by Arnold and his contemporaries was clearly hierarchical. They did not seek structural changes in the society but wished to effect reforms in the quality of life of its members through a change of heart, a cultural regeneration. Society was attacked because it was not upholding the moral principles which purportedly that society claimed to be essential to its existence. This approach to the problems of modern industrial society precluded any consideration of the extent to which they may be endemic to the very structure of that society.

William Morris was equally concerned with the way of life of the people, but he was not restricted by this concern to a cultural critique. His ideas were initially formulated in a similar mould to Arnold with strong allegiances to the romantic movement in poetry. But he transcended many of the strictures of this tradition in his later work, while continuing to affirm his deep commitment to a humanistic vision of society. He rejected the assumption of a hierarchically structured society associated with the literary tradition, and as a socialist worked to promote its radical transformation.

Significantly, the concept of culture played no role in Morris's ideas. Unlike other intellectuals of this period, Morris displayed no particular interest (at least, in his later work) in elaborating notions of the specialness of the intellectual's or artist's role in society. He shared with John Ruskin, the mentor of his youth, an increasing sense of disenchantment with beliefs that might set the artist apart from the rest of society. This did not signify any less preoccupation with art, but they became convinced of the primacy of changing society, if art were to flourish.

As the nineteenth century drew to a close, the concept of culture and its associated claims of the relationship between art and society disappeared from intellectual discourse. Two alternative views of this relationship emerged as predominant amongst literary and artistic circles. Aestheticism was the logical outcome of the romantic tendencies in the concept of culture. The withdrawal of the artists from society and the assertion of the principle of 'art for art's sake' expressed an unyielding belief in the superior reality of the artist's world. This alternative did not attract significant or long-term support amongst English artists or intellectuals. The Bloomsbury group stands out in English cultural history not so much for the talent of its members, but for the eccentricity of their claims. The Pre-Raphaelites were the only notable precursors to this group and their leanings towards aestheticism were always tempered by a degree of social awareness.

The other alternative sought by literary and artistic intellectuals was socialism. As pursued by H. G. Wells and George Bernard Shaw this socialism displayed the virile nature of English Fabianism at this stage in its development. But it was not particularly radical in its outlook even then: it was preoccupied with parliamentary politics. Fabianism was as much part of the English liberal tradition, particularly in its utilitarian form, as an inheritor of the socialism of the nineteenth century. Wells and Shaw rejected Fabianism at different stages in their lives, both of them resorting to notions akin to Plato's philosopher kings. These ideals, though demonstrating a hierarchical vision of society similar to the one expressed by the concept of culture, did not entail a belief in the superior reality of the artistic imagination. Wells and Shaw, though of different mind on many issues, both spoke of art as simply a powerful mechanism for the promulgation of ideas.

In the 1930s with science gaining increased confidence in its voice and demands for specialization pervading all areas of intellectual inquiry, literary intellectuals attempted to revivify the concept of culture. Once again it formed the central focus of a powerful critique of modern industrial society. Suggestions of this move were first apparent in the 1920s, but it gained momentum in the next decade with the work of F. R. Leavis. He extended the type of criticisms made by Arnold of the supreme individualism and materialism of the society to challenge the new cultural institutions of his age. The mass media were vilified for their exploitation of the cheap response, their use of applied psychology to manipulate the audience and their lack of critical standards.

In Arnold's writings the concept of culture affirmed a hierarchical vision of society. What was implicit in this context was made explicit by this new generation of cultural critics. F. R. Leavis and T. S. Eliot, in particular, proclaimed their first allegiance to culture, to the preservation of the traditions of society, rather than to democracy. Arnold had admitted no such choice. He advocated the continued existence of classes in the society to serve specific functions in the promotion of culture. Leavis and Eliot were far more defensive in advocating a similar view of the necessity of élites in the society to preserve and revive the best of past traditions or the traditional culture.

Leavis interpreted culture as a moral force in society in terms similar to those of the romantic poets of the early nineteenth century. With special access to the realm of truth, the artistic imagination was a force for the betterment of society. But Leavis could give the concept of culture none of the vitality or confidence that Arnold expressed in his writings. In Leavis's work the concept lacked coherence; at times it appeared to be the pursuit of an ideal and at other times it was identified with the actual objects or artefacts whose appreciation should promote this pursuit. Similarly, Eliot attempted to manipulate two concepts and, through their conflation, validate his claims for the necessity of an hereditary élite. The concept of culture had lost its vision and its cogency for the literary intellectuals; it no longer evinced a conviction that they could claim a special place in society.

Morris studied the past to learn from its methods in art and life; Leavis turned to the past to lament that anything had ever changed. Leavis revealed more than the lingering regrets of Arnold who did little other than chide the aristocracy for their lack of vision and glance at American society with some apprehension. Americanization for Leavis contained a far greater threat; it exemplified the industrialism, materialism and fragmentation of modern industrial society that threatened the very existence of the traditional culture. Yet Leavis refused to examine the extent to which those processes might be connected with the whole basis of the organization of society. He saw his stance on this issue as one of specific opposition to any form of social thought that might be linked with Marxism. He despised this mode of thought at least as much as he was tormented by the question of the quality of life in mass society.

In the years prior to the Second World War left-wing political thought was a powerful force in intellectual circles. But the issue which animated a wide range of writers was the problematic nature of the intellectual's role in society. This concern represented a significant organizing principle in all their work, although its centrality varied considerably in the writings of one intellectual to the next. Bertrand Russell, for example, in his attack on the 'tyranny of the herd' was insisting on the overriding necessity of the intellectual's detachment from society. Similarly, George Orwell, though committed to introducing poetry to a mass audience, was adamant that the intellectual should retain a position of autonomy in the society. In every instance, these writers declared the specialness of the intellectuals' contribution to society.

Raymond Williams in the 1950s and 1960s sought to re-work the romantic literary tradition of social criticism on an egalitarian framework. He owed much to the humanist critique of the literary intellectuals in the formulation of his ideas and felt more in common with that tradition than with the tradition of socialist thought in England. But he rejected any suggestion of a hierarchical vision of society in his writings on culture. Drawing on his Welsh working-class background, Williams proposed a concept of a common culture. Through this concept he hoped to provide a basis for the promotion of excellence in the society and to institute this quest as the preserve of everyone, not just a select group in the society.

Williams articulated a common concern amongst a number of intellectuals in the 1950s. It was a concern, as he expressed it, with the lived experience of social change. Richard Hoggart examined this question in terms of the changing pattern of life of the working class in the twentieth century. Williams himself analysed the way in which the literary intellectuals in their moral critique of society have provided a valuable testimony of reactions to the social changes of industrialism and democracy.

Williams and Hoggart are the successors to the humanist literary tradition through their commitment to its moral critique of society and the preoccupation with the quality of life of its members. Williams redefined 'culture' in terms of patterns learned and created in the mind and the means of communication within a social group. He envisaged the restructuring of the cultural institutions of education and the mass media in order to promote the evolution of a common culture. As the basis for effective communication between all members of society, Williams believed that a common culture would be intimately related to the elimination of class divisions in the society.

In the late 1960s Williams discarded the question of cultural change as the central consideration in his work to examine culture within a framework of social control or domination. Through this shift in focus, Williams turned to the task of exploring the possibilities of a Marxist cultural theory. The concept of hegemony derived from Gramsci's work acquired special significance in his inquiry into the way in which culture was an aspect of the process of domination of one class over another, just as much as the basis of communication within a social group. But Williams also sought to avoid reducing culture to a total dependence on the economic structure of society, by proposing concepts such as 'emergent cultural elements' and 'residual cultural elements' as analytical tools.

Williams has continued this project in his later writings, refining his theoretical propositions in terms of concepts such as 'structures of feeling' and 'culture'. The transition in his work coincided with his political disenchantment with the Labour Party and parliamentary reformism. Yet his greater commitment to Marxism in his analysis of society and its culture does not signal a complete transformation of the framework of his thought. This feature of his later work entails a number of limitations in his approach to a theory of culture. The particular value of creative activity in society and the specialness of art as a realm of human activity remain dominant issues in Williams's writings. Similarly, his analysis of society concentrates on the cultural level, neglecting any investigation of the economic level of society. And finally, he continues to employ concepts such as 'structures of feeling' that emphasize social cohesion, thereby deflecting attention away from the deep-rooted social conflict in society.

## Cultural studies

In the 1970s interest in the humanist literary tradition has become more widespread. It no longer remains largely the preserve of literary intellectuals, but has become the background material for studies of a range of contemporary and historical questions. Though these studies appear of a more academic orientation without the overriding sense of vision intrinsic to the writings particularly of Arnold and Leavis, they are nevertheless characterized by a strong sense of commitment. Without attempting to summarize the various movements in cultural studies in England in the 1970s, a number of trends can be outlined as highlighting its central concerns amongst particular schools of thought.

Raymond Williams in his work during the 1960s and 1970s attempts to examine the extent to which culture is as much about ways of conflict as about ways of life in the society. His conceptual framework indicates that he has not succeeded in fully confronting this issue. E. P. Thompson in his work on the popular history of the eighteenth and nineteenth centuries in England provides a counterbalance to Williams's work. These two men are contemporaries who share a fundamental concern with the lived experience of social change. Yet just as Williams and Hoggart were ignorant of each other's work until they published their first books in the field of cultural studies almost simultaneously, so were Williams and Thompson ignorant of each other's work in the 1950s though working in related areas of interest.[1]

In the 1970s Thompson has been inserted in the humanist tradition of the literary intellectuals. This appropriation of his work stems from a number of its central features. As Williams points out, this literary tradition demonstrates a particular experience of social change. Thompson records the experience of social change from a different perspective in the nineteenth century, for example, in his study *The Making of the English Working Class* (1963). Further, Thompson indicates his strong allegiance to certain aspects of this romantic literary tradition through his great tribute to William Morris in the writing of his intellectual biography and the later additions to that work. But perhaps most significantly, Thompson shares with this tradition a 'culturalist' orientation to the study of society. Such a framework entails a preoccupation with the values and attitudes of the people whose history is studied and an acceptance of their own representations of their experiences as the substance of historical accounts. Though the notion of class is fundamental to Thompson's work, his analysis is confined to the cultural and political levels of society; economic questions play a minor role.

This criticism of Thompson's work is made by the very people who have asserted his significance as a counterbalancing element in the humanist literary tradition. In particular, the Centre for Contemporary Cultural Studies at the University of Birmingham draws on Thompson's work in theoretical and empirical studies. Their concern with Thompson's culturalism lies at the heart of their own theoretical problems, for, as an institution established to study culture, it will inevitably have a continuing struggle not to be ensnared by its own project.[2]

The Centre for Contemporary Cultural Studies provides a valuable focus for examining many of the trends in the study of cultural questions in England. They have been prolific as a group in the production of papers, articles, and so on, but they have also been responsible for creating a great deal of the interest in that field. The Centre was formed in 1964 under the directorship of Richard Hoggart. Though theoretically the work of the Centre has diverged considerably from earlier concerns since his departure in 1973, Hoggart's impact at this level can still be discerned. In particular he left a legacy of interest in sub-cultures and sub-cultural analysis which continues to add strength to the Centre's theoretical analyses. Though the question of the relationship between sub-cultures and the dominant culture remains unresolved, its presence resists an over-formalization of the notions of culture or cultural hegemony.

To attempt to summarize the activities of the Centre is an impossible task for a number of reasons. As an academic institution it has stressed cooperative work by staff and students and it has been prolific in its production of papers over the years. This feature of its work makes it an overwhelming task for anyone to attempt to describe specific developments. Moreover, the production of working papers has meant that evidence of the intellectual lineage within the Centre is scattered. The most direct evidence is obtainable from the Centre's journal *Working Papers in Cultural Studies* and their *Stencilled Occasional Papers*. But to search for such a lineage would misrepresent the changes over the years as being straightforward stages and the Centre as a monolithic institution in which everyone held the same opinions.

Rather than risk such errors, a number of points of divergence from the humanist literary tradition will suffice to indicate the direction of the Centre's work, particularly in the 1970s under the directorship of Stuart Hall. First, the Centre has emphasized the analysis of class as being fundamental to the study of culture. A striking feature of the literary tradition was the extent to which these writers depoliticized class. Up until Williams's work this attempt emerged in the depiction of classes according to particular 'natural' functions in the society. This mystification was not at all unusual amongst intellectuals, the most obvious example being in the popular representation of education as establishing a new structure of élites in the society. Though Williams rejected this connection between class and function, he did not succeed in escaping its import. By discussing culture in terms of communication, he contributed to the depoliticization of the concept of class. In his early work at least Williams argued in terms of the possibility of breaking down the divisions between classes through the establishment of a common culture; he did not recognize classes as fundamental economic divisions. The problem of class, he believed, could be solved through communication. Particularly in their work of the mid-1970s, the Centre has sought to examine class at the economic level as well as the cultural level, though they have had some difficulties in reconciling this theoretical task with their interest in class as lived experience.[3]

The second area in which the Centre has departed from the romantic literary tradition relates to the centrality of the question of the role of art in society. This question plays no part in the Centre's work either explicitly or implicitly, whereas the concept of culture of the literary tradition has always been contained by that question. In its very conception the question of the role of art in society seeks to affirm its specialness as a human activity. In Arnold's work the concept of culture articulated a belief in the superior reality of art and the special function of the artistic imagination in society. Similarly, Raymond Williams sought a special function for the artistic imagination as the basis of his concept of a common culture. In so doing he eluded any inquiry into the class basis of the selective culture and the extent to which the traditional art of the society is an expression of the values, the interests, of the dominant class. Though Williams has attempted to move away from the question of the role of art in society, he continues to reveal residues of this framework in his discussion of concepts such as 'emergent cultural elements'. This question appears to play no role in the work of the Centre in the 1970s; art is examined rather in terms of material production.

The third way in which the Centre has departed from the romantic literary tradition is in its rejection of a moral critique of society. This feature of thought is intimately connected with the desire to avoid a 'culturalist' orientation. Its criticisms of society look beyond the way in which people live their lives, to an investigation into the structures that support that way of life. Further, the Centre has not accepted the humanistic concerns of that tradition as unproblematic. It has been heavily influenced by the anti-humanism of the French Marxists, such as Louis Althusser, who have declared the humanist framework, among other things, an affirmation of the bourgeois approach to the individual.

Finally, the Centre's work differs from the literary tradition in its emphasis on theoretical concerns. English social thought has been generally characterized by its aversion to abstract theoretical ideas; the literary intellectuals were no exception. The Centre has emphasized the need for theoretical rigour in its work. This has led in the mid-1970s to a concern that they may have swung too far in this direction amongst at least certain members of the Centre.[4] But theoretical interests have not precluded their undertaking concrete studies of historical and contemporary issues (though at times these may have been devalued).

These points of departure only indicate certain aspects of the Centre's work. They represent significant shifts in the field of cultural studies and provide some indication of the continuing significance of this area of English social thought. These moves by the Centre for Contemporary Cultural Studies have not been unique to that group. There are a number of other writers in England who share similar interests. For example, Terry Eagleton, who was a student of Raymond Williams, has worked in the field of Marxist cultural theory from an anti-humanist framework. He too was heavily influenced by Althusser; but just as the Centre has moved on to other theoretical interests, so has Eagleton. Stephen Heath, on the other hand, represents a significant trend towards the study of semiotics. Heath forms part of the group associated with the journals *Screen* and *Screen Education*, which focus on a theoretical understanding of the cinema.

Interest in cultural studies is burgeoning in a number of different contexts. This phenomenon is vital for preventing stultifying debates around rigidly defined theoretical positions. Theoretical analysis has made a significant contribution to the development of cultural studies as a vital area of social thought in

England in the 1970s. The danger lies in these concerns obscuring the importance of concrete investigations in the elaboration of theoretical positions. But, more significantly, the tradition associated with the concept of culture promoted a vigorous critique of society. Despite its limitations, this critique has been the source of its vitality over a considerable period of time. It is crucial that this focus be retained.

# Notes

## Chapter 1 Introduction: intellectuals and their ideas

1 Raymond Williams, *Culture and Society*, Harmondsworth, Penguin, 1968.
2 Matthew Arnold, *Culture and Anarchy*, ed. J. Dover Wilson, Cambridge University Press, 1963, p. 6.
3 Zygmunt Bauman, *Culture as Praxis*, London, Routledge & Kegan Paul, 1973, p. 9.
4 W. J. Bate, *From Classic to Romantic*, New York, Harper, 1961, p. 10.
5 Ibid., p. 24.
6 Williams, *Culture and Society*, p. 56.
7 G. A. Theodorson and A. G. Theodorson, *A Modern Dictionary of Sociology*, London, Methuen, 1969, p. 210.
8 J. Bensman and R. Lilienfield, *Craft and Consciousness*, New York, Wiley, 1973, p. 241.
9 J. P. Nettl, 'Ideas, Intellectuals, and Structures of Dissent', in P. Rieff, ed., *On Intellectuals*, New York, Doubleday, 1969, p. 63.
10 Ibid., p. 81; Nettl is quoting from an article in French by Edgar Morin.
11 Bensman and Lilienfield, *Craft and Consciousness*, p. 259.
12 Karl Mannheim, *Essays on the Sociology of Culture*, London, Routledge & Kegan Paul, 1956, p. 159.
13 Edward Shils, *The Intellectuals and the Powers and Other Essays*, University of Chicago Press, 1972, p. 2.
14 Ibid., p. 17.
15 Pierre Bourdieu, 'Intellectual Field and Creative Project', in M. F. D. Young, ed., *Knowledge and Social Control*, London, Collier-Macmillan, 1971.
16 Ibid., p. 170.
17 Ibid., p. 175.
18 Ibid., pp. 162–5.
19 Antonio Gramsci, *Selections from the Prison Notebooks*, Quinton Hoare and Geoffrey Nowell Smith, ed. and trans., New York, International Publishers, 1971, p. 5.

20 Ibid., p. 7.
21 Ibid., p. 10.
22 P. L. Nokes, 'What Kind of Applied Social Sciences?', *Universities Quarterly*, vol. 28, no. 2, 1974, p. 140.
23 Perry Anderson, 'Components of the National Culture', in Alexander Cockburn and Robin Blackburn, eds, *Student Power*, Harmondsworth, Penguin, 1969, pp. 224–5 (his italics).
24 Gareth Stedman Jones, 'History: the poverty of Empiricism', in Robin Blackburn, ed., *Ideology in Social Sciences*, Bungay, Suffolk, Fontana, 1973, pp. 103–4.
25 E. P. Thompson, 'The Peculiarities of the English', in Ralph Miliband and John Saville, eds, *The Socialist Register 1965*, London, Merlin Press, 1965, p. 312.
26 Ibid., p. 333.
27 Ibid., p. 342.
28 Robert Gray, 'Bourgeois Hegemony in Victorian Britain', in Jon Bloomfield, ed., *Class, Hegemony and Party*, London, Lawrence & Wishart, 1977, p. 75.
29 Ibid., p. 85.
30 Malcolm Bradbury, *The Social Context of Modern Literature*, Oxford, Basil Blackwell, 1971, p. 18.
31 Nokes, 'What Kind of Applied Social Sciences?', p. 142.
32 William Wordsworth, 'The Prelude', *The Poetical Works of Wordsworth*, London, Oxford University Press, 1964, p. 582.

**Chapter 2 Matthew Arnold**

1 He himself in his *Notebooks* discussed with some regret what he saw as the waning of his poetic inspiration quite early in his life: Matthew Arnold, *The Notebooks of Matthew Arnold*, H. F. Lowry, Karl Young, and W. H. Dunn, eds, London, Oxford University Press, 1952.
2 Matthew Arnold, 'Democracy', introduction to 'The Popular Education of France', *The Complete Prose Works of Matthew Arnold*, II, R. H. super, ed., Ann Arbor, University of Michigan Press, 1962, p. 7. All references to Arnold's work, where possible, will be taken from these volumes, hereafter cited as *Works*.
3 See Lionel Trilling, *Matthew Arnold*, London, Unwin Books, 1963.
4 Arnold, 'Democracy', p. 14.
5 Matthew Arnold, *Culture and Anarchy*, ed., J. Dover Wilson, Cambridge University Press, 1963, p. 84.
6 Arnold, 'Democracy', p. 17.
7 Trilling, *Matthew Arnold*, p. 171.
8 Ibid.
9 Arnold, 'Democracy', p. 18.
10 W. F. Connell, *The Educational Thought and Influence of Matthew Arnold*, London, Routledge & Kegan Paul, 1950, p. 276.
11 Arnold, 'Democracy', pp. 26–7.
12 Connell, *Educational Thought*, p. 81.
13 Arnold's notions of 'right reason' and 'best self' can be seen as similar

to concepts developed by other socio-political thinkers such as Rousseau's 'the general will'. These concepts are generally vague.

14 Trilling, *Matthew Arnold*, p. 255.

15 It should be noted that Matthew Arnold's concept of the state does not bear great resemblance to Plato's Republic.

16 Arnold, 'Democracy', pp. 5–6.

17 Matthew Arnold, 'Friendship's Garland', *Works*, vol. V, p. 15.

18 Matthew Arnold, 'A French Eton', *Works*, vol. II, p. 292.

19 Arnold, 'Friendship's Garland', p. 19.

20 Ibid., pp. 21–2.

21 Ibid., p. 18.

22 Ibid., p. 329.

23 Arnold, 'A French Eton', p. 292.

24 Arnold, *Culture and Anarchy*, p. 70.

25 See for example, *The Saturday Review*, vol. XVIII, 3 Dec., 1864, pp. 683–5.

26 Matthew Arnold, 'The Bishop and the Philosopher', *Works*, vol. III, pp. 43–4.

27 Arnold, 'Democracy', p. 8.

28 Richard Johnson is one of a number of authors who analyses moves towards compulsory education in the nineteenth century, in terms of 'class cultural control'. See for example, 'Education Policy and Social Control in Early Victorian England', *Past and Present*, vol. 49, 1970, pp. 96–119.

29 Trilling, *Matthew Arnold*, pp. 277–91.

30 See the chapter 'Our Liberal Practitioners' in Arnold's *Culture and Anarchy*.

31 Fred G. Walcott, *The Origins of Culture and Anarchy*, University of Toronto Press, 1970.

32 Arnold reveals this particularly in his letters. See for example, *Letters of Matthew Arnold*, vol. II, ed. G. W. Russell, New York, Macmillan, 1895, p. 222.

33 Arnold, 'Democracy', p. 10.

34 H. Sidgwick appears to be the first to refer to him in this manner.

35 Matthew Arnold, *Reports on Elementary Schools*, 1852–1882, ed. F. S. Marvin, London, HMSO, 1908, pp. 16–17; cf. Charles Dickens's criticism of this same feature of Victorian schools in his novel *Hard Times* (1854).

36 Arnold, *Culture and Anarchy*, p. 6.

37 Ibid., pp. 44–5.

38 Ibid., p. 200.

39 For example, Arnold's fight against the Revised Code for education.

40 Raymond Williams in *Culture and Society*, Harmondsworth, Penguin, 1968, p. 128, argues that Arnold's involvement in social issues shows that his policy was not one of cultivated inaction. This view does not take into account the explicit statements arguing for cultivated inaction which Arnold makes at the end of *Culture and Anarchy*.

41 Frederic Harrison, 'Culture a Dialogue', *The Fortnightly Magazine*, vol. ii, 1867, p. 606.

42 Matthew Arnold, 'Literature and Science', in *Discourses in America*, London, Macmillan, 1896, pp. 124–9.
43 K. I. Palmer, 'Matthew Arnold's Perception of Culture and the Implications of that Perception for his Educational Writings', unpublished M.Ed. Thesis, University of Melbourne, 1976, p. 60.
44 Arnold, *Culture and Anarchy*, p. 132.
45 E. Alexander, *Matthew Arnold and John Stuart Mill*, New York, Columbia University Press, 1965, p. 52.
46 Arnold, *Culture and Anarchy*, p. 48.
47 Matthew Arnold, 'Literature and Dogma', *Works*, vol. VI, p. 407.
48 See for example, Matthew Arnold, *Letters*, vol. I, pp. 454–5.
49 Arnold, 'Literature and Dogma', p. 370.
50 Alexander, *Matthew Arnold and John Stuart Mill*, p. 52.
51 Connell, Letter to the author, July 1974.
52 G. H. Bantock, *Freedom, Authority and Education*, London, Faber, 1970, p. 90.
53 Arnold, *Culture and Anarchy*, p. 64.
54 Arnold, 'A French Eton', pp. 316–17.
55 Arnold, *Culture and Anarchy*, p. 53.
56 Ibid., pp. 53–4.
57 Quote from J. H. Newman, 'On the Scope and Nature of University Education', 1852, pp. 197–8, quoted in Raymond Williams, *Culture and Society*, p. 121.
58 See Connell, *Educational Thought*, p. 27.
59 Matthew Arnold, 'School and Universities on the Continent', *Works*, vol. IV, p. 304.
60 Arnold, 'Democracy', pp. 20–6.
61 Ibid., p. 26.
62 Arnold also accused the Public Schools of this weakness: Arnold, 'Schools and Universities on the Continent'.
63 Ibid., p. 319.
64 Ibid., p. 328.
65 Arnold assumed that the education of the populace, or masses, should only be carried out in elementary schools. Hence, when he referred to 'popular education' he was referring to the education provided for this segment of the population, carried out in the elementary schools.
66 Arnold was apprehensive about attacking his superior, Lowe, but he felt justified because of earlier attacks on Inspectors made by Lowe himself. See Arnold, *Letters*, vol. I, pp. 159–60.
67 Arnold, *Reports on Elementary Schools*, pp. 90–101.
68 Ibid.
69 *First Report to the Royal Commission on the Elementary Education Acts, 1886*, C. 4863, A. 5825.
70 Arnold, *Letters*, vol. I, pp. 194–7.
71 Connell interprets Arnold's position on the payment by results principle differently. He suggests that Arnold did actually wish to retain payment by results because of his desire to retain individual examinations. See Connell, *Educational Thought*, pp. 226–7.
The interpretation offered above appears to be more useful in

explaining Arnold's stance before the Cross Commission. In addition Connell's interpretation does not appear to explain the vehement opposition to the Revised Code and individual examinations which Arnold expressed in his *Letters*. See March, 1862, p. 189.

72 Arnold, *Reports on Elementary Schools*, 1876, p. 171.
73 Ibid. (1874).
74 G. H. Bantock, 'Matthew Arnold, H.M.I.', *Scrutiny*, vol. XVIII, 1951–2, p. 42.
75 Arnold, 'A French Eton', pp. 324–5.

**Chapter 3 Arnold's contemporaries**

1 This phrasing of the question is generally claimed to be first stated by Thomas Carlyle.
2 Noel Annan, 'The Intellectual Aristocracy', in J. H. Plumb, ed., *Studies in Social History*, London, Longmans, 1955. An example of inter-marriage in these networks was the fact that Matthew Arnold's niece, Julia, was one of Thomas Huxley's daughters-in-law.
3 J. S. Mill, *Essays on Politics and Culture*, ed. Gertrude Himmelfarb, New York, Anchor Books, 1963, pp. 200–1.
4 Gertrude Himmelfarb, 'Introduction' to J. S. Mill, *Essays on Politics and Culture*, pp. ix–xviii.
5 Ibid., p. 260.
6 Ibid., p. 195.
7 Ibid., p. 62.
8 J. S. Mill, 'Inaugural Lecture to St. Andrews, 1867', *John Stuart Mill. A selection of his works*, ed. J. M. Robson, Toronto University Press, 1966, pp. 413–19.
9 Raymond Williams, *Culture and Society*, Harmondsworth, Penguin, 1968, pp. 76–83.
10 Mill, *Essays on Politics and Culture*, p. 264.
11 Ibid., pp. 61–7.
12 Ibid., p. 72.
13 Ibid., pp. 380–4.
14 Ibid., pp. 75–6.
15 Herbert Spencer, *The Man versus the State*, Harmondsworth, Penguin, 1969, p. 148.
16 Ibid., pp. 1–4; p. 43.
17 Herbert Spencer, *Essays in Education*, London, Dent, 1941, p. 9.
18 Ibid., p. 63.
19 Ibid., p. 32.
20 Ibid., pp. 62–83.
21 Also published during this year: J. S. Mill, *On Liberty* and Samuel Smiles, *Self Help*.
22 Spencer, *Essays in Education*, p. 4.
23 Ibid., p. 7.
24 See David Layton, *Science for the People*, London, Allen & Unwin, 1973.

25 T. H. Huxley, *Method and Results, Essays*, vol. I, London, Macmillan, 1898, p. 261.
26 Ibid., p. 278.
27 Leonard Huxley, *Life and Letters of Thomas Henry Huxley*, vol. I, London, Macmillan, 1903, p. 461.
28 Cyril Bibby, *Scientist Extraordinary—T. H. Huxley*, Oxford, Pergamon, 1972, p. 90.
29 T. H. Huxley, *Science and Education, Essays*, vol. III, London, Macmillan, 1905, p. 143.
30 Ibid., p. 36.
31 Leonard Huxley, Letter from T. H. Huxley to W. P. Clayton, November, 1892, vol. II, p. 305.
32 See W. E. Houghton, *The Victorian Frame of Mind*, New Haven, Yale University Press, 1959; and Asa Briggs, *The Age of Improvement*, London, Longmans, 1959, p. 445.
33 Huxley, *Science and Education*, p. 65.
34 See 'A Liberal Education; and where to find it', *Science and Education*.
35 Layton, *Science for the People*, p. 143.
36 Huxley, *Science and Education*, p. 77.
37 Layton, *Science for the People*, pp. 159–60.
38 Huxley, *Science and Education*, p. 86.
39 The meaning of this term was beginning to change at this time. See P. W. Musgrave, *Society, History and Education*, London, Methuen, 1970.
40 Huxley, *Science and Education*, pp. 413–26.
41 Ibid., p. 91.
42 Ibid., p. 261.
43 Bibby, *Scientist Extraordinary*, p. 125.
44 Important figures in the Pre-Raphaelite Brotherhood were Edward Burne-Jones, Dante Gabriel Rossetti, W. Holman Hunt, Ford Madox Brown, and J. E. Millais.
45 John Ruskin, *Unto this Last*, London, Harrap, 1866, p. 23.
46 John Ruskin, *Sesame and Lilies*, Kent, Allen & Unwin, 1880.
47 Quentin Bell, *Ruskin*, London, Oliver & Boyd, 1963, p. 49.
48 John Ruskin, *Fors Clavigera*, Letter VII, Kent, Allen & Unwin, 1871, pp. 4–6.
49 Ruskin, *Unto this Last*, pp. 119–20.
50 For example, his letters *Fors Clavigera* were addressed to 'The workmen and labourers of Great Britain'.
51 Ruskin, *Sesame and Lilies*, p. 152.
52 John Ruskin, *The Crown of Wild Olive*, London, Allen & Unwin, 1941, p. 73.
53 Ibid., p. 74.
54 Ruskin, *Sesame and Lilies*, pp. 166–8.
55 Ruskin alluded to these failings, ibid., pp. 124–33.
56 See Annan, 'The Intellectual Aristocracy', p. 251. Chapter 2 discusses these features of the English literary intellectuals in the mid-Victorian period in greater detail.

57 Ruskin, *The Crown of Wild Olive*, p. 76.
58 Ruskin, *Sesame and Lilies*, pp. 99–100. His preoccupation with females in this case seems to be as much an indication of his private life and its problems as any theoretical leaning.
59 Ibid., p. 87.
60 William Morris, *On Art and Socialism*, ed. Holbrook Jackson, London, John Lehmann, 1947.
61 Edward Thompson, 'Romanticism, Moralism and Utopianism: the Case of William Morris', *New Left Review*, vol. 99, 1976, p. 98.
62 Morris, *On Art and Socialism*, p. 275.
63 Ibid., p. 278.
64 Ibid., pp. 134–5.
65 Ibid., p. 138.
66 Ibid., p. 50.
67 Ibid., p. 36.
68 Ibid., pp. 66–7.
69 Ibid., p. 98.
70 Holbrook Jackson, 'Introduction' to William Morris, *On Art and Socialism*, pp. 8–9.
71 Malcolm Bradbury, *The Social Context of Modern Literature*, Oxford, Basil Blackwell, 1971, pp. 41–2.
72 Thompson, 'Romanticism, Moralism and Utopianism', pp. 108–9.
73 Louis Althusser and his followers have been particularly responsible for developing this critique of humanism in its various forms.
74 Morris, *On Art and Socialism*, pp. 195–6.

**Chapter 4 Entr'acte: 1890–1920**

1 See George Dangerfield, *The Strange Death of Liberal England*, London, Paladin, 1972.
2 Clive Bell, *Civilization: An Essay*, London, Chatto & Windus, 1928, p. 221.
3 Samuel Hynes, *The Edwardian Turn of Mind*, Princeton University Press, 1968, p. 311.
4 Holbrook Jackson, *The Eighteen Nineties*, New York, Capricorn books, 1966, pp. 17–18.
5 Ibid., p. 65.
6 John Gross, *The Rise and Fall of the Man of Letters*, Harmondsworth, Penguin, 1973, p. 232.
7 Jackson, *The Eighteen Nineties*, p. 46.
8 Graham Hough, 'English Criticism', in C. B. Cox and A. G. Dyson, eds, *The Twentieth Century Mind*, London, Oxford University Press, 1972, p. 475.
9 Jackson, *The Eighteen Nineties*, p. 196.
10 Ibid., pp. 66–7.
11 See A. M. McBriar, *Fabian Socialism and English Politics, 1884–1918*, Cambridge University Press, 1962, p. 98.
12 For example, when the *Lusitania* sank he refused to be as emotional

about this as others. He did not see it to be any worse than the slaughtering of men in the front lines of World War I.

13 G. B. Shaw, *An Intelligent Woman's Guide to Socialism, Capitalism, Sovietism and Fascism*, Harmondsworth, Penguin, 1971, p. 240.
14 G. B. Shaw, Preface to *Major Barbara*, Harmondsworth, Penguin, 1960, p. 22.
15 Ibid., pp. 20–1.
16 G. B. Shaw, Preface to *Back to Methuselah*, Harmondsworth, Penguin, 1954, p. 14.
17 Louis Crampton, introduction to Bernard Shaw, *The Road to Equality*, Boston, Beacon Press, 1971, p. xxvii.
18 Colin Wilson, *Bernard Shaw. A Reassessment*, London, Hutchinson, 1969, p. 113.
19 McBriar, *Fabian Socialism*, p. 161.
20 Wilson, *Bernard Shaw*, pp. 35–6.
21 G. B. Shaw, 'The Fabian Society: What it has done; and How it has Done it', London, *Fabian Tract*, no. 41, 1892, pp. 3–4.
22 Shaw, *The Road to Equality*, p. 300.
23 Ibid., p. 301.
24 Ibid., p. 282.
25 Sidney and Beatrice Webb, *Industrial Democracy*, London, Longmans, 1897, pp. 844–9.
26 H. G. Wells, *Experiment in Autobiography*, London, Gollancz, 1934, p. 737.
27 Ibid., p. 721. In 1916 Wells was an ardent advocate of the League of Nations idea, but the form it actually took disappointed him greatly. He saw it as merely an arena for statesmen, not really intent on working for world peace.
28 Wells went to one of these, his mother having pretensions towards being a member of the lower middle class. She had been a lady's maid.
29 Ibid., p. 93.
30 Shaw, *The Road to Equality*, p. 289.
31 H. G. Wells, *An Englishman Looks at the World*, London, Cassell, 1914, p. 79.
32 Ibid.
33 Ibid.
34 H. G. Wells, *A Modern Utopia*, London, Odhams Press, n.d., p. 141.
35 Wells, *An Englishman . . .*, p. 49.
36 Ibid., p. 81.
37 Wells, *Experiment in Autobiography*, p. 245.
38 H. G. Wells, *Mankind in the Making*, London, Chapman & Hall, 1903, pp. 7–8.
39 Ibid., pp. 389–90.
40 Wells, *Experiment in Autobiography*, pp. 651–2. It should be noted that Wells was only an outsider to a certain extent. In his autobiography he describes his increasing acceptance in the social and intellectual circles of the time. He was only an outsider from the actual political positions of power.
41 Michael Sadler, a member of the Bryce Commission into Secondary

education (1894–5), was another intellectual who was heavily influenced by Matthew Arnold. Sadler's ideas, though presented less publicly, were more coherent and thoughtfully expressed than Masterman. Yet he exhibited the same disturbing lack of an overriding vision as did Masterman.

42 Donald Read, 'History: Political and Democratic', in Cox and Dyson, *The Twentieth Century Mind*, p. 21.
43 C. F. G. Masterman, *The Condition of England*, London, Methuen, 1960, p. 65.
44 Ibid., p. 204.
45 Beatrice Webb in *My Apprenticeship*, London, Longmans Green, 1926, provides an insightful description of an attempt to fill this need.
46 Masterman, *The Condition of England*, p. 202.
47 Hynes, *The Edwardian Turn of Mind*, p. 64.
48 Masterman, *The Condition of England*, p. 233.
49 Michael Holroyd, *Lytton Strachey and the Bloomsbury Group*, Harmondsworth, Penguin, 1971, p. 53.
50 Ibid., p. 54.
51 Bell, *Civilization*, p. 81.
52 Ibid., p. 91.
53 Ibid., pp. 208–9.
54 Ibid., p. 205.
55 Ibid., p. 227.

**Chapter 5 F. R. Leavis**

1 Discussion of Leavis's social and educational ideas is confined to the main three publications: P. W. Musgrave, '*Scrutiny* and Education', *British Journal of Educational Studies*, vol. XXI, 1973, pp. 273–6; 'Culture, Education and Society', a special issue of *The Universities Quarterly*, 1975; and Paul Filmer, 'Literary Study as Liberal Education and as Sociology in the Work of F. R. Leavis' in Chris Jencks, ed., *Rationality, Education and the Social Organization of Knowledge*, London, Routledge & Kegan Paul, 1977, pp. 55–85. David Holbrook has contributed work of practical application of Leavis's educational ideas.
2 Terry Eagleton, *Criticism and Ideology*, London, New Left Books, 1976, p. 14.
3 Ronald Hayman points out that when Leavis undertook his doctoral thesis with Quiller-Couch it was still considered unnecessary for lecturers in English Literature courses to have qualifications in that field. Ronald Hayman, *Leavis*, London, Heinemann, 1976, p. 5.
4 F. R. Leavis, *Education and the University*, London, Chatto & Windus, 1961, p. 147.
5 Ibid., p. 22.
6 F. R. Leavis and Denys Thompson, *Culture and Environment*, London, Chatto & Windus, 1960, pp. 1–2.
7 Raymond Williams, *Culture and Society*, Harmondsworth, Penguin, 1968, p. 251.

8 F. R. Leavis, *Nor Shall My Sword*, London, Chatto & Windus, 1972, p. 88.
9 Williams, *Culture and Society*, p. 253.
10 Leavis and Thompson, *Culture and Environment*, pp. 62–3.
11 See Eagleton, *Criticism and Ideology*, for a further discussion of Williams's debt to Leavis, pp. 24–38.
12 F. R. Leavis, *Nor Shall My Sword*, p. 209.
13 Ibid., p. 211.
14 Ibid., p. 169.
15 Q. D. Leavis, *Fiction and the Reading Public*, London, Chatto & Windus, 1965, p. 190.
16 Ibid., p. 264.
17 See, for example, Kenneth Trodd, 'Report from the Younger Generation', *Essays in Criticism*, vol. XIV, 1964.
18 F. R. Leavis, *Education and the University*, p. 24.
19 F. R. Leavis, 'Under which King, Bezonian?', *Scrutiny*, vol. I, 1932, pp. 207–10.
20 Trodd, 'Report from the Younger Generation', p. 30.
21 F. R. Leavis, *Education and the University*, p. 143.
22 Ibid.
23 Ibid., p. 34.
24 Leavis and Thompson, *Culture and Environment*, p. 82.
25 F. R. Leavis, 'What's Wrong with Criticism?', *Scrutiny*, vol. I, 1932, p. 135.
26 F. R. Leavis, 'The Literary Mind', *Scrutiny*, vol. I, 1932, p. 31.
27 F. R. Leavis, *English Literature in our Time and the University*, London, Chatto & Windus, 1969, p. 2.
28 F. R. Leavis, 'The Responsible Critic: or the Function of Criticism at any Time', *Scrutiny*, vol. XIX, 1952, p. 179.
29 F. R. Leavis, 'What's Wrong with Criticism?', pp. 137–8.
30 F. R. Leavis, *Nor Shall My Sword*, p. 185.
31 F. R. Leavis, *Education and the University*, p. 106.
32 F. R. Leavis, *Revaluation*, Harmondsworth, Penguin, 1964, p. 10.
33 Rene Wellek, 'Literary Criticism and Philosophy', *Scrutiny*, vol. V, 1937, p. 376.
34 F. R. Leavis, *The Common Pursuit*, p. 213.
35 Perry Anderson, 'Components of the National Culture', in A. Cockburn and R. Blackburn, eds, *Student Power*, Harmondsworth, Penguin, 1969, p. 271.
36 Eagleton, *Criticism and Ideology*, p. 15.
37 F. R. Leavis, *English Literature* . . ., p. 47.
38 Vincent Buckley, *Poetry and Morality*, London, Chatto & Windus, 1961, p. 184.
39 Anderson, 'Components . . .', p. 269.
40 F. R. Leavis, *Education and the University*, p. 16.
41 F. R. Leavis, 'The *Scrutiny* Movement in Education', *Scrutiny*, vol. II, 1933, Addendum, p. 110.
42 Leavis and Thompson, *Culture and Environment*, p. 5.
43 F. R. Leavis, *English Literature* . . ., p. 66.

44 F. R. Leavis, *Nor Shall My Sword*, pp. 150–1.
45 C. P. Snow, *The Two Cultures*, New York, Mentor, 1963, p. 20.
46 F. R. Leavis, *Nor Shall My Sword*, p. 56.
47 F. R. Leavis, *Education and the University*, pp. 25–8.
48 F. R. Leavis, 'Retrospect of a Decade', *Scrutiny*, vol. IX, 1940, p. 72.
49 F. R. Leavis, 'A Retrospect', *Scrutiny*, vol. XX, 1952, p. 7.
50 George Steiner, *Language and Silence*, Harmondsworth, Penguin, 1969, pp. 238–9.
51 S. W. Dawson, '*Scrutiny* and the Idea of a University', *Essays in Criticism*, vol. XIV, 1964, p. 3.
52 Ibid., pp. 8–9.

**Chapter 6 Leavis's contemporaries**

1 Neal Wood, *Communism and British Intellectuals*, New York, Columbia University Press, 1959, p. 80.
2 Stuart Samuels, 'English Intellectuals and Politics in the 1930s', in Phillip Rieff, ed., *On Intellectuals*, New York, Doubleday, 1969.
3 D. H. Lawrence, 'Democracy', *Phoenix*, Surrey, Windmill Press, 1970, p. 718.
4 Raymond Williams, *Culture and Society*, Harmondsworth, Penguin, 1968, p. 209.
5 D. H. Lawrence, 'Democracy', p. 718.
6 See Richard Aldington, *Portrait of a Genius, But . . .*, New York, Collier Books, 1967, p. 8.
7 D. H. Lawrence, 'Education of the People', *Phoenix*, p. 609.
8 Williams, *Culture and Society*, p. 232.
9 D. H. Lawrence, 'Nottingham and Mining Countryside', *Phoenix*, pp. 135–8.
10 See Aldington, op. cit., for example: pp. 285–7.
11 Lawrence, 'Education of the People', p. 602.
12 Lawrence, 'Democracy', p. 701.
13 Lawrence, 'Education of the People', p. 650. The fascist tendencies in Lawrence's development of these ideas about the supremacy of the individuals are revealed in his novel *Kangaroo* (1923).
14 Ibid., p. 612.
15 D. H. Lawrence, 'Why the Novel Matters', *Phoenix*, p. 535.
16 Lawrence, 'Education of the People', p. 609. Lawrence does not necessarily equate the membership of these two groups.
17 D. H. Lawrence, 'The Novel and the Feelings', *Phoenix*, p. 755.
18 Ibid., pp. 759–60.
19 Lawrence, 'Education of the People', pp. 604–7.
20 Ibid., p. 617.
21 T. S. Eliot, 'The Wasteland', *Selected Poems*, London, Faber, 1964, p. 64.
22 T. S. Eliot, *The Idea of a Christian Society*, London, Faber, 1962, pp. 31–4.
23 Ibid., pp. 35–8.
24 Ibid., p. 38.

25 Ibid., p. 42.
26 T. S. Eliot, *Notes Towards the Definition of Culture*, London, Faber, 1967, p. 42.
27 Ibid.
28 T. B. Bottomore, *Elites and Society*, London, C. A. Watts & Co., 1964, p. 141.
29 Pierre Bourdieu, 'Systems of Education and Systems of Thought', in Michael F. D. Young, ed., *Knowledge and Control*, London, Collier-Macmillan, 1971, p. 197.
30 Allen Austin, *T. S. Eliot, The Literary and Social Criticism*, Bloomington, Indiana University Press, 1971, pp. 80–1.
31 Eliot, *Notes Towards* . . ., p. 99.
32 Ibid., p. 16.
33 Williams, *Culture and Society*, pp. 228–9.
34 Ibid., p. 229.
35 Eliot, *Notes Towards* . . ., pp. 106–7.
36 Ibid., p. 31.
37 Williams, *Culture and Society*, p. 236.
38 Pierre Bourdieu, 'Cultural Reproduction and Social Reproduction', in R. Brown, ed., *Knowledge, Education and Social Change*, London, Tavistock, 1973, pp. 80–1.
39 Eliot, *Notes Towards* . . ., pp. 107–8.
40 Eliot, *The Idea of a Christian Society*, pp. 39–40.
41 Aldous Huxley, 'On Handicraft', *On Art and Artists*, London, Chatto & Windus, 1960, pp. 96–7.
42 Bertrand Russell, *Education and the Social Order*, London, Unwin Books, 1970, p. 49.
43 Bertrand Russell, *The Autobiography of Bertrand Russell I*, London, Allen & Unwin, 1971, p. 162.
44 Russell, *Education* . . ., pp. 92–3.
45 Bertrand Russell, *Authority and the Individual*, London, Unwin Books, 1965, p. 29.
46 Russell, *Education* . . ., pp. 138–42.
47 Russell, *Authority* . . ., pp. 67–74.
48 Russell, *The Autobiography* . . ., 2, p. 75.
49 Russell, *Education* . . ., p. 49.
50 Bertrand Russell, *The Impact of America on European Civilization*, Boston, The Beacon Press, 1951, p. 17. It should be noted that Russell was painfully aware of this feature of American life because of his own persecution there in 1940.
51 Bertrand Russell, *Sceptical Essays*, London, Unwin Books, 1970, p. 97.
52 Russell, *Education* . . ., p. 95.
53 Joe Park, *Bertrand Russell on Education*, London, Allen & Unwin, 1964, p. 42.
54 For example see: Robert Skidelsky, *English Progresssive Schools*, Harmondsworth, Penguin, 1969, p. 153.
55 Russell, *Education* . . ., p. 117.
56 Ibid., p. 12.
57 Russell, *Authority* . . ., p. 29.

58 Russell, *Education* . . ., p. 51.
59 Christopher Caudwell, *Studies in a Dying Culture*, New York, Monthly Review Press, 1972, p. xxi.
60 Ibid., p. 9.
61 Christopher Caudwell, *Further Studies in a Dying Culture*, New York, Monthly Review Press, 1972, p. 120.
62 Sol Yurick, Introduction to *Studies in a Dying Culture*, p. 15.
63 George Orwell, 'Why I Write', *Collected Essays*, London, Mercury Books, 1961, p. 424.
64 Alan Sandison, *The Last Man in Europe*, London, Macmillan, 1974.
65 Williams, *Culture and Society*, p. 284.
66 George Orwell, *The Road to Wigan Pier*, Harmondsworth, Penguin, 1972, p. 138.
67 Ibid., p. 157.
68 John Gross, *The Rise and Fall of the Man of Letters*, Harmondsworth, Penguin, 1973, p. 288.
69 Orwell, *The Road to Wigan Pier*, p. 203.
70 Gross, *The Rise and Fall of the Man of Letters*, p. 288.
71 Orwell, *The Road to Wigan Pier*, p. 190.
72 Ibid., pp. 149–50.
73 George Orwell, 'Writers and Leviathan', *Collected Essays*, pp. 428–9.
74 Williams, *Culture and Society*, p. 280.
75 Gross, op. cit., p. 287.
76 Orwell, 'Writers and Leviathan', pp. 429–30.
77 Gross, *The Rise and Fall*, p. 291.
78 Orwell, *The Road to Wigan Pier*, pp. 143–4.
79 George Orwell, 'Poetry and the Microphone', *Collected Essays*, p. 306.
80 R. H. Tawney, *Religion and the Rise of Capitalism*, London, John Murray, 1926, which was an economic, social history, heavily influenced by Max Weber's work; and *The Acquisitive Society*, London, Bell, 1937, and *Equality*, London, Allen & Unwin, 1952, both of which expressed Tawney's socialist commitments.
81 R. H. Tawney, *The Radical Tradition*, ed. R. Hinder, Harmondsworth, Penguin, 1966, pp. 87–8. His practical approach is no doubt a reflection of his considerable practical involvement in educational matters. Apart from his work on the WEA, his speeches and articles for the Labour Party and affiliated bodies, he was also one of the major formulators of the Hadow Report which was to form the basis of the 1944 Education Act.
82 Ross Terrill, *R. H. Tawney and His Times*, London, André Deutsch, 1973, p. 136.
83 Tawney, *Equality*, p. 38.
84 Ibid., p. 27.
85 Tawney, *The Acquisitive Society*, pp. 53–4.
86 Ibid., p. 32.
87 Ibid., p. 169.
88 Tawney, *Equality*, p. 20.
89 Tawney, *The Acquisitive Society*, pp. 234–5.
90 Tawney, *Equality*, p. 81.

91 Terrill, *R. H. Tawney and his Times*, p. 195. Terrill instances Perry Anderson and E. P. Thompson amongst these writers.

**Chapter 7 Raymond Williams**

1 Perry Anderson, 'The Left in the Fifties', *New Left Review*, no. 29, 1965, p. 14.
2 Tom Nairn, 'The Twilight of the British State', *New Left Review*, no. 101–2, 1977, p. 22.
3 Anderson, 'The Left in the Fifties', p. 14.
4 Raymond Williams, *Culture and Society*, Harmondsworth, Penguin, 1968, p. 289.
5 Ibid., p. 301.
6 Terry Eagleton, 'Criticism and Politics: The Work of Raymond Williams', *New Left Review*, no. 95, 1976, p. 13.
7 Raymond Williams, *Communications*, Harmondsworth, Penguin, 1971, p. 120.
8 Raymond Williams, *The Long Revolution*, Harmondsworth, Penguin, 1971, p. 118.
9 Andrew Miller, 'Socio-Cultural Theories of Education and the Sociology of Education', in Donald E. Edgar, ed., *Sociology of Australian Education*, Sydney, McGraw-Hill, 1975, p. 435.
10 Raymond Williams and Richard Hoggart, 'Working Class Attitudes', *New Left Review*, no. 1, 1960, pp. 27–8.
11 Raymond Williams, *The Country and the City*, London, Chatto & Windus, 1973, pp. 44–5.
12 Williams, *The Long Revolution*, p. 133.
13 E. P. Thompson, 'The Long Revolution. I', *New Left Review*, no. 9, 1961, pp. 24–5.
14 Quinton Hoare, 'Education: Programmes and Men', *New Left Review*, no. 32, 1965, p. 50.
15 Barry Smith, 'A Historian's Comments upon *Culture and Society* and *The Long Revolution*', *The Melbourne Historical Journal*, vol. 8, 1969, p. 32.
16 Anderson, 'The Left in the Fifties', p. 17.
17 Williams, *Communications*, p. 127.
18 Raymond Williams, 'Notes on British Marxism since the War', *New Left Review*, no. 100, 1976–7, p. 73.
19 Ibid., p. 89.
20 Williams, *Culture and Society*, p. 17.
21 Williams, *The Long Revolution*, p. 66.
22 Ibid., p. 55.
23 Ernest Gellner, 'Concepts and Society', in Dorothy Emmet and Alistair MacIntyre, eds, *Sociological Theory and Philosophical Analysis*, London, Macmillan, 1970, pp. 139–41.
24 Williams, *Communications*, p. 97.
25 Raymond Williams, 'Culture and Revolution: A Response', in Terry Eagleton and Brian Wicker, eds, *From Culture to Revolution*, London, Sheed & Ward, 1968, p. 308.

26 Williams, *Culture and Society*, p. 314.
27 Raymond Williams, 'The British Left', *New Left Review*, no. 3, 1965, p. 23.
28 Raymond Williams, 'Towards a Socialist Society', in Perry Anderson and Robin Blackburn, eds, *Towards Socialism*, Harmondsworth, Penguin, 1965, pp. 389–90.
29 Raymond Williams, 'Literature and Sociology: in Memory of Lucien Goldmann', *New Left Review*, no. 67, 1971, p. 9.
30 Eagleton, 'Criticism and Politics . . .', p. 22.
31 Raymond Williams, *Marxism and Literature*, Oxford University Press, 1977, p. 194.
32 Ibid., pp. 108–9.
33 Raymond Williams, 'Base and Superstructure in Marxist cultural theory', *New Left Review*, no. 82, 1973, p. 9.
34 Raymond Williams, ed., *May Day Manifesto, 1968*, Harmondsworth, Penguin, 1968, pp. 34–5.
35 Williams, *The Country . . .*, pp. 304–5.
36 Williams, *The Long Revolution*, p. 375.
37 Williams, *Communications*, pp. 127–37.
38 Williams, *May Day . . .*, p. 35.
39 Williams, *The Long Revolution*, p. 364.
40 Hoare, 'Education: Programmes and Men', pp. 40–52.
41 Williams, *Marxism and Literature*, pp. 117–18.

**Chapter 8 Williams's contemporaries**

1 Richard Hoggart, Guest of honour talk for the Australian Broadcasting Commission (Typescript), 20.10.74, p. 3.
2 Richard Hoggart, *Speaking to Each Other*, Vol. One, Harmondsworth, Penguin, 1973, p. 239.
3 Richard Hoggart, *Speaking to Each Other*, Vol. Two, Harmondsworth, Penguin, 1973, p. 18.
4 George Steiner, *In Bluebeard's Castle*, London, Faber, 1971, p. 64.
5 *Report of the Committee on Broadcasting 1960* (presented June, 1962), IX–X, p. 271.
6 Hoggart, *Speaking . . .*, Vol. One, p. 195.
7 Ibid., p. 243.
8 Ibid.
9 Ibid., p. 102.
10 Ibid., p. 101.
11 Ibid., p. 60.
12 Tibor Szamuily, 'Comprehensive Inequality', in C. B. Cox and A. E. Dyson, eds, *Black Paper Two*, London, Dent, 1969, p. 51.
13 Hoggart, *Speaking . . .*, Vol. One, p. 64.
14 Ibid., pp. 101–2.
15 Richard Hoggart, *The Uses of Literacy*, Harmondsworth, Penguin, 1969, p. 340.
16 Ibid., p. 339.
17 Ibid., p. 148.

18 Ibid., p. 248.
19 Ibid., p. 102.
20 Richard Wollheim, 'Culture and Socialism', *Fabian Tract* no. 331, London, 1961, p. 2.
21 Ibid., p. 14.
22 Ibid., p. 45.
23 Hoggart, *Speaking* . . ., Vol. One, p. 117.
24 G. H. Bantock, *Culture, Industrialisation and Education*, London, Routledge & Kegan Paul, 1968, p. 2.
25 Edward B. Tylor, *Primitive Culture*, Vol. I, London, John Murray, 1891, p. 1.
26 Bantock, *Culture, Industrialisation and Education*, p. 86.
27 Ibid., p. 65.
28 G. H. Bantock, 'Current Dilemmas in the Education of the Elite', *Melbourne Studies in Education*, Melbourne University Press, 1972, p. 5.
29 G. H. Bantock, *Education, Culture and the Emotions*, London, Faber, 1967, p. 162.
30 Ibid., p. 122.
31 Ibid., p. 130.
32 See for example: G. H. Bantock, *Freedom and Authority in Education*, London, Faber, 1970, p. 178.
33 Bantock, *Education, Culture and the Emotions*, p. 132.
34 Bantock, 'Current Dilemmas . . .', p. 8.
35 Bantock, *Education, Culture and the Emotions*, p. 134.
36 Bantock, 'Current Dilemmas . . .', p. 3.
37 Bantock, *Education in an Industrial Society*, 2nd Edition, London, Faber, 1973, p. 181.
38 G. H. Bantock, 'Equality and Education', Bryan Wilson, ed., *Education, Equality and Society*, London, Allen & Unwin, 1975, pp. 149–50.
39 Bantock, *Culture, Industrialisation and Education*, p. 77.
40 Bantock, *Education in an Industrial Society*, pp. 4–5.
41 Ibid., p. 70.
42 See for example: C. B. Cox, 'In Praise of Examinations', *Fight for Education A Black Paper*, London, The Critical Quarterly Society, 1968, p. 36.
43 A. M. Hardie, 'Let's return to Sanity', *Fight for Education*, p. 57.
44 Bantock, *Freedom and Authority in Education*, p. 202.
45 R. S. Peters, *Ethics and Education*, London, Allen & Unwin, 1968, p. 45.
46 Ibid., p. 159.
47 Bantock, *Education, Culture and the Emotions*, pp. 144–5.
48 R. S. Peters, 'What is an Educational Process?', R. S. Peters, ed., *The Concept of Education*, London, Routledge & Kegan Paul, 1968, pp. 5–6.
49 R. S. Peters, 'Education as Initiation', R. D. Archambault, ed., *Philosophical Analysis and Education*, London, Routledge & Kegan Paul, 1965, p. 110.

50 Peters, 'Education and the Educated Man', *Proceedings of the Annual Conference, The Philosophy of Education Society of Great Britain*, January, 1970.
51 Peters, *Ethics and Education*, p. 16.
52 David Adelstein, 'The Philosophy of Education or the Wisdom and Wit of R. S. Peters', in T. Pateman, ed., *Counter Course*, Harmondsworth, Penguin, 1972, p. 138.
53 Peters, 'What is an Educational Process?', p. 9.
54 Ernest Gellner, *Words and Things*, Harmondsworth, Penguin, 1968, p. 277.
55 Adelstein, 'The Philosophy of Education . . .', p. 120.
56 Ibid., p. 130.
57 Peters, 'Education and the Educated Man', p. 9.

**Chapter 9 Conclusion: cultural studies**

1 E. P. Thompson, 'Romanticism, Moralism and Utopianism: the Case of William Morris', *New Left Review*, vol. 99, 1976, p. 84.
2 Richard Johnson alludes to this problem in a working paper on cultural theory (1977); see also Gregor McClellan, '"Ideology" and "Consciousness": Some Problems in Marxist Historiography', *Stencilled Occasional Papers*, Centre for Contemporary Cultural Studies, September, 1976.
3 This aspect of the Centre's work has been examined in the critique by Rosalind Coward, 'Class, "Culture" and the Social Formation', *Screen*, Spring 1977, 18, no. 1, pp. 75–106.
4 Richard Johnson, for example, has expressed this concern in memos etc. to the general meeting of the Centre.

# Select bibliography

*Note*: This bibliography contains a selection of works considered most useful in studying the writers and issues examined in this book. Further references can be obtained throughout the notes to the text.

Adelstein, David, 'The Philosophy of Education or the Wisdom and Wit of R. S. Peters', T. Pateman, ed., *Counter Course*, Harmondsworth, Penguin, 1972.

Anderson, Perry, 'Origins of the Present Crisis', *New Left Review*, no. 23, 1964, pp. 27–53.

Anderson, Perry, 'The Left in the Fifties', *New Left Review*, no. 29, 1965, pp. 3–18.

Anderson, Perry, 'Components of the National Culture', Alexander Cockburn and Robin Blackburn, eds, *Student Power*, Harmondsworth, Penguin, 1969, pp. 214–84.

Annan, Noel, 'The Intellectual Aristocracy', J. H. Plumb, ed., *Studies in Social History*, London, Longmans, 1955, pp. 243–84.

Arnold, Matthew, *Culture and Anarchy*, J. Dover Wilson, ed., Cambridge University Press, 1963.

Arnold, Matthew, *The Complete Works of Matthew Arnold*, R. H. Super, ed., 12 vols, Ann Arbor, University of Michigan Press, 1962.

Bantock, G. H., *Education, Culture and the Emotions*, London, Faber, 1967.

Bantock, G. H., *Culture, Industrialisation and Education*, London, Routledge & Kegan Paul, 1968.

Bantock, G. H., *Education in an Industrial Society*, 2nd Edn, London, Faber, 1973.

Bate, W. J., *From Classic to Romantic*, New York, Harper, 1961.

Bauman, Zygmunt, *Culture as Praxis*, London, Routledge & Kegan Paul, 1973.

Bell, Clive, *Civilization: An Essay*, London, Chatto & Windus, 1928.

Bensman, J. and R. Lilienfield, *Craft and Consciousness*, New York, Wiley, 1973.

Berger, John, *Ways of Seeing*, London, British Broadcasting Commission and Penguin, 1972.
Bibby, Cyril, *Scientist Extraordinary—T. H. Huxley*, Oxford, Pergamon, 1972.
Bottomore, T. B., *Elites and Society*, London, C. A. Watts and Co., 1964.
Bourdieu, Pierre, 'Intellectual Field and Creative Project', Michael Young, ed., *Knowledge and Social Control*, London, Collier-Macmillan, 1971, pp. 161–88.
Bourdieu, Pierre, 'Cultural Reproduction and Social Reproduction', R. Brown, ed., *Knowledge, Education and Social Change*, London, Tavistock, 1973, pp. 71–112.
Bradbury, Malcolm, *The Social Context of Modern Literature*, Oxford, Basil Blackwell, 1971.
Bramson, Leon, *The Political Context of Sociology*, Princeton University Press, New Jersey, 1961.
Bramson, N. and Heinemann, M., *Britain in the Nineteen Thirties*, London, Weidenfeld and Nicolson, 1971.
Buckley, Vincent, *Poetry and Morality*, London, Chatto & Windus, 1961.
Caudwell, Christopher, *Studies and Further Studies in a Dying Culture*, New York, Monthly Review Press, 1972.
Connell, W. F., *The Educational Thought and Influence of Matthew Arnold*, London, Routledge & Kegan Paul, 1950.
Coward, Rosalind, 'Class, "Culture" and the Social Formation', *Screen*, Spring 1977, 18, no. 1, pp. 75–106.
'Culture, Education and Society', a special issue of *The Universities Quarterly*, 1975.
Currie, Robert, *Genius: An Ideology in Literature*, London, Chatto & Windus, 1974.
Dangerfield, George, *The Strange Death of Liberal England*, London, Paladin, 1972.
Dawson, S. W., '*Scrutiny* and the Idea of a University', *Essays in Criticism*, vol. XIV, 1964, pp. 1–9.
Eagleton, Terry, 'Criticism and Politics: The Work of Raymond Williams', *New Left Review*, no. 95, 1976, pp. 3–23.
Eagleton, Terry, *Criticism and Ideology*, London, New Left Books, 1976.
Eliot, T. S., *The Idea of a Christian Society*, London, Faber, 1962.
Eliot, T. S., *Notes Towards the Definition of Culture*, London, Faber, 1967.
Filmer, Paul, 'The Literary Imagination and the Explanation of Socio-Cultural Change in Modern Britain', *Archives Europienes de Sociologie*, vol. 10, 1969, pp. 271–91.
Gellner, Ernest, *Words and Things*, Harmondsworth, Penguin, 1968.
Gramsci, Antonio, *Selections from the Prison Notebooks*, Quinton Hoare and Geoffrey Nowell Smith, eds. and trans., New York, International Publishers, 1971.
Gray, Robert, 'Bourgeois Hegemony in Victorian Britain', Jon Bloomfield, ed., *Class, Hegemony and Party*, London, Lawrence & Wishart, 1977, pp. 73–93.

Green, Michael, 'Raymond Williams and Cultural Studies', *Working Papers in Cultural Studies 6*, Centre for Contemporary Cultural Studies, Autumn 1974, pp. 31–48.

Gross, John, *The Rise and Fall of the Man of Letters*, Harmondsworth, Penguin, 1973.

Hall, Stuart and Jefferson, Tony (eds), *Resistance Through Rituals: Youth Subcultures in Post War Britain*, London, Hutchinson, 1976.

Hayman, Ronald, *Leavis*, London, Heinemann, 1976.

Hoare, Quinton, 'Education: Programmes and Men', *New Left Review*, no. 32, 1965, pp. 40–52.

Hoggart, Richard, *The Uses of Literacy*, Harmondsworth, Penguin, 1969.

Hoggart, Richard, *Speaking to Each Other,* 2 Vols, Harmondsworth, Penguin, 1973.

Holroyd, Michael, *Lytton Strachey and the Bloomsbury Group*, Harmondsworth, Penguin, 1971.

Houghton, W. E., *The Victorian Frame of Mind*, New Haven, Yale University Press, 1959.

Huxley, Leonard, *Life and Letters of Thomas Henry Huxley*, 2 Vols, London, Macmillan, 1903.

Huxley, T. H., *Method and Results, Essays*, Vol. I, London, Macmillan, 1898.

Huxley, T. H., *Science and Education, Essays*, Vol. III, London, Macmillan, 1905.

Hynes, Samuel, *The Edwardian Turn of Mind*, Princeton University Press, 1968.

Hynes, Samuel, *The Auden Generation, Literature and Politics in England in the 1930s*, London, The Bodley Head, 1976.

Jackson, Holbrook, *The Eighteen Nineties*, New York, Capricorn Books, 1966.

Johnson, Richard, 'Educational Policy and Social Control in early Victorian England', *Past and Present*, vol. 49, 1970, pp. 96–119.

Johnson, Richard, 'Barrington Moore, Perry Anderson and English Social Development', *Working Papers in Cultural Studies 9*, Centre for Contemporary Cultural Studies, Spring 1976, pp. 7–28.

Lawrence, D. H., *Phoenix*, Surrey, Windmill Press, 1970.

Layton, David, *Science for the People*, London, Allen & Unwin, 1973.

Leavis, F. R., 'The Literary Mind', *Scrutiny*, I, 1932, pp. 20–32.

Leavis, F. R., 'What's Wrong with Criticism?', *Scrutiny*, vol. I, 1932, pp. 132–46.

Leavis, F. R., 'Under Which King, Bezonian?', *Scrutiny*, vol. I, 1932, pp. 205–14.

Leavis, F. R., 'A Retrospect', *Scrutiny*, vol. XX, 1952, pp. 1–26.

Leavis, F. R., 'The Responsible Critic: or the Functions of Criticism at any Time', *Scrutiny*, vol. XIX, 1952, pp. 162–83.

Leavis, F. R., *Education and the University*, London, Chatto & Windus, 1961.

Leavis, F. R., *English Literature in Our Time and the University*, London, Chatto & Windus, 1969.

Leavis, F. R., *Nor Shall My Sword*, London, Chatto & Windus, 1972.

Leavis, F. R. and Denys Thompson, *Culture and Environment*, London, Chatto & Windus, 1960.

Leavis, Q. D., *Fiction and the Reading Public*, London, Chatto & Windus, 1965.

Lucas, John, ed., *Literature and Politics in the Nineteenth Century*, London, Unwin Books, 1971.

McBriar, A. M., *Fabian Socialism and English Politics, 1884–1918*, Cambridge University Press, 1962.

McClennan, Gregor, '"Ideology" and "Consciousness": Some Problems in Marxist Historiography', *Stencilled Occasional Papers*, Centre for Contemporary Cultural Studies, University of Birmingham, September, 1976.

Mannheim, Karl, *Essays on the Sociology of Culture*, London, Routledge & Kegan Paul, 1956.

Masterman, C. F. G., *The Condition of England*, London, Methuen, 1960.

Mathieson, Margaret, *The Preachers of Culture*, London, Allen & Unwin, 1975.

Mill, J. S., *Essays on Politics and Culture*, ed. Gertrude Himmelfarb, New York, Anchor Books, 1963.

Mill, J. S., *John Stuart Mill. A Selection of his works*, ed. J. M. Robson, Toronto University Press, 1966.

Miller, Andrew, 'Socio-Cultural Theories of Education and the Sociology of Education', Donald E. Edgar, ed., *Sociology of Australian Education*, Sydney, McGraw-Hill, 1975, pp. 423–44.

Morris, William, *On Art and Socialism*, Holbrook Jackson, ed., London, John Lehmann, 1947.

Musgrave, P. W., '*Scrutiny* and Education', *British Journal of Educational Studies*, vol. XXI, 1973, pp. 253–7.

Nairn, Tom, 'The Twilight of the British State', *New Left Review*, nos. 101–2, 1977, pp. 3–61.

Nettl, J. P., 'Ideas, Intellectuals, and Structures of Dissent', P. Rieff, ed., *On Intellectuals*, New York, Doubleday, 1969, pp. 53–122.

Nokes, P. L., 'What Kind of Applied Social Sciences?', *Universities Quarterly*, vol. 28, no. 2, 1974.

Orwell, George, *Collected Essays*, London, Mercury Books, 1961.

Orwell, George, *The Road to Wigan Pier*, Harmondsworth, Penguin, 1972.

Peters, R. S., 'Education as Initiation', R. D. Archambault, ed., *Philosophical Analysis and Education*, London, Routledge & Kegan Paul, 1965.

Peters, R. S., *Ethics and Education*, London, Allen & Unwin, 1968.

Peters, R. S., 'What is an Educational Process?', R. S. Peters, ed., *The Concept of Education*, London, Routledge & Kegan Paul, 1968.

Ruskin, John, *Unto this Last*, London, Harrap, 1866.

Ruskin, John, *Fors Clavigera*, Kent, Allen & Unwin, 1871.

Ruskin, John, *Sesame and Lilies*, Kent, Allen & Unwin, 1880.

Russell, Bertrand, *The Impact of America on European Civilization*, Boston, The Beacon Press, 1951.

Russell, Bertrand, *Authority and the Individual*, London, Unwin Books, 1965.
Russell, Bertrand, *Education and the Social Order*, London, Unwin Books, 1970.
Russell, Bertrand, *Sceptical Essays*, London, Unwin Books, 1970.
Russell, Bertrand, *The Autobiography of Bertrand Russell*, 3 Vols, London, Allen & Unwin, 1971.
Sandison, Alan, *The Last Man in Europe*, London, Macmillan, 1974.
Shaw, George Bernard, 'The Fabian Society: What It Has Done; and How It Has Done It', *Fabian Tract*, no. 41, London, 1892.
Shaw, George Bernard, Preface to *Back to Methuselah*, Harmondsworth, Penguin, 1954.
Shaw, George Bernard, *Major Barbara*, Harmondsworth, Penguin, 1971.
Shaw, George Bernard, *An Intelligent Woman's Guide to Socialism, Capitalism, Sovietism and Fascism*, Harmondsworth, Penguin, 1971.
Shils, Edward, *The Intellectuals and the Powers and Other Essays*, Chicago University Press, 1972.
Snow, C. P., *The Two Cultures*, New York, Mentor, 1963.
Spencer, Herbert, *The Man versus The State*, Harmondsworth, Penguin, 1969.
Spencer, Herbert, *Essays in Education*, London, Dent, 1941.
Stedman Jones, Gareth, 'History: the Poverty of Empiricism', Robin Blackburn, ed., *Ideology in Social Sciences*, Bungay, Suffolk, Fontana, 1973, pp. 96–118.
Steiner, George, *Language and Silence*, Harmondsworth, Penguin, 1969.
Tawney, Richard, *The Acquisitive Society*, London, Bell, 1937.
Tawney, Richard, *The Radical Tradition*, ed. Rita Hinder, Harmondsworth, Penguin, 1966.
Tawney, Richard, *Equality*, London, Allen & Unwin, 1952.
Terrill, Ross, *R. H. Tawney and His Times*, London, André Deutsch, 1973.
Thompson, E. P., 'The Peculiarities of the English', Ralph Miliband and John Saville, eds, *The Socialist Register 1965*, London, Merlin Press, 1965, pp. 311–62.
Thompson, E. P., 'Romanticism, Moralism and Utopianism: the Case of William Morris', *New Left Review*, vol. 99, 1976, pp. 83–111.
Thompson, E. P., *William Morris, Romantic to Revolutionary*, London, Merlin Press, 1977.
Trilling, Lionel, *Matthew Arnold*, London, Unwin Books, 1963.
Tylor, Edward B., *Primitive Culture*, vol. 1, London, John Murray, 1891.
Vaizey, John, '"Scrutiny" and Education', *Essays in Criticism*, XIV, 1964, pp. 36–42.
Walcott, Fred G., *The Origins of Culture and Anarchy*, University of Toronto Press, 1970.
Wells, H. G., *Mankind in the Making*, London, Chapman & Hall, 1903.
Wells, H. G., *An Englishman Looks at the World*, London, Cassell, 1914.
Wells, H. G., *Experiment in Autobiography*, London, Gollancz, 1934.
Wells, H. G., *A Modern Utopia*, London, Odhams Press, n.d.

White, Allan, 'From Culture to Culture. The Disputed Passage', *Cambridge Review*, 96, May, 1975, pp. 129–31.
Wilson, Colin, *Bernard Shaw. A Reassessment*, London, Hutchinson, 1969.
Williams, Raymond, *Border Country*, Harmondsworth, Penguin, 1964.
Williams, Raymond, *Second Generation*, London, Chatto & Windus, 1964.
Williams, Raymond, *Culture and Society*, Harmondsworth, Penguin, 1968.
Williams, Raymond, *The Long Revolution*, Harmondsworth, Penguin, 1971.
Williams, Raymond, *Communications*, Harmondsworth, Penguin, 1962.
Williams, Raymond, 'Towards a Socialist Society', Perry Anderson and Robin Blackburn, eds, *Towards Socialism*, Harmondsworth, Penguin, 1965.
Williams, Raymond, 'The British Left', *New Left Review*, no. 30, 1965, pp. 18–26.
Williams, Raymond, 'Culture and Revolution. a Response', Terry Eagleton and Brian Wicker, eds, *From Culture to Revolution*, London, Sheed & Ward Ltd., 1968.
Williams, Raymond (ed.), *May Day Manifesto, 1968*, Harmondsworth, Penguin, 1968.
Williams, Raymond, 'Literature and Sociology: in Memory of Lucien Goldmann', *New Left Review*, no. 67, 1971, pp. 3–18.
Williams, Raymond, *Orwell*, London, Fontana-Collins, 1971.
Williams, Raymond, 'Base and Superstructure in Marxist Cultural Theory', *New Left Review*, no. 82, 1973, pp. 3–16.
Williams, Raymond, *The Country and the City*, London, Chatto & Windus, 1973.
Williams, Raymond, *Television, Technology and Cultural Form*, London, Fontana, 1974.
Williams, Raymond, *Marxism and Literature*, Oxford University Press, 1977.
Wollheim, Richard, 'Culture and Socialism', *Fabian Tract*, 331, London, 1961.
Wood, Neal, *Communism and British Intellectuals*, New York, Columbia University Press, 1959.

# Index

# Routledge Social Science Series

Routledge & Kegan Paul London, Henley and Boston

39 Store Street, London WC1E 7DD
Broadway House, Newtown Road,
Henley-on-Thames, Oxon RG9 1EN
9 Park Street, Boston, Mass. 02108

# Contents



*Authors wishing to submit manuscripts for any series in this catalogue should send them to the Social Science Editor, Routledge & Kegan Paul Ltd, 39 Store Street, London WC1E 7DD*

●*Books so marked are available in paperback*
*All books are in Metric Demy 8vo format (216 × 138mm approx.)*

# International Library of Sociology

*General Editor* John Rex

## GENERAL SOCIOLOGY

**Barnsley, J. H.** The Social Reality of Ethics. *464 pp.*
**Brown, Robert.** Explanation in Social Science. *208 pp.*
● Rules and Laws in Sociology. *192 pp.*
**Bruford, W. H.** Chekhov and His Russia. *A Sociological Study. 244 pp.*
**Burton, F.** and **Carlen, P.** Official Discourse. *On Discourse Analysis, Government Publications, Ideology. About 140 pp.*
**Cain, Maureen E.** Society and the Policeman's Role. *326 pp.*
● **Fletcher, Colin.** Beneath the Surface. *An Account of Three Styles of Sociological Research. 221 pp.*
**Gibson, Quentin.** The Logic of Social Enquiry. *240 pp.*
**Glucksmann, M.** Structuralist Analysis in Contemporary Social Thought. *212 pp.*
**Gurvitch, Georges.** Sociology of Law. *Foreword by Roscoe Pound. 264 pp.*
**Hinkle, R.** Founding Theory of American Sociology 1883-1915. *About 350 pp.*
**Homans, George C.** Sentiments and Activities. *336 pp.*
**Johnson, Harry M.** Sociology: *a Systematic Introduction. Foreword by Robert K. Merton. 710 pp.*
● **Keat, Russell** and **Urry, John.** Social Theory as Science. *278 pp.*
**Mannheim, Karl.** Essays on Sociology and Social Psychology. *Edited by Paul Keckskemeti. With Editorial Note by Adolph Lowe. 344 pp.*
**Martindale, Don.** The Nature and Types of Sociological Theory. *292 pp.*
● **Maus, Heinz.** A Short History of Sociology. *234 pp.*
**Myrdal, Gunnar.** Value in Social Theory: *A Collection of Essays on Methodology. Edited by Paul Streeten. 332 pp.*
**Ogburn, William F.** and **Nimkoff, Meyer F.** A Handbook of Sociology. *Preface by Karl Mannheim. 656 pp. 46 figures. 35 tables.*
**Parsons, Talcott,** and **Smelser, Neil J.** Economy and Society: *A Study in the Integration of Economic and Social Theory. 362 pp.*
**Podgórecki, Adam.** Practical Social Sciences. *About 200 pp.*
**Raffel, S.** Matters of Fact. *A Sociological Inquiry. 152 pp.*
● **Rex, John.** (Ed.) Approaches to Sociology. *Contributions by Peter Abell,* Sociology and the Demystification of the Modern World. *282 pp.*
● **Rex, John** (Ed.) Approaches to Sociology. *Contributions by Peter Abell, Frank Bechhofer, Basil Bernstein, Ronald Fletcher, David Frisby, Miriam Glucksmann, Peter Lassman, Herminio Martins, John Rex, Roland Robertson, John Westergaard and Jock Young. 302 pp.*
**Rigby, A.** Alternative Realities. *352 pp.*
**Roche, M.** Phenomenology, Language and the Social Sciences. *374 pp.*
**Sahay, A.** Sociological Analysis. *220 pp.*

**Strasser, Hermann.** The Normative Structure of Sociology. *Conservative and Emancipatory Themes in Social Thought. About 340 pp.*
**Strong, P.** Ceremonial Order of the Clinic. *About 250 pp.*
**Urry, John.** Reference Groups and the Theory of Revolution. *244 pp.*
**Weinberg, E.** Development of Sociology in the Soviet Union. *173 pp.*

## FOREIGN CLASSICS OF SOCIOLOGY

● **Gerth, H. H.** and **Mills, C. Wright.** From Max Weber: *Essays in Sociology. 502 pp.*
● **Tönnies, Ferdinand.** Community and Association. *(Gemeinschaft and Gesellschaft.) Translated and Supplemented by Charles P. Loomis. Foreword by Pitirim A. Sorokin. 334 pp.*

## SOCIAL STRUCTURE

**Andreski, Stanislav.** Military Organization and Society. *Foreword by Professor A. R. Radcliffe-Brown. 226 pp. 1 folder.*
**Carlton, Eric.** Ideology and Social Order. *Foreword by Professor Philip Abrahams. About 320 pp.*
**Coontz, Sydney H.** Population Theories and the Economic Interpretation. *202 pp.*
**Coser, Lewis.** The Functions of Social Conflict. *204 pp.*
**Dickie-Clark, H. F.** Marginal Situation: *A Sociological Study of a Coloured Group. 240 pp. 11 tables.*
**Giner, S.** and **Archer, M. S.** (Eds.). Contemporary Europe. *Social Structures and Cultural Patterns. 336 pp.*
● **Glaser, Barney** and **Strauss, Anselm L.** Status Passage. *A Formal Theory. 212 pp.*
**Glass, D. V.** (Ed.) Social Mobility in Britain. *Contributions by J. Berent, T. Bottomore, R. C. Chambers, J. Floud, D. V. Glass, J. R. Hall, H. T. Himmelweit, R. K. Kelsall, F. M. Martin, C. A. Moser, R. Mukherjee, and W. Ziegel. 420 pp.*
**Kelsall, R. K.** Higher Civil Servants in Britain: *From 1870 to the Present Day. 268 pp. 31 tables.*
● **Lawton, Denis.** Social Class, Language and Education. *192 pp.*
**McLeish, John.** The Theory of Social Change: *Four Views Considered. 128 pp.*
● **Marsh, David C.** The Changing Social Structure of England and Wales, 1871-1961. *Revised edition. 288 pp.*
**Menzies, Ken.** Talcott Parsons and the Social Image of Man. *About 208 pp.*
● **Mouzelis, Nicos.** Organization and Bureaucracy. *An Analysis of Modern Theories. 240 pp.*
**Ossowski, Stanislaw.** Class Structure in the Social Consciousness. *210 pp.*
● **Podgórecki, Adam.** Law and Society. *302 pp.*
**Renner, Karl.** Institutions of Private Law and Their Social Functions. *Edited, with an Introduction and Notes, by O. Kahn-Freud. Translated by Agnes Schwarzschild. 316 pp.*

**Rex, J.** and **Tomlinson, S.** Colonial Immigrants in a British City. *A Class Analysis. 368 pp.*

**Smooha, S.** Israel: Pluralism and Conflict. *472 pp.*

**Wesolowski, W.** Class, Strata and Power. *Trans. and with Introduction by G. Kolankiewicz. 160 pp.*

**Zureik, E.** Palestinians in Israel. *A Study in Internal Colonialism. 264 pp.*

## SOCIOLOGY AND POLITICS

**Acton, T. A.** Gypsy Politics and Social Change. *316 pp.*

**Burton, F.** Politics of Legitimacy. *Struggles in a Belfast Community. 250 pp.*

**Etzioni-Halevy, E.** Political Manipulation and Administrative Power. *A Comparative Study. About 200 pp.*

● **Hechter, Michael.** Internal Colonialism. *The Celtic Fringe in British National Development, 1536–1966. 380 pp.*

**Kornhauser, William.** The Politics of Mass Society. *272 pp. 20 tables.*

**Korpi, W.** The Working Class in Welfare Capitalism. *Work, Unions and Politics in Sweden. 472 pp.*

**Kroes, R.** Soldiers and Students. *A Study of Right- and Left-wing Students. 174 pp.*

**Martin, Roderick.** Sociology of Power. *About 272 pp.*

**Myrdal, Gunnar.** The Political Element in the Development of Economic Theory. *Translated from the German by Paul Streeten. 282 pp.*

**Wong, S.-L.** Sociology and Socialism in Contemporary China. *160 pp.*

**Wootton, Graham.** Workers, Unions and the State. *188 pp.*

## CRIMINOLOGY

**Ancel, Marc.** Social Defence: *A Modern Approach to Criminal Problems. Foreword by Leon Radzinowicz. 240 pp.*

**Athens, L.** Violent Criminal Acts and Actors. *About 150 pp.*

**Cain, Maureen E.** Society and the Policeman's Role. *326 pp.*

**Cloward, Richard A.** and **Ohlin, Lloyd E.** Delinquency and Opportunity: *A Theory of Delinquent Gangs. 248 pp.*

**Downes, David M.** The Delinquent Solution. *A Study in Subcultural Theory. 296 pp.*

**Friedlander, Kate.** The Psycho-Analytical Approach to Juvenile Delinquency: *Theory, Case Studies, Treatment. 320 pp.*

**Gleuck, Sheldon** and **Eleanor.** Family Environment and Delinquency. *With the statistical assistance of Rose W. Kneznek. 340 pp.*

**Lopez-Rey, Manuel.** Crime. *An Analytical Appraisal. 288 pp.*

**Mannheim, Hermann.** Comparative Criminology: *a Text Book. Two volumes. 442 pp. and 380 pp.*

**Morris, Terence.** The Criminal Area: *A Study in Social Ecology. Foreword by Hermann Mannheim. 232 pp. 25 tables. 4 maps.*

**Podgorecki, A.** and **Łos, M.** *Multidimensional Sociology. About 380 pp.*

**Rock, Paul.** Making People Pay. *338 pp.*

● **Taylor, Ian, Walton, Paul,** and **Young, Jock.** The New Criminology. *For a Social Theory of Deviance. 325 pp.*

● **Taylor, Ian, Walton, Paul** and **Young, Jock.** (Eds) Critical Criminology. *268 pp.*

## SOCIAL PSYCHOLOGY

**Bagley, Christopher.** The Social Psychology of the Epileptic Child. *320 pp.*

**Brittan, Arthur.** Meanings and Situations. *224 pp.*

**Carroll, J.** Break-Out from the Crystal Palace. *200 pp.*

● **Fleming, C. M.** Adolescence: Its Social Psychology. *With an Introduction to recent findings from the fields of Anthropology, Physiology, Medicine, Psychometrics and Sociometry. 288 pp.*

● The Social Psychology of Education: *An Introduction and Guide to Its Study. 136 pp.*

**Linton, Ralph.** The Cultural Background of Personality. *132 pp.*

● **Mayo, Elton.** The Social Problems of an Industrial Civilization. *With an Appendix on the Political Problem. 180 pp.*

**Ottaway, A. K. C.** Learning Through Group Experience. *176 pp.*

**Plummer, Ken.** Sexual Stigma. *An Interactionist Account. 254 pp.*

● **Rose, Arnold M.** (Ed.) Human Behaviour and Social Processes: *an Interactionist Approach. Contributions by Arnold M. Rose, Ralph H. Turner, Anselm Strauss, Everett C. Hughes, E. Franklin Frazier, Howard S. Becker et al. 696 pp.*

**Smelser, Neil J.** Theory of Collective Behaviour. *448 pp.*

**Stephenson, Geoffrey M.** The Development of Conscience. *128 pp.*

**Young, Kimball.** Handbook of Social Psychology. *658 pp. 16 figures. 10 tables.*

## SOCIOLOGY OF THE FAMILY

**Bell, Colin R.** Middle Class Families: *Social and Geographical Mobility. 224 pp.*

**Burton, Lindy.** Vulnerable Children. *272 pp.*

**Gavron, Hannah.** The Captive Wife: *Conflicts of Household Mothers. 190 pp.*

**George, Victor** and **Wilding, Paul.** Motherless Families. *248 pp.*

**Klein, Josephine.** Samples from English Cultures.

1. Three Preliminary Studies and Aspects of Adult Life in England. *447 pp.*
2. Child-Rearing Practices and Index. *247 pp.*

**Klein, Viola.** The Feminine Character. *History of an Ideology. 244 pp.*

**McWhinnie, Alexina M.** Adopted Children. *How They Grow Up. 304 pp.*

● **Morgan, D. H. J.** Social Theory and the Family. *About 320 pp.*

● **Myrdal, Alva** and **Klein, Viola.** Women's Two Roles: *Home and Work. 238 pp. 27 tables.*

**Parsons, Talcott** and **Bales, Robert F.** Family: Socialization and Interaction Process. *In collaboration with James Olds, Morris Zelditch and Philip E. Slater. 456 pp. 50 figures and tables.*

## SOCIAL SERVICES

**Bastide, Roger.** The Sociology of Mental Disorder. *Translated from the French by Jean McNeil. 260 pp.*

**Carlebach, Julius.** Caring For Children in Trouble. *266 pp.*

**George, Victor.** Foster Care. *Theory and Practice. 234 pp.*

Social Security: *Beveridge and After. 258 pp.*

**George, V.** and **Wilding, P.** Motherless Families. *248 pp.*

● **Goetschius, George W.** Working with Community Groups. *256 pp.*

**Goetschius, George W.** and **Tash, Joan.** Working with Unattached Youth. *416 pp.*

**Heywood, Jean S.** Children in Care. *The Development of the Service for the Deprived Child. Third revised edition. 284 pp.*

**King, Roy D., Ranes, Norma V.** and **Tizard, Jack.** Patterns of Residential Care. *356 pp.*

**Leigh, John.** Young People and Leisure. *256 pp.*

● **Mays, John.** (Ed.) Penelope Hall's Social Services of England and Wales. *About 324 pp.*

**Morris, Mary.** Voluntary Work and the Welfare State. *300 pp.*

**Nokes, P. L.** The Professional Task in Welfare Practice. *152 pp.*

**Timms, Noel.** Psychiatric Social Work in Great Britain (1939-1962). *280 pp.*

● Social Casework: *Principles and Practice. 256 pp.*

## SOCIOLOGY OF EDUCATION

**Banks, Olive.** Parity and Prestige in English Secondary Education: a Study in Educational Sociology. *272 pp.*

● **Blyth, W. A. L.** English Primary Education. *A Sociological Description.* 2. Background. *168 pp.*

**Collier, K. G.** The Social Purposes of Education: *Personal and Social Values in Education. 268 pp.*

**Evans, K. M.** Sociometry and Education *158 pp.*

● **Ford, Julienne.** Social Class and the Comprehensive School. *192 pp.*

**Foster, P. J.** Education and Social Change in Ghana. *336 pp. 3 maps.*

**Fraser, W. R.** Education and Society in Modern France. *150 pp.*

**Grace, Gerald R.** Role Conflict and the Teacher. *150 pp.*

**Hans, Nicholas.** New Trends in Education in the Eighteenth Century. *278 pp. 19 tables.*

● Comparative Education: *A Study of Educational Factors and Traditions. 360 pp.*

● **Hargreaves, David.** Interpersonal Relations and Education. *432 pp.*

● Social Relations in a Secondary School. *240 pp.*

School Organization and Pupil Involvement. *A Study of Secondary Schools.*

- ● **Mannheim, Karl** and **Stewart, W.A.C.** An Introduction to the Sociology of Education. *206 pp.*
- ● **Musgrove, F.** Youth and the Social Order. *176 pp.*
- ● **Ottaway, A. K. C.** Education and Society: An Introduction to the Sociology of Education. *With an Introduction by W. O. Lester Smith. 212 pp.*
- **Peers, Robert.** Adult Education: *A Comparative Study. Revised edition. 398 pp.*
- **Stratta, Erica.** The Education of Borstal Boys. *A Study of their Educational Experiences prior to, and during, Borstal Training. 256 pp.*
- ● **Taylor, P. H., Reid, W. A.** and **Holley, B. J.** The English Sixth Form. *A Case Study in Curriculum Research. 198 pp.*

## SOCIOLOGY OF CULTURE

- **Eppel, E. M.** and **M.** Adolescents and Morality: *A Study of some Moral Values and Dilemmas of Working Adolescents in the Context of a changing Climate of Opinion. Foreword by W. J. H. Sprott. 268 pp. 39 tables.*
- ● **Fromm, Erich.** The Fear of Freedom. *286 pp.*
- ● The Sane Society. *400 pp.*
- **Johnson, L.** The Cultural Critics. *From Matthew Arnold to Raymond Williams. 233 pp.*
- **Mannheim, Karl.** Essays on the Sociology of Culture. *Edited by Ernst Mannheim in co-operation with Paul Kecskemeti. Editorial Note by Adolph Lowe. 280 pp.*
- **Zijderfeld, A. C.** On Clichés. *The Supersedure of Meaning by Function in Modernity. About 132 pp.*

## SOCIOLOGY OF RELIGION

- **Argyle, Michael** and **Beit-Hallahmi, Benjamin.** The Social Psychology of Religion. *About 256 pp.*
- **Glasner, Peter E.** The Sociology of Secularisation. *A Critique of a Concept. About 180 pp.*
- **Hall, J. R.** The Ways Out. *Utopian Communal Groups in an Age of Babylon. 280 pp.*
- **Ranson, S., Hinings, B.** and **Bryman, A.** Clergy, Ministers and Priests. *216 pp.*
- **Stark, Werner.** The Sociology of Religion. *A Study of Christendom.*
  - Volume II. *Sectarian Religion. 368 pp.*
  - Volume III. *The Universal Church. 464 pp.*
  - Volume IV. *Types of Religious Man. 352 pp.*
  - Volume V. *Types of Religious Culture. 464 pp.*
- **Turner, B. S.** Weber and Islam. *216 pp.*
- **Watt, W. Montgomery.** Islam and the Integration of Society. *320 pp.*

## SOCIOLOGY OF ART AND LITERATURE

**Jarvie, Ian C.** Towards a Sociology of the Cinema. *A Comparative Essay on the Structure and Functioning of a Major Entertainment Industry. 405 pp.*

**Rust, Frances S.** Dance in Society. *An Analysis of the Relationships between the Social Dance and Society in England from the Middle Ages to the Present Day. 256 pp. 8 pp. of plates.*

**Schücking, L. L.** The Sociology of Literary Taste. *112 pp.*

**Wolff, Janet.** Hermeneutic Philosophy and the Sociology of Art. *150 pp.*

## SOCIOLOGY OF KNOWLEDGE

**Diesing, P.** Patterns of Discovery in the Social Sciences. *262 pp.*

● **Douglas, J. D.** (Ed.) Understanding Everyday Life. *370 pp.*

**Glasner, B.** Essential Interactionism. *About 220 pp.*

● **Hamilton, P.** Knowledge and Social Structure. *174 pp.*

**Jarvie, I. C.** Concepts and Society. *232 pp.*

**Mannheim, Karl.** Essays on the Sociology of Knowledge. *Edited by Paul Kecskemeti. Editorial Note by Adolph Lowe. 353 pp.*

**Remmling, Gunter W.** The Sociology of Karl Mannheim. *With a Bibliographical Guide to the Sociology of Knowledge, Ideological Analysis, and Social Planning. 255 pp.*

**Remmling, Gunter W.** (Ed.) Towards the Sociology of Knowledge. *Origin and Development of a Sociological Thought Style. 463 pp.*

## URBAN SOCIOLOGY

**Aldridge, M.** The British New Towns. *A Programme Without a Policy. About 250 pp.*

**Ashworth, William.** The Genesis of Modern British Town Planning: *A Study in Economic and Social History of the Nineteenth and Twentieth Centuries. 288 pp.*

**Brittan, A.** The Privatised World. *196 pp.*

**Cullingworth, J. B.** Housing Needs and Planning Policy: *A Restatement of the Problems of Housing Need and 'Overspill' in England and Wales. 232 pp. 44 tables. 8 maps.*

**Dickinson, Robert E.** City and Region: *A Geographical Interpretation. 608 pp. 125 figures.*

The West European City: *A Geographical Interpretation. 600 pp. 129 maps. 29 plates.*

**Humphreys, Alexander J.** New Dubliners: *Urbanization and the Irish Family. Foreword by George C. Homans. 304 pp.*

**Jackson, Brian.** Working Class Community: *Some General Notions raised by a Series of Studies in Northern England. 192 pp.*

● **Mann, P. H.** An Approach to Urban Sociology. *240 pp.*

**Mellor, J. R.** Urban Sociology in an Urbanized Society. *326 pp.*

**Morris, R. N.** and **Mogey, J.** The Sociology of Housing. *Studies at Berinsfield. 232 pp. 4 pp. plates.*

**Rosser, C.** and **Harris, C.** The Family and Social Change. *A Study of Family and Kinship in a South Wales Town. 352 pp. 8 maps.*

● **Stacey, Margaret, Batsone, Eric, Bell, Colin** and **Thurcott, Anne.** Power, Persistence and Change. *A Second Study of Banbury. 196 pp.*

## RURAL SOCIOLOGY

**Mayer, Adrian C.** Peasants in the Pacific. *A Study of Fiji Indian Rural Society. 248 pp. 20 plates.*

**Williams, W. M.** The Sociology of an English Village: *Gosforth. 272 pp. 12 figures. 13 tables.*

## SOCIOLOGY OF INDUSTRY AND DISTRIBUTION

**Dunkerley, David.** The Foreman. *Aspects of Task and Structure. 192 pp.*

**Eldridge, J. E. T.** Industrial Disputes. *Essays in the Sociology of Industrial Relations. 288 pp.*

**Hollowell, Peter G.** The Lorry Driver. *272 pp.*

● **Oxaal, I., Barnett, T.** and **Booth, D.** (Eds) Beyond the Sociology of Development. *Economy and Society in Latin America and Africa. 295 pp.*

**Smelser, Neil J.** Social Change in the Industrial Revolution: *An Application of Theory to the Lancashire Cotton Industry, 1770–1840. 468 pp. 12 figures. 14 tables.*

**Watson, T. J.** The Personnel Managers. *A Study in the Sociology of Work and Employment. 262 pp.*

## ANTHROPOLOGY

**Brandel-Syrier, Mia.** Reeftown Elite. *A Study of Social Mobility in a Modern African Community on the Reef. 376 pp.*

**Dickie-Clark, H. F.** The Marginal Situation. *A Sociological Study of a Coloured Group. 236 pp.*

**Dube, S. C.** Indian Village. *Foreword by Morris Edward Opler. 276 pp. 4 plates.*

India's Changing Villages: *Human Factors in Community Development. 260 pp. 8 plates. 1 map.*

**Firth, Raymond.** Malay Fishermen. *Their Peasant Economy. 420 pp. 17 pp. plates.*

**Gulliver, P. H.** Social Control in an African Society: a Study of the Arusha, Agricultural Masai of Northern Tanganyika. *320 pp. 8 plates. 10 figures.*

Family Herds. *288 pp.*

**Jarvie, Ian C.** The Revolution in Anthropology. *268 pp.*

**Little, Kenneth L.** Mende of Sierra Leone. *308 pp. and folder.*

Negroes in Britain. *With a New Introduction and Contemporary Study by Leonard Bloom. 320 pp.*

**Madan, G. R.** Western Sociologists on Indian Society. *Marx, Spencer, Weber, Durkheim, Pareto. 384 pp.*

**Mayer, A. C.** Peasants in the Pacific. *A Study of Fiji Indian Rural Society. 248 pp.*

**Meer, Fatima.** Race and Suicide in South Africa. *325 pp.*

**Smith, Raymond T.** The Negro Family in British Guiana: *Family Structure and Social Status in the Villages. With a Foreword by Meyer Fortes. 314 pp. 8 plates. 1 figure. 4 maps.*

## SOCIOLOGY AND PHILOSOPHY

**Barnsley, John H.** The Social Reality of Ethics. *A Comparative Analysis of Moral Codes. 448 pp.*

**Diesing, Paul.** Patterns of Discovery in the Social Sciences. *362 pp.*

● **Douglas, Jack D.** (Ed.) Understanding Everyday Life. *Toward the Reconstruction of Sociological Knowledge. Contributions by Alan F. Blum, Aaron W. Cicourel, Norman K. Denzin, Jack D. Douglas, John Heeren, Peter McHugh, Peter K. Manning, Melvin Power, Matthew Speier, Roy Turner, D. Lawrence Wieder, Thomas P. Wilson and Don H. Zimmerman. 370 pp.*

**Gorman, Robert A.** The Dual Vision. *Alfred Schutz and the Myth of Phenomenological Social Science. About 300 pp.*

**Jarvie, Ian C.** Concepts and Society. *216 pp.*

**Kilminster, R.** Praxis and Method. *A Sociological Dialogue with Lukács, Gramsci and the early Frankfurt School. About 304 pp.*

● **Pelz, Werner.** The Scope of Understanding in Sociology. *Towards a More Radical Reorientation in the Social Humanistic Sciences. 283 pp.*

**Roche, Maurice.** Phenomenology, Language and the Social Sciences. *371 pp.*

**Sahay, Arun.** Sociological Analysis. *212 pp.*

**Slater, P.** Origin and Significance of the Frankfurt School. *A Marxist Perspective. About 192 pp.*

**Spurling, L.** Phenomenology and the Social World. *The Philosophy of Merleau-Ponty and its Relation to the Social Sciences. 222 pp.*

**Wilson, H. T.** The American Ideology. *Science, Technology and Organization as Modes of Rationality. 368 pp.*

# International Library of Anthropology

*General Editor* Adam Kuper

**Ahmed, A. S.** Millenium and Charisma Among Pathans. *A Critical Essay in Social Anthropology. 192 pp.*

Pukhtun Economy and Society. *About 360 pp.*

**Brown, Paula.** The Chimbu. *A Study of Change in the New Guinea Highlands. 151 pp.*

**Foner, N.** Jamaica Farewell. *200 pp.*

**Gudeman, Stephen.** Relationships, Residence and the Individual. *A Rural Panamanian Community. 288 pp. 11 plates, 5 figures, 2 maps, 10 tables.*

The Demise of a Rural Economy. *From Subsistence to Capitalism in a Latin American Village. 160 pp.*

**Hamnett, Ian.** Chieftainship and Legitimacy. *An Anthropological Study of Executive Law in Lesotho. 163 pp.*

**Hanson, F. Allan.** Meaning in Culture. *127 pp.*

**Humphreys, S. C.** Anthropology and the Greeks. *288 pp.*

**Karp, I.** Fields of Change Among the Iteso of Kenya. *140 pp.*

**Lloyd, P. C.** Power and Independence. *Urban Africans' Perception of Social Inequality. 264 pp.*

**Parry, J. P.** Caste and Kinship in Kangra. *352 pp. Illustrated.*

**Pettigrew, Joyce.** Robber Noblemen. *A Study of the Political System of the Sikh Jats. 284 pp.*

**Street, Brian V.** The Savage in Literature. *Representations of 'Primitive' Society in English Fiction, 1858–1920. 207 pp.*

**Van Den Berghe, Pierre L.** Power and Privilege at an African University. *278 pp.*

# International Library of Social Policy

*General Editor* Kathleen Jones

**Bayley, M.** Mental Handicap and Community Care. *426 pp.*

**Bottoms, A. E.** and **McClean, J. D.** Defendants in the Criminal Process. *284 pp.*

**Butler, J. R.** Family Doctors and Public Policy. *208 pp.*

**Davies, Martin.** Prisoners of Society. *Attitudes and Aftercare. 204 pp.*

**Gittus, Elizabeth.** Flats, Families and the Under-Fives. *285 pp.*

**Holman, Robert.** Trading in Children. *A Study of Private Fostering. 355 pp.*

**Jeffs, A.** Young People and the Youth Service. *About 180 pp.*

**Jones, Howard,** and **Cornes, Paul.** Open Prisons. *288 pp.*

**Jones, Kathleen.** History of the Mental Health Service. *428 pp.*

**Jones, Kathleen,** with **Brown, John, Cunningham, W. J., Roberts, Julian** and **Williams, Peter.** Opening the Door. *A Study of New Policies for the Mentally Handicapped. 278 pp.*

**Karn, Valerie.** Retiring to the Seaside. *About 280 pp. 2 maps. Numerous tables.*

**King, R. D.** and **Elliot, K. W.** Albany: Birth of a Prison—End of an Era. *394 pp.*

**Thomas, J. E.** The English Prison Officer since 1850: *A Study in Conflict. 258 pp.*

**Walton, R. G.** Women in Social Work. *303 pp.*

● **Woodward, J.** To Do the Sick No Harm. *A Study of the British Voluntary Hospital System to 1875. 234 pp.*

# International Library of Welfare and Philosophy

*General Editors* Noel Timms and David Watson

● **McDermott, F. E.** (Ed.) Self Determination in Social Work. *A Collection of Essays on Self-determination and Related Concepts by Philosophers and Social Work Theorists. Contributors: F. B. Biestek, S. Bernstein, A. Keith-Lucas, D. Sayer, H. H. Perelman, C. Whittington, R. F. Stalley, F. E. McDermott, I. Berlin, H. J. McCloskey, H. L. A. Hart, J. Wilson, A. I. Melden, S. I. Benn. 254 pp.*

● **Plant, Raymond.** Community and Ideology. *104 pp.*

**Ragg, Nicholas M.** People Not Cases. *A Philosophical Approach to Social Work. About 250 pp.*

● **Timms, Noel** and **Watson, David.** (Eds) Talking About Welfare. *Readings in Philosophy and Social Policy. Contributors: T. H. Marshall, R. B. Brandt, G. H. von Wright, K. Nielsen, M. Cranston, R. M. Titmuss, R. S. Downie, E. Telfer, D. Donnison, J. Benson, P. Leonard, A. Keith-Lucas, D. Walsh, I. T. Ramsey. 320 pp.*

● (Eds). Philosophy in Social Work. *250 pp.*

● **Weale, A.** Equality and Social Policy. *164 pp.*

# Primary Socialization, Language and Education

*General Editor* Basil Bernstein

**Adlam, Diana S.,** *with the assistance of Geoffrey Turner and Lesley Lineker.* Code in Context. *About 272 pp.*

**Bernstein, Basil.** Class, Codes and Control. *3 volumes.*

● 1. *Theoretical Studies Towards a Sociology of Language. 254 pp.*

2. *Applied Studies Towards a Sociology of Language. 377 pp.*

● 3. *Towards a Theory of Educational Transmission. 167 pp.*

**Brandis, W.** and **Bernstein, B.** Selection and Control. *176 pp.*

**Brandis, Walter** and **Henderson, Dorothy.** Social Class, Language and Communication. *288 pp.*

**Cook-Gumperz, Jenny.** Social Control and Socialization. *A Study of Class Differences in the Language of Maternal Control. 290 pp.*

● **Gahagan, D. M** and **G. A.** Talk Reform. *Exploration in Language for Infant School Children. 160 pp.*

**Hawkins, P. R.** Social Class, the Nominal Group and Verbal Strategies. *About 220 pp.*

**Robinson, W. P.** and **Rackstraw, Susan D. A.** A Question of Answers. *2 volumes. 192 pp. and 180 pp.*

**Turner, Geoffrey J.** and **Mohan, Bernard A.** A Linguistic Description and Computer Programme for Children's Speech. *208 pp.*

## Reports of the Institute of Community Studies

**Baker, J.** The Neighbourhood Advice Centre. A Community Project in Camden. *320 pp.*

● **Cartwright, Ann.** Patients and their Doctors. *A Study of General Practice. 304 pp.*

**Dench, Geoff.** Maltese in London.*A Case-study in the Erosion of Ethnic Consciousness. 302 pp.*

**Jackson, Brian** and **Marsden, Dennis.** Education and the Working Class: *Some General Themes raised by a Study of 88 Working-class Children in a Northern Industrial City. 268 pp. 2 folders.*

**Marris, Peter.** The Experience of Higher Education. *232 pp. 27 tables.*

● Loss and Change. *192 pp.*

**Marris, Peter** and **Rein, Martin.** Dilemmas of Social Reform. *Poverty and Community Action in the United States. 256 pp.*

**Marris, Peter** and **Somerset, Anthony.** African Businessmen. *A Study of Entrepreneurship and Development in Keyna. 256 pp.*

**Mills, Richard.** Young Outsiders: *a Study in Alternative Communities. 216 pp.*

**Runciman, W. G.** Relative Deprivation and Social Justice. *A Study of Attitudes to Social Inequality in Twentieth-Century England. 352 pp.*

**Willmott, Peter.** Adolescent Boys in East London. *230 pp.*

**Willmott, Peter** and **Young, Michael.** Family and Class in a London Suburb. *202 pp. 47 tables.*

**Young, Michael** and **McGeeney, Patrick.** Learning Begins at Home. *A Study of a Junior School and its Parents. 128 pp.*

**Young, Michael** and **Willmott, Peter.** Family and Kinship in East London. *Foreword by Richard M. Titmuss. 252 pp. 39 tables.*

The Symmetrical Family. *410 pp.*

# Reports of the Institute for Social Studies in Medical Care

**Cartwright, Ann, Hockey, Lisbeth** and **Anderson, John J.** Life Before Death. *310 pp.*

**Dunnell, Karen** and **Cartwright, Ann.** Medicine Takers, Prescribers and Hoarders. *190 pp.*

**Farrell, C.** My Mother Said. . . . *A Study of the Way Young People Learned About Sex and Birth Control. 200 pp.*

# Medicine, Illness and Society

*General Editor* W. M. Williams

**Hall, David J.** Social Relations & Innovation. *Changing the State of Play in Hospitals. 232 pp.*

**Hall, David J.,** and **Stacey, M.** (Eds) Beyond Separation. *234 pp.*

**Robinson, David.** The Process of Becoming Ill. *142 pp.*

**Stacey, Margaret** *et al.* Hospitals, Children and Their Families. *The Report of a Pilot Study. 202 pp.*

**Stimson G. V.** and **Webb, B.** Going to See the Doctor. *The Consultation Process in General Practice. 155 pp.*

# Monographs in Social Theory

*General Editor* Arthur Brittan

● **Barnes, B.** Scientific Knowledge and Sociological Theory. *192 pp.*

**Bauman, Zygmunt.** Culture as Praxis. *204 pp.*

● **Dixon, Keith.** Sociological Theory. *Pretence and Possibility. 142 pp.*

**Meltzer, B. N., Petras, J. W.** and **Reynolds, L. T.** Symbolic Interactionism. *Genesis, Varieties and Criticisms. 144 pp.*

● **Smith, Anthony D.** The Concept of Social Change. *A Critique of the Functionalist Theory of Social Change. 208 pp.*

# Routledge Social Science Journals

**The British Journal of Sociology.** *Editor – Angus Stewart; Associate Editor – Leslie Sklair. Vol. 1, No. 1 – March 1950 and Quarterly. Roy. 8vo. All back issues available. An international journal publishing original papers in the field of sociology and related areas.*

**Community Work.** *Edited by David Jones and Marjorie Mayo. 1973. Published annually.*

**Economy and Society.** *Vol. 1, No. 1. February 1972 and Quarterly. Metric Roy. 8vo. A journal for all social scientists covering sociology, philosophy, anthropology, economics and history. All back numbers available.*

**Ethnic and Racial Studies.** *Editor – John Stone. Vol. 1 – 1978. Published quarterly.*

**Religion. Journal of Religion and Religions.** *Chairman of Editorial Board, Ninian Smart. Vol. 1, No. 1, Spring 1971. A journal with an inter-disciplinary approach to the study of the phenomena of religion. All back numbers available.*

**Sociology of Health and Illness.** *A Journal of Medical Sociology. Editor – Alan Davies; Associate Editor – Ray Jobling. Vol. 1, Spring 1979. Published 3 times per annum.*

**Year Book of Social Policy in Britain, The.** *Edited by Kathleen Jones. 1971. Published annually.*

## Social and Psychological Aspects of Medical Practice

*Editor* Trevor Silverstone

**Lader, Malcolm.** Psychophysiology of Mental Illness. *280 pp.*

● **Silverstone, Trevor** and **Turner, Paul.** Drug Treatment in Psychiatry. *Revised edition. 256 pp.*

**Whiteley, J. S.** and **Gordon, J.** Group Approaches in Psychiatry. *256 pp.*

Printed in Great Britain by
Lowe & Brydone Printers Limited, Thetford, Norfolk 1278